WHAT THEY DON'T TEACH YOU AT TEACH YOU AT HARVARD BUSINESS SCHOOL ABOUT EXECUTIVE TRAVEL

By the same author

WHAT THEY DON'T TEACH YOU AT HARVARD BUSINESS SCHOOL

THE TERRIBLE TRUTH ABOUT LAWYERS

WHAT THEY *STILL* DON'T TEACH YOU AT HARVARD BUSINESS SCHOOL

THE 110% SOLUTION

ON NEGOTIATING

ON SELLING

WHAT THEY DON'T TEACH YOU AT HARVARD BUSINESS SCHOOL ABOUT EXECUTIVE TRAVEL

HIT THE

GROUND RUNNING

Mark H. McCormack

DOVE
B O O K S

ISBN 0-7871-0684-4

Printed in the United States of America

Dove Books
8955 Beverly Boulevard
West Hollywood, CA 90048

Distributed by Penguin USA

Text design by Hespenheide Design
Cover design and layout by Rick Penn-Kraus

First Printing: July 1996

10 9 8 7 6 5 4 3 2 1

To my trusted personal assistants, secretaries, and associates—especially Laurie Roggenburk, Sarah Wooldridge, Fumiko Matsuki, Penny Thompson, and Michelle Lane, who tirelessly worked throughout the year to make sure that I "Hit the Ground Running" wherever I might be in the world; and also to those who have filled these roles during the past thirty years including Mary Wenzel, Ayn Robbins, Nancy Grey, Doris Jones, Judy Chilcote, Vicky Micatrotto, Jean Barnes, Sally Anne Pickard, Elaine de Spoelberch, Penny Clark, Mary Ann Badalamenti, and a host of others. Finally and especially to my father, Ned Hume McCormack, who taught me the first things I ever learned about travel and who showed me how enjoyable it can be.

Acknowledgments

Writing this book would have been impossible without the help of many people. My gratitude and thanks:

To John Meyer, Jose Luis Ferrando, Todd McCormack, Steven Flanders, Eric Drossart, Michel Masquelier, Ivo Cozzini, Fred Adams, Peter Townsend, Tony Barry, Laurence St. John, Alastair Johnston, Peter Henke, Jacques Heyer, Marc Biver, Breck McCormack, Richard Avory, Timo Lumme, Cino Marchese, Kappy Flanders, Cliff Minshull, John Beddington, David and Jeannie Evans, Leslie McCormack, Erik van Dillen, Lars Sternmarker, Jim Curley, and Kazuo Kondo for their knowledge of what is excellent and true in various ports of call around the world.

To Herve Houdre, Mike Baverstock, Michael Gray, Bob Anderson, Marvin Bush, Sir Christopher Lewinton, Ian Wooldridge, Michael Parkinson, Sir David Frost, Gino Santin, Anton Mosimann, Bill Fugazy, and Melvyn Hartzel for sharing their personal travel secrets.

To Gretchen Mayfield for her fleet fingers at the word processor.

To Digby Diehl, an insightful and responsive collaborator, without whom this book could never have been completed.

Table of Contents

Preface
Less Haste, More Speed

You have undoubtedly seen Mr. Haste—that harried, self-important business traveler elbowing his way up to the front of the plane seconds after the wheels touch down. Hauling bulging carry-ons, sweating profusely, and often babbling into a mobile phone, he charges up the jetway, literally running to catch a taxi to his first appointment. This guy looks like a confused, rumpled maniac. He tells anyone who will listen how much he hates travel. He thinks that he is a road warrior who's running ahead of the pack. He thinks that he knows how to hit the ground running. He's got it all wrong.

There is a real difference between haste and speed. My concept of *Hit the Ground Running* is derived from the carefully planned, precisely executed landings made by the U.S. 101st and 82nd airborne assault divisions during World War II. Our paratroopers studied the terrain, reviewed their plans of attack in detail, made pinpoint parachute jumps, stayed in communication with each other, and re-formed their units rapidly to maximize efficiency. They spent as little time in the drop zone as possible. They were fast, but seldom rushed. They hit the ground running because they knew where they were going, what their mission was, and how to do it.

They were also ready for anything. Before leaving, they had made certain that they were fully equipped to deal with a myriad of "what-ifs" in case things didn't go according to plan. One of the reasons I decided to write this book is that over the past thirty years, my friends and associates have noticed that I not only get to flights and meetings on time in cities all over the world, but I get there ready to do business.

Over the years, other executives often have asked me how I have managed to avoid "travel burnout." In fact, I still look forward to every trip as an opportunity to help my company—and to expand my own horizons. Associates always call me for tips on hotels and restaurants when they are heading to new cities. And colleagues have pressed me for my "secrets" of efficient travel. It's not that I am somehow immune to jet lag, gate holds, weather delays, cancellations, missed connections, bad food, lost luggage, lost reservations, surly cabbies with no sense of direction, and all the other pitfalls that bedevil other business travelers. It's just that I have learned to manage them. At some point in the history of our company, I started collecting some of this hard-won advice in a company manual, telling our executives, for example, How to Travel in Tokyo. We have done this for three dozen cities where we maintain an office, and you'll find some of these "secrets" in this book.

The second and more important reason for this book is that over the past thirty years I have seen travel become the key to business success in my own life. I began my management firm with one client (Arnold Palmer, bless him) and one small office in Cleveland, Ohio. Today, International Management Group represents sports, music, and entertainment celebrities all over the world, including: Gary Player, Ivan Lendl, Martina Navratilova, Chris Evert, Monica Seles, Jim Courier, Andre Agassi, Joe Montana, Herschel Walker, Wayne Gretzky, Isabelle and Paul Duchesnay, Brian Orser, Jean-Claude Killy, Alberto Tomba, Jackie Stewart, Dennis Conner, Bart Conner, Bela Karoly, Itzhak Perlman, Andre Watts, Sir Neville Marriner, James Galway, Bob Costas, John Madden, Greg Gumbel, and Michael Parkinson.

IMG has managed and continues to manage various commercial activities for many of the world's foremost sports events, including the Winter Olympics (both the '92 Olympics at Albertville, France, and the '94 Olympics at Lillehammer, Norway), Wimbledon, the Australian, Italian, and German Open tennis championships, World Cup Skiing, the Augusta Masters golf tournament, the America's Cup, and the World Gymnastics Championships.

We also organize and present sporting and cultural events around the world, everything from the ATP World Championship tennis tournament in Frankfurt, to the Johnnie Walker World Championship of Golf in Jamaica, to the Grand Prix of Cleveland motor race, to *An Evening with José Carreras* in Bath.

From a one-office/one-client establishment in the 1960s, IMG has grown to become a multinational enterprise encompassing sixty-one offices in nineteen countries with over 1,500 full-time employees.

The Importance of the Global Perspective

I tell you all this not to brag, but to impress upon you the fact that travel and the broadened outlook it engenders will become increasingly important to all companies in the coming years. We are just beginning to see the emergence of a global business environment. The businesses that will survive and thrive in the 1990s and beyond must take an international perspective.

All of us are dealing constantly with other cultures and other vocabulary. Even when the language is the same, as is the case with England and the United States, the means of expression can be very different. A British friend of mine told me that our house in Orlando, Florida, although it was a very big house, was very homely. I was not offended; the man was paying me a compliment: in England "homely" means "homey." In America it means "ugly."

Another Englishman described a golfer's putt as very "nervy." "Nervy" in Britain means "nervous." "Nervy" in America means "gutsy." They're total opposites. George Bernard Shaw wasn't wrong when he said that "England and America are two countries separated by a common language."

These are just two tiny examples of the shades of meaning that occur between cultures. To understand what's going in business and in life in general, you have to catch the conversational nuances, which are highly variable from one part of the world to another. Although you can study books on business etiquette in the Far East or social customs in France or Italy, it's like trying to learn to play tennis by reading about it without ever getting out on the court with a racket in your hand. There's no better way to become more global yourself than by traveling and immersing yourself in another culture.

I think that doing so gives you a leg up on business dealings with people outside your geographic area and indeed on life in general. You don't really know and understand other people until you've been in their environment, talked to them, and learned from them. I'm always learning as I travel, not just from business associates, but from cab drivers, bellboys, and headwaiters. Travel not only gives you new insights on people in other nations and other regions of your own country, it also freshens your outlook on your own backyard.

Because of IMG's worldwide reach, I've become one of a new breed, a rapidly growing category of traveler: *the global commuter.* I have learned how to feel "at home" in many different countries—and in the air. A sedentary month for me is one when I fly fewer than 10,000 miles, the equivalent of four trips between London and Los Angeles. Last year I logged over 225,000 miles on business travel—just as I have for each of the past thirty years. I have eaten meals in more than 5,000 restaurants on six continents and stayed in hundreds of hotels in every major city.

Unlike the travel journalists who write books about travel, I have paid my own tab—always seeking the best value for myself and my company. My travel is always arranged with the practical aim of accomplishing business. I certainly am not a promoter or an apologist for the travel industry, as you will see in the following pages. However, I am not a dewy-eyed sentimentalist about "the good old days" of travel, either. In almost every area, the travel experience has improved in both comfort and efficiency over the years I have been on the road.

The "Good Old Days"

Thirty years ago is far enough back for many people to think of them as "the good old days." However, in travel as in other areas of life, the rosy memory of the "good old days" obscures the fact that for the traveling executive, those "good old days" weren't very good at all. When I started traveling on business, the flight from Sydney to Tokyo on an Electra prop-jet took twenty-six hours. We had to stop in Darwin and in Hong Kong, where we had to get off the plane for about five hours.

For those who have not been through as many takeoffs and landings as I have, I'll try to describe how far we've come since those first twenty-six-hour airborne marathons, and how much easier these last 225,000 miles were for me than the first 225,000 I racked up. Travel is a very change-intensive industry, and the speed of that change has been accelerating. It is very different today than it was even five years ago. It has changed, and by and large it has changed for the better.

Even taking terrorism into account, flying is a lot safer than it used to be. The equipment is more reliable, and computers help airlines establish regular maintenance and replacement schedules. Travelers are also far less vulnerable to the vagaries of weather systems and other natural phenomena.

I remember trying get an appointment with John DeLorean when he was head of Chevrolet. He was a friend, but his schedule was tightly booked and he was very hard to see. My schedule was busy too, but finally we set up a meeting in Detroit. I flew to Detroit from New York, but when we got there we were told that the airport was fogbound and we couldn't get in. We landed in Chicago instead.

When we finally got in I called DeLorean, of course. Since there were no phones on board back then, until I called and explained he thought I'd stood him up. Although he understood what had happened to me, he had no openings in his agenda any time soon. Our meeting had to be postponed for several months.

Today that just doesn't happen very often. With the advancement of computer technology in flight routing, instrument landings, and advancements in aircraft design, weather is much less a factor than it was. Bad weather, which commonly affected about twenty percent of our flights, now only rarely causes delays.

The airports themselves have become far more user-friendly. Not long ago they had all the appeal of a dingy bus station, oriented far more toward planes and baggage than toward people. The newest terminals are light, airy places that can handle large volumes of passengers quickly and efficiently. Airline frequent flyer clubs are very pleasant and offer wide-screen televisions, bars, complimentary drinks and hors d'oeuvres, and a chance for some real privacy in what can be a very public place.

Baggage comes off the plane more quickly than it did, and preferred baggage gets there even faster. Although it most assuredly is far from perfect, the computerized reservation process, including the ability to request a particular seat and to order a special meal, has become more efficient over the past few years. Clearing Customs, which was formerly very trying, is usually speedy now and no longer the brutalizing experience of just a few years ago.

Hotels have changed as well. The grand hotels have always been remarkable, but I believe that the experience for the average traveler has become better, because the quality of the average hotel room has been vastly improved. Now there's twenty-four-hour room service, pressing service, shoeshine service—everything you need for maintenance on the road. In the "good old days" before I could afford to stay in better hotels, it was not uncommon for the rooms to be dirty and outfitted with plumbing and electricity that worked fitfully, if at all.

There is also the new, enlarged role of the telephone in business life. Thirty years ago they were almost prehistoric. An international call was an adventure, and not a pleasant one at that. When we first began representing South Africa's Gary Player I tried to place a call from Johannesburg to the United States. There was no such thing as direct dialing. You had to call an overseas operator, and they were always engaged. It would take hours to reach one. Once you got one, you had to book a time to make your phone call. In effect you had to make an appointment with the operator to call someone, something no business person would put up with today. The connection, if the call actually went through, was often dismal.

The Specialness of Travel

Although no one misses these aspects of the "good old days," the one wonderful thing that too many of us seem to have lost from those days of long ago is a sense of the specialness of travel. In the past, a large part of that specialness was the wonder that you could do it at all. Except for entertainers and sports teams, frequent business travel was relatively uncommon. It used to be that a trip was something that you saved up for vacation. A family stayed home all year and went on one or two eagerly awaited long trips a year. However, the vacation experience did not truly begin until they arrived at their destination. People lived in a state of suspended animation while en route—the travel itself wasn't part of the experience.

Today the rigors of the past are long forgotten, and the business-as-usual nature of travel, for business and for pleasure, is both what's right and what's wrong with it. Travel is so commonplace that people no longer look forward to it. Too many travelers start anticipating the hassle with the baggage, the hassle of standing in line, the delays, the uncomfortable seats, and lousy food. They don't compare their experience to the way travel used to be, but rather to the comfort and convenience of staying at home or in the office.

I firmly believe that expectations create their own reality. Those who constantly measure the adventurous experience of travel against the comfortable familiarity of staying home are doomed to perpetual disappointment. People who approach travel wringing their hands with trepidation in effect sabotage themselves. Because they are not looking forward to their trip, they don't plan adequately for it. In a very real sense, the fact that they leave expecting the worst goes a long way toward guaranteeing a bad experience.

On the other hand, if you look at travel as an invigorating or exhilarating possibility, you can create that immensely positive reality as well. Your outlook helps you make what could be a drudgery-type business trip into an experience that you can remember with pleasure.

Unlike many frequent flyers, I still genuinely enjoy traveling. I'm traveling at least as much as I'm at home. I look forward to it, and I plan some joy and positive experience into each trip. I travel for a living and in a sense I live to travel. I'm not Pollyanna, but I've never lost that sense of the specialness of travel, and that's one of the reasons why I still love life on the road.

The Positive Aspects of Business Travel

How do you approach every business trip with a positive attitude? First you have to realize that going to see someone in any business dynamic is in and of itself a positive thing. There is nobody in business who doesn't appreciate it when someone makes the effort to come see them. It doesn't matter whether it's across the ocean, or from New York to Chicago, or from New York to Princeton, New Jersey. In all of my previous books—from *What They Don't Teach You at Harvard Business School* to *On Selling*—I have emphasized the importance of that person-to-person contact. In a global business environment driven by fax machines and cellular telephones, the personal touch takes on even greater value. "You can't fax a handshake," the executive travel motto at Boeing Aircraft, says it all.

Far too many business travelers counterbalance that highly positive aspect of a trip by thinking about the negatives—the hassles of travel itself. Business travel can be fun, enjoyable, and relaxing, even as it accomplishes its business objectives. I believe that putting some enjoyment into business travel makes good business sense.

Hit the Ground Running is designed to help the executive traveler make travel, which is essential, a positive experience. It contains my best advice on how to put the enjoyment back into business travel, plus insider tips on enjoyable travel experiences in twenty-five worldwide business destinations.

Chapter I
Travel Should Be a
Life-Enhancing Pleasure

Travelers are always discoverers, especially those who travel by air. There are no signposts in the sky to show that a man [or a woman] has passed that way before.

Anne Morrow Lindbergh

I can still recall the thrill of traveling with my parents on long train trips as a child. My father was in the publishing business—farm journals and magazines. We lived in Chicago, but Dad traveled frequently on business to New York and Topeka, Kansas, and occasionally to Washington, D.C., to see Senator Capper, who owned the publishing company. My mother used to take vacation trips every year and would often plan out her trips years ahead of time. She knew what she was going to be doing every minute. She would figure out which hotels were the good ones and which rooms in those hotels were the most quiet. She knew what tours she was going to be on and where she would eat. She was an amazing traveler.

Whole worlds of new sights and smells, new people, new experiences opened up to me on those trips with my parents. I switched from watching the American landscape flashing by outside to studying the array of other passengers on the train with equal fascination. I returned from each journey like an explorer—laden with treasures and filled with exotic tales. At home, when my parents would begin to discuss another trip, I always reacted with enthusiastic excitement.

Traveling out beyond the narrow confines of our own homes and neighborhoods is a childhood thrill that most of us remember with great pleasure. But for many adults, years of hectic, repetitious, mandatory business trips have taken the pleasure out of travel. The majority of business people regard travel as an unpleasant duty, a drudgery that comes with the territory. You can see their long faces at boarding gates and baggage carousels all over the world.

Contemporary Travel Is No Bed of Roses

There is a lot of evidence to support the unhappy folks who feel that business travel is a misery. Long periods away from friends and families, traffic-jammed highways, crowded airport terminals, uncomfortable airplane flights, bad food, lack of exercise, impersonal hotel rooms, stressful schedules, hostile "service industry" personnel, sleepless nights, shrinking expense accounts—the litany of legitimate complaints goes on. There are very real impediments to enjoying business travel.

There are impediments to enjoying other aspects of life, too. However, I enjoy my life, my business, and my frequent travel. Perhaps that is because I constantly reexamine my goals and objectives to be assured of where I am headed and to enjoy the satisfaction of accomplishing those goals. I design my life, my work, and my travel to be enjoyable. Sometimes that means redefining impediments, problems, or hassles as "problem-solving opportunities" which challenge my resourcefulness. Sometimes that means redistributing my work or travel load over a schedule with extra hours added to it. Sometimes—as much as a corporate executive hates to admit it—that means spending extra money. Ultimately I find that enjoyment in almost any area of life has a lot to do with my own attitude.

Attitude Adjustment

If you are reading this book, you are already committed to finding ways to make your own travel more effective and pleasant. I want to show you how this can be done at all levels of business experience. I will demonstrate how modest adjustments in your goal definitions, your thinking, your scheduling, and your travel strategies can reap big rewards in satisfaction and efficiency. There's no magic to my methods. In fact, much of what you will read in this book is common sense judgment that could be applied to many areas of endeavor. In my book, *What They Don't Teach You at Harvard Business School,* I pointed out the sort of simple ideas that get lost in the abstractions of marketing theories and management techniques. The same common-sense approach to planning your business travel works, too. You just have to apply it.

Willingness to change, to learn, to adjust old attitudes is always more difficult than you think. You may have to consider the possibility that you are setting yourself up for misery with your present travel techniques. You may have to confront the fact that like most people, you waste valuable time that could be better used. You may have to consider that you have stuck yourself in an unpleasant rut. So get ready to examine your attitudes towards travel, to reorganize your travel planning, to maximize your travel efficiency, to add some new experiences to your schedule, and to take responsibility for making your business travel fun again.

The Six Most Common Complaints About Business Travel

In surveys of business travelers worldwide, the same complaints appear year after year. I suspect you will agree with most of them. I certainly do. But after we grumble together, let's consider how the savvy executive deals with these problems.

- Separation from home, family, and daily routines
- Stress of unfamiliar surroundings and hassle of life on the road
- Time wasted in transit and standing in lines
- Discomfort of airplane seats and hotel accommodations
- Bad food
- Expense account pressure

The "Dorothy" Syndrome

Most of this book will deal with getting the most out of business travel by attacking Items 2–6 on the above list, but I believe it is important here to address the number one issue—separation from family.

As Dorothy discovered in *The Wizard of Oz*, even the most magical travel experience is unpleasant if you miss your home and family. According to a study of 700 business travelers conducted by Harvard University psychiatrist Barrie Greiff, M.D., for Hyatt Hotels, separation from home and family is one of the primary dissatisfactions of life on the road. Everyone misses their loved ones, and even grownups are subject to homesickness. The study found that the perceived conflict between career and family is difficult for most people to handle.

Because my wife, Betsy Nagelsen, plays professional tennis and I am able determine my own travel schedule, I'm fortunate that she can accompany me on many of my trips. For executives with young children, however, I realize that this is not possible. Although repeated long absences will strain family relationships under almost any circumstances, there are ways for the traveling executive to **take a little of home with you, and leave a little of yourself at home.**

Schedule Your Trips Carefully

Marvin Bush, son of former president George Bush and an investment banker in Washington, D.C., plans his travel to avoid family dislocations. "I travel about five days a month, but I don't like to miss things at home," he says. "I've got two kids, aged seven and three. There is no meeting that's more important to me than an event that's important to my children—a birthday, a school play, the first soccer game. Unless it's *really* something that can't be changed, I tell associates and business partners that I just can't be there at that time. Nine times out of ten, the meeting can be rescheduled. That way, when I do go away, I can leave with a clean conscience."

No Surprise Departures

Real travel benefits come from planning ahead. This advance planning also benefits family members who will stay at home. Kids do much better adjusting to the absence of a parent when they have time to anticipate that absence. **Announce your trip to your family** as far in advance as you know of it. Especially with small children, mention your trip repeatedly. Use your trip as a way to teach them about things they will learn about in school:

- Count down the weeks and days on a calendar
- Get out a globe or an atlas and show them where they live and where you are going
- If you are traveling overseas, show them your passport and foreign currency

I don't advocate this for everyone, but one dedicated dad even lets his kids help him pack. A child's packing certainly won't win any awards for efficiency or neatness, but it doesn't take much manual dexterity to put shoes into a flannel shoe bag, take a prefolded shirt from the laundry and put it in the outside pocket of your carry-on bag, or make sure that your toothbrush and toothpaste are in your toiletries kit. Psychologists suggest that by helping with packing, children become acclimated to your departure—and the idea of your eventual return.

Pieces of Home

Although spouses and children must cope with the absence of a loved one from familiar surroundings, don't underestimate the potential effects of homesickness on you, the business traveler. Take a small album of family snapshots along, and keep it updated. I have an associate whose wife always puts a going-away card or other memento in his luggage—somewhere. From time to time the location is obvious, but more often she's very cleverly hidden it. She also has their daughter make a card for Dad and tucks that into the suitcase as well.

Pieces of You

In the same vein, a traveling executive who is also a mother leaves little evidences of her own eventual return in unexpected places—a new set of crayons in a kindergartner's lunchbox, a good luck charm in a basketball shoe or ballet slipper, a note in her husband's sock drawer, a tape-recorded message to "clean your room" in an older child's Walkman. Most traveling parents bring back presents for family members. These don't need to be extravagant—some business travelers find a collectible item such as a doll or baseball cap or food item and begin building a collection that they add to with each trip.

The most personal piece of yourself you can give to your family while you're away, however, is your voice. Before leaving, **make a date for a phone call,** and make sure you keep it.

Rethinking Time Away From Home

There is no doubt that separation from home, family, and personal contacts is a far more emotional issue for business people than concern about being away from the office. Parents, particularly parents of young children, are already filled with guilt about not spending enough time with their kids. Working couples often resent how often work keeps them apart, and travel will only exacerbate this problem. Unmarried young professionals are more susceptible to homesickness, the need for contact with friends, and simply the comfortable surroundings of their homes than they would care to admit.

Although family and friends should come first, career is an important part of most people's lives. And a career that requires business travel can share space with those personal connections, if you have a clear assessment of your life objectives and design your life to attain them. If travel makes you more effective in your work, then that same travel makes you a more effective breadwinner with a more secure future for your family. The well-balanced business traveler sees his or her time on the road as part of a life plan that has room for many objectives.

Opportunities for Personal Growth

I'm in my sixties now and I have already lived a very active and interesting life, but there is not a day I can remember that I haven't tried to learn something new. Sometimes new insights arise from the daily flow of information and people I encounter in my travels. Sometimes my natural curiosity will lead me into a new area. Sometimes I am taken by surprise in some new— and, I hope, pleasant—way. But most often, I learn something new every day because I plan to.

For example, over many years of traveling to New York City, I have developed a list of favorite restaurants I return to regularly. I enjoy the food and service, and the restaurant managers have come to know me over the years. But I realized that this comfortable rut was keeping me from having new dining experiences in a city with thousands of restaurants. So I made a private rule for myself that for every time I went back to one of my old favorites, I had to try three new restaurants.

Have I had some disappointments? Naturally. I have also had many new dishes that I never tried before, seen new wine lists, and enjoyed a variety of unusual restaurant ambiances. A few of those new places have even been added to my "favorites" list.

I don't even regret the disappointments, because usually I learned something new about what does (or doesn't) make a restaurant work.

I believe in the value of business meetings over meals. Seeing your business associates in surroundings outside of their offices often gives you a different relationship with them. I think you can tell something about a person by how he or she orders a meal or deals with the social amenities of seating at a table. By going to restaurants that I have not tried before, I take a bit of a risk. But the opportunity to combine a new dining experience with a business discussion gives "added value" to my life.

There are dozens of other examples of how travelers can enhance their lives while on business trips. I try to arrange a game of golf if I am traveling to a destination with a particularly good golf course. I'll seek out information about theatres, concerts, or museum shows in cities where I am doing business. Sometimes I just want to take a break from my business routine for a quick visit to a historic or cultural monument. I have a friend who tries to visit the zoo in whatever city he is visiting. Does that sound silly for a grown man? Not to me. This opportunity for self-fulfillment gives him a bit of exercise, a respite from the stress of a hectic schedule, and something to look forward to in every destination.

Breaking Routines, Creating Small Adventures

For business travelers who have trapped themselves in an unpleasant routine, one of the best exercises I can suggest is to **define pleasure for yourself.** Try making a list of the things that you like to do and see how they might fit into your travel plans. Some suggestions:

- Reading a good novel
- Listening to music on a CD player (not the airlines' ten channels of Muzak)

- Writing in a journal
- Playing video games or computer bridge or crossword puzzles
- Seeing some architectural highpoints of a city
- Looking up old friends or classmates

At this point, I can almost hear some of my readers objecting: "My company doesn't send me on trips to enjoy a tourist's vacation. I don't have time to entertain myself. I barely have time to get to all of the meetings I must attend in a day!" Possibly so. However, when it comes to busy schedules, there are few people who can surpass me.

I own my company and I want to maximize every business opportunity I have. I also know that I will have a more positive attitude if I have given myself a late-morning half hour to stroll through a historic neighborhood en route to a business lunch. I know that I will arrive more refreshed, more alert, more relaxed than if I had just come from another business meeting. To me, that is time well spent—and all too many people who think that they have busy, efficient schedules waste valuable time that could be devoted to such moments of self-fulfillment.

Finding Precious Hours by Eliminating Wasted Time in Your Schedule

Business people who complain that there is a great deal of wasted time in the travel process are correct. And, usually, they are to blame for the waste. Even the most capable business people lose time, energy, money, and opportunities for personal growth and pleasure on the road because they are not nearly as effective and efficient while traveling as they are at home.

The most common cause of wasted time is poor planning. Managers who know how to keep a tight and efficient schedule in their offices seem to fall apart on the road. In Chapter II, I explain the basics of planning and suggest some time-saving tricks that have worked well for me. For starters, however, let's spell out The Business Traveler's Golden Rule: **Never stand in line.**

Never Stand in Line

When friends complain about how much time they waste standing in lines at airports or hotels, I can only shake my head in amazement. With sensible planning, there is no reason a business traveler should ever have to stand in line. Before you depart for the airport, you should have your tickets and probably your boarding passes in your pocket. Ideally, you have packed everything you need in carry-on luggage. If not, on domestic flights, use the curbside baggage check. Have a tip, at least a dollar per bag, visible in your hand. Service will be quick.

If there is no other alternative to bringing luggage or identification documents to the check-in desk—luggage or passports for an international flight, for example—you will need to be a bit more creative. In later chapters, I will give you the details of how business travelers can take advantage of frequent flyer clubs and airlines' Special Services divisions to avoid the long lines of tourists at the main airport ticketing desks. However, my point is that there are a variety of ways to deal with this hurdle, and you must consider them before you embark or you will be left standing there while the USC Marching Band checks in.

Long before you arrive at the departure gate for your flight, you should have confirmed your seat assignment through a travel agent or a call to the airline. If you are not already a member of the airline club, your travel agent can often arrange for you to be admitted on a one-time guest pass. There, you can check in, have a cup of coffee, and wait for your flight in the civilized atmosphere of a lounge hidden from the noise and chaos of the gate waiting area. Also, the club desk will issue boarding passes if you don't already have them. If you have extra time, in the club business areas you have easy access to telephones, computers, or faxes to continue doing business.

Excuse Me, I Think You're in My Seat

In general, I prefer to board the plane as soon as possible. I always inquire with the airline about preboarding privileges. Sometimes preboarding is routinely offered to first-class and business-class travelers; sometimes the Special Services division can assist. This allows me to be certain I have possession of my assigned seat, to let the flight attendants know about any special requests I might have, to get organized for the flight, and get to work. Other experienced travelers tell me that they wait until the rush is over and board at the last minute. They avoid standing in the jetway (if they have not been able to arrange preboarding), but they risk the possibility of finding another passenger holding a boarding card with the identical seat number sitting in their seat. How this happens as frequently as it does in the computer era is difficult to explain. But it happens, and you don't want it to happen to you—in this instance, unfortunately, possession is nine-tenths of the law.

Forget the Red Carpet—Show Me to the Room

The same travel strategies I use in dealing with airlines apply to hotels. Check information about the location and facilities of the hotels in a city you are visiting. Make direct arrangements with the hotel desk. Make sure that the hotel knows who you are, and what you want in your room, and that you will have "express check-in." Almost every hotel is familiar with the business traveler's complaint about long check-in lines, and most of them are prepared to get you in and out quickly if you provide them with credit information in advance. Sometimes this entails joining the hotel chain's "frequent guest club," usually at no cost.

Solving Life's Little Puzzles

I certainly don't like to find myself in potentially time-wasting situations any more than the next traveler does, but I have learned to react to them as one of Life's Little Puzzles. Instead of getting angry or aggravated—which might be reasonable enough reactions in a travel hassle—I find myself searching my memory bank, alerting my mental resources, preparing to meet a challenge. Keeping cool and coming up with unconventional solutions to those annoying problems has proven effective. I remind myself that I have already avoided many pitfalls of the traveler's life. If I can deal with this glitch in the program, my trip will continue smoothly. And generally it does.

What enables me to solve this sampling of Life's Little Problems more calmly and efficiently than the person with smoke coming out of his or her ears? Attitude. I'm confident that I have the resources and the know-how to come up with an answer. I'm on a roll of positive travel experiences. I'm having a good trip and one harried, overworked desk clerk is not going to get in my way. **Don't get angry. Get creative.** (Trying to Get Even with a belated letter of complaint is rarely satisfying.)

Set Your Own Agenda

Ultimately you are in control of your own business travel experiences. If you establish the self-fulfilling prophecy that your next trip will be a hectic misery (just like all the rest), there's no doubt that a cloud of gloom will follow your footsteps. However, if you would like to make your next trip fun, enjoyable, and relaxing—even as it accomplishes your business objectives—then you've come to the right book.

In the following chapters I will teach you some travel tricks from my experiences and give you the strategic tools to develop your own plans for more productive and pleasurable trips. I'm going to urge you to take charge of this area of your life, to set your own agenda, and to see how putting some enjoyment into business travel makes good business sense. I'm going to show you how to "personalize" your travel and to let your friends in other cities improve your business. I'm going to force you to think carefully about when to enjoy travel luxuries—and when to skip them. I'm going to demonstrate how you keep your focus on your business objectives on the road, despite distractions. Most of all, I'm going to teach you about detailed, meticulous planning—the not-so-secret weapon of my success.

Chapter II
Planning the Business Trip—
Do You Hit the Road, or
Does the Road Hit You?

Good travel planning can avert many travel disasters, but there is often little that even the most agile executive traveler can do to salvage problems created by poor or incomplete planning. Sadly, many executives believe they've "planned" everything once they have airline tickets, a hotel reservation, and ground transportation. However, virtually no input of their own has gone into the decisions about what airline they are flying, what flight they are on, what hotel they are staying at, what room they receive, or what ground transportation they will be using when they arrive. Most executives rely on secretaries or aides who book reservations for plane trips, hotels, and rental cars and type out an itinerary. For the hit-the-ground-running business traveler, this is far from sufficient.

This chapter demonstrates exactly what comprehensive planning for a business trip entails, how to gather information and do your spadework before leaving, how to know which travel arrangements can be delegated, and which details to handle yourself. It will also discuss how to avoid being a travel victim by forcing others to be prepared—how to schedule meetings for your own convenience, how to schedule time for personal reward and enjoyment, and how to pack. In this chapter I discuss a bit of how to get a better price break on some aspects of travel. However, I'll deal more with that in Chapter VII, "Insider Techniques in the Trenches."

The business traveler is a successful executive who has learned how to delegate authority. In making travel arrangements, however, many executives err by leaving the details of their trip to lower-level staff, or to unsophisticated travel agents. In this electronic age, many executives have never *seen* their travel agent. A corporate travel office is a little more concerned, because they are more readily held accountable, but often the personnel that staff it are not nearly as knowledgeable or demanding as you are yourself.

Travel planning is not trivial or menial—it's the difference between a grim trip and an enjoyable one. The executive traveler knows that choice of hotel rooms and flight times should never be left entirely up to someone who is not getting on the plane, not familiar with the executive's travel preferences, or not familiar enough with travel destinations to intelligently be of help.

For example, someone who has never traveled to London's Heathrow Airport on an overnight flight doesn't realize that many of these flights land at the same time in the early morning. There could be a thousand people waiting to go through Immigration. There are, of course, ways to beat this problem, but many travel bookers aren't going to be familiar with them.

The first rule of trip planning sounds obvious but is all too often ignored: **Know something about where you are going.** The executive traveler maintains an active interest in travel in general and in his or her most frequent destinations in particular.

I make a point of maintaining an up-to-date library of travel guides from a variety of sources. Most larger cities have bookstores which specialize in travel guides. I regularly read newsletters and magazines like *Andrew Harper's Hideaway Report, Passport, Savoir Faire* (put out by Air France), *Condé Nast Traveler*, and *Frequent Flyer*, which keep better tabs on rapidly changing conditions than guidebooks that are updated annually at best.

I also keep a "go to" file for each city I visit, whether it's New York, Houston, Seattle, or Singapore. When I see an article about a hotel I'd like to stay at or an interesting new restaurant, I either clip the article or make a note in the file.

Block Out Your Time

The second rule of planning a trip is the one that is most often overlooked: **Block out your time.** Too often, overburdened executives don't start thinking about what they are going to do at their destination until they are on the plane. But if you organize your days on the road before you leave, you can meet all your business objectives and also have time to plan some fun into the trip. By "fun" I don't mean a boozy good time in the hotel cocktail lounge. Fun to me means something which nourishes and enriches you personally, on the inside. It may be culturally rewarding, such as taking in a new musical on Broadway, or educational, such as touring the antebellum mansions north of New Orleans, or pure relaxation, such as tacking on an extra day to a trip to San Francisco to enjoy the Wine Country.

I can visualize a lot of you shaking your heads at this—there's no time for this kind of activity when you travel, and to do these things is somehow "cheating" the company. Wrong. That's what real executive travel is all about. There is time for these activities if you plan them into your trip, if you are efficient in the use of your time during the business day, and if you know how to avoid being a victim at the airport and hotel. This enables you to conserve your most valuable resource, your time, and make it work to your own advantage.

When Saving Time, Think Small

Time saved in small increments all adds up. For example, our New York office is located on 71st Street between Madison and Fifth Avenues. Traffic on Madison flows one-way uptown (north); Fifth is one-way downtown (south). When I'm leaving for the airport, ordinarily I'll have the car or cab wait for me in front of my hotel or office. Our front door on 71st in New York, however, is just thirty yards west of Madison. If the car is going to pick me up in front of the building, the driver has to circle the entire block—down to Fifth, wait for a light, get into the

Fifth Avenue traffic, wait for another light, and circle around to be headed in the right direction (uptown) to get to the airport. It can take as much as ten minutes just to get back to where you were before, and all for thirty yards. For that ten minutes, it's worth it to me to go downstairs, walk the thirty yards and meet the car pointed in the right direction, heading north up Madison. With that extra ten minutes, I can stay in a meeting a little longer, make a couple of phone calls, or finish dictating a memo. If I can engineer a few more of these ten-minute timesavers into each day, I can get in a little tennis, some worthwhile leisure reading, or a nap.

Long before you step on the plane, you should have made your choices about the use of your time. You should have made a calendar for yourself of your activities during your trip, including all your meetings, lunches, and dinners.

The first thing I try to do when I know I have a trip is to prioritize the people that I really want to see. Some people are hard to get a hold of, so I get in contact with them first, and let them know when I'll be in town, as far in advance as possible. I put people who I really want to see but who generally are more available next, followed by people who might be nice to see, and by people in my own office staff who can work around my schedule. I do this weeks, even months in advance of my trip.

Use Who You Are

Rule number three is one that business travelers perhaps don't realize or fully understand: **Use who you are.** Many executives underestimate how much clout they have with hotels, airlines, and restaurants, in part because they leave the details of their trip to aides who have little clout themselves.

Let me make it clear how much power you have. As a business traveler, you are the very client and customer that airlines, restaurants, and hotels value most. Business travelers are repeat customers, and repeat customers are highly prized, especially in these difficult times. The effort to secure repeat customers is at the foundation of any frequent flyer or frequent stayer program. It's an attempt to establish your loyalty to a particular airline or hotel chain.

You really are number one, not just with Hertz, but with everyone else in the travel industry. Executives on the road are the major profit generators for a large segment of the industry. Without the business traveler, hotels would be largely empty Monday through Friday; better restaurants would go belly up; and airlines would be stuck trying to turn a profit on deeply discounted coach fares for families of five in plaid Bermuda shorts. Only about one-fifth of the passengers on a full flight sit in business or first-class. These passengers, however, bring in as much as two-thirds of the revenue for the airlines, according to *Traveler* magazine. Your position as the preferred customer gives you added clout when making reservations, but it's your job to know how to use it.

Making Reservations

Using a Travel Agent

Most people, even sophisticated business travelers, don't really understand how travel agents work. Just because you don't have to pay them a commission doesn't mean that these folks are working for free. Travel agents have to make their money somehow. If the traveler isn't paying the agency's commission, someone else is.

Who? The airlines you fly and hotels where you spend the night. In most businesses it's customary to believe that you work for the people who pay your salary or commission. Travel agents are unusual in that they work not for the vendors of travel services who pay them, but for clients—business executives and other travelers—who don't.

Because of the highly complex airline fare system, even independent travel agents are dependent on computerized reservation systems. These systems are owned in whole or in part by various airlines, and many have a built-in bias in favor of the flagship carrier. If you call a travel agent for information about an early flight tomorrow to New York from San Francisco, and the agent informs you that the first flight out is a United flight, it's a pretty good bet that their agency computer is hooked into the Apollo system, which is owned by United Airlines. If the first flight mentioned is an American flight, it's probable that their computer is part of the Sabre system, which is owned by American Airlines. United's Apollo and American's Sabre reservations systems list their own flights ahead of flights of their competitors leaving at the same time. When an agent starts reading you a list of options, these are the flights that will be at the top of the list. This doesn't make the system "evil" or "corrupt," it just means that you as a travel consumer should know which system your agent uses and whose flights are going to get top billing.

Pick Your Travel Agent as Carefully as Your Surgeon

You should audition a travel agent like a doctor before surgery. How does the executive traveler find a good travel agency? At a minimum, your agency should be a member of ASTA (the American Society of Travel Agents), and should be fully automated. It goes without saying that executive travel should be a sizable part of their business. Booking a business trip through an agency that specializes in cruises or in adventure vacation trips to remote destinations is not unlike consulting a neurosurgeon to remove a wart, or a gynecologist for a coronary bypass. When you find a business-oriented travel agency, let them know your standards and how they must perform. If you're a volume traveler, the agency needs to know what you will and will not accept, and what the conditions of your continued business will be.

No matter what the credentials of the agency, from the perspective of the executive traveler, your travel agency is only as good as the agent who is handling your account. There should be just a couple of agents within a firm handling travel arrangements for your business, unless your company is large or your travel plans are very intricate and change frequently.

Two Travel Agents Are Better Than One

Once you have found a reliable agency, it's best not to rely on one agent exclusively. Having more than one agent who knows your business is good self-defense. If your agent moves on and someone unfamiliar is handling your account, you have every right to question him or her closely to make sure they are experienced enough to do the job. If the new agent is unsatisfactory, talk to the owner of the agency and ask to be assigned to a more seasoned travel veteran. Failing that, take your business elsewhere.

Good travel agents are part tightwad, and know how to navigate the maze of fares to get you the best possible flight at the best possible rate. Get to know your travel agent, and make sure he or she has a computerized up-to-date personal profile of your travel preferences and dislikes. Give your agent feedback when you get back from a destination you've never visited before—not just if something went wrong, but if things went terrific, too.

The very best travel agent for the executive traveler is also part bulldog, part geographer, part *artiste*, part computer genius, and part mindreader. That agent knows whether you meant Portland, Oregon, or Portland, Maine; the Plaza or the Plaza Athenée; Paris, Texas, or Paris, France; Orly or Charles de Gaulle; Cairo, Illinois, or Cairo, Egypt; 8 A.M. or 8 P.M.; Lima, Ohio, or Lima, Peru; O'Hare or Midway, *or knows enough to ask if the instructions are unclear.* Because these kinds of misunderstandings are not uncommon, **always look at your tickets *before* you leave the travel agency.**

Booking Your Flight, or, There and Back Again

You Are Your Own Best Travel Agent

Even the best travel agent in the best travel agency can't work miracles without your active participation. Although I rely on my inhouse staff and on travel agencies for ticketing, my best travel agent looks me in the bathroom mirror every morning. I know my needs and my travel plans better than anyone else—or at least I ought to. Only I know how much leeway there is in my itinerary, or whether going a day sooner or a day later makes more sense than my original target flight date. I can determine whether flying through Oakland rather than San Francisco will save me a couple of hours. I can choose whether I'd prefer to take the train overnight or sleep in a hotel and catch a plane in the morning. I will almost always give myself more options than an agent with a multitude of clients, any number of whom may be clamoring for service at the same time. In that regard I am a travel agent with a clientele of one—me.

Although I am a demanding traveler, I am probably the easiest client my travel agency has. Frequently I'll even have my staff make the reservations directly with the airline, so that all the agency has to do is issue my ticket. If you handle your flight arrangements in this manner, it's essential that you get your locator number from your airline. The locator number is generally a six letter or six letter and number code. It's the way the computer finds you in the system. Once you give that code to the travel agency, that's all the information they need to write up your ticket. This means that all you have to do is pick up your ticket and boarding pass at the agency—without standing in line. Again, however, **always look at your tickets *before* you leave the travel agency.** The time to discover a ticketing mistake is as soon as possible after it's been made. If a staff assistant or family member is picking up the ticket, make sure that they know what the ticket is supposed to say before they walk out the door.

The Skyguide: *The Executive Traveler's Best Friend*

I find my preferred flight in the *Skyguide*, which is the executive traveler's best friend. No business traveler should be without it. The *Skyguide* lists commercial flights of all airlines serving North America, including flights to major overseas destinations. An annual subscription costs $45, but the first time the

Skyguide gets you out of a jam at the airport when a flight is delayed, it's worth every penny.

The *Skyguide* gives you power because it gives you control over information about potential flights. Your choices are in front of you. With the *Skyguide*, I don't have to ask the travel agent what time the flights are leaving, I tell them what flight I want. How do I know which flight I want? Very often I'm not entirely sure, so I try to leave myself some options.

Don't Be a Victim of Airline Scheduling

I'm a great double booker of flights, or triple or quadruple booker. For executives, celebrities, and other travelers with uncertain schedules, it's an act of self-defense and quite common. On a recent trip to Los Angeles, I thought I was leaving on Thursday morning, but I also booked myself on a Thursday noon and Friday morning flight on the same airline. I always use different initials or slightly different spellings of my last name so they don't pick me up on the computer.

Airlines hate this, of course, but business travelers continue to do it because from our perspective it's better to double book than to get stuck or not get the flight that we want. It's a matter of attitude: The executive traveler plans ahead to use airlines, hotels, and restaurants to suit his or her own convenience, rather than being trapped as a "victim" of procedures and policies designed for the convenience of service providers.

Schedule requirements narrow the choices of which airlines I fly to particular destinations, but they are not the only considerations. Think creatively about where you clear U.S. Customs. Almost anywhere is better than New York. If you are a U.S. citizen returning to the northeast or north central United States and need to make a connecting flight, you are far better off flying into Canada and connecting than flying into Kennedy and connecting. Canadian Customs from Europe is much easier and quicker. For our staff returning to Cleveland, it's about the same timewise to fly London/New York/Cleveland as to fly London/Toronto/Cleveland. However, Toronto Customs is much easier than New York Customs. It's a much more pleasant place to fly into. Toronto considers you a transit passenger. Moreover, having been a transit passenger in Toronto, you are now cleared by American Customs when you land in Cleveland as if you were coming from Canada rather than coming from Europe. It's a much smoother homecoming.

Some Gates Are More Convenient Than Others

I can also save a lot of time and avoid unpleasantness by picking the airline with the most convenient gate and terminal. If I'm flying into O'Hare in Chicago, I'll use Delta because their gates are about 60 yards from curbside. Those assigned to United and American are miles away. If you have to change planes, it's worse. It always seems as if someone with a sadistic sense of humor has maximized the distance between your arrival gate and your departure gate—arrival Concourse H, Gate 12; departure Concourse K, Gate 16, about half a mile away. In New York's LaGuardia, Delta and Northwest have their own terminal, as does USAir, which recently opened LaGuardia's newest and most efficient terminal. The baggage claim is quicker and more modern. If you are being met, pick-up at the exit is also much more convenient.

Fly the Flag

On international flights, my general rule is: **fly the flag,** meaning the airline homebased in my destination. For overtaxed foreign airports, it makes it more likely that I'll escape one of my pet hates—being bused to a plane whose "gate" is in the middle of the tarmac. When you think about it, it's just common sense. Air France will have more pull at DeGaulle than British Airways. Coming into Tokyo, Japan Airlines will almost always have a better gate than Delta.

As an additional benefit, since most citizens tend to fly the airline of their own nationality, these flights usually carry fewer foreign visitors. So what? So large numbers of Japanese citizens are lined up in that part of Customs and Immigration reserved for returning nationals, while the much smaller group of foreigners (including me) is going through a much shorter Customs and Immigration queue. These are factors that pay time benefits for the executive traveler, factors that aides and travel agents don't ordinarily consider.

Fly Against the Hub

Within the United States, however, it doesn't follow that you'll get better service at an airline's hub airport. In fact, my general rule within the United States is **fly against the hub.** The Hub Theory of airline management is designed to cut personnel costs for the airlines. As such, it works to their benefit, not necessarily to yours. Often too many flights from a single airline converge on a hub city at the same time. Frequently there aren't enough baggage handlers to process the luggage from all flights expeditiously. You are usually better off on an airline that doesn't have tons of flights coming into a particular city than on one of eight flights landing at the same time. You have a much better chance of getting your bags sooner if the baggage from your flight is the only luggage being offloaded.

Fly Alternative Airports

The *Skyguide* also gives you information about alternative airports. I'm a big fan of alternative airports. They generally are less congested, and often are more convenient to your ground destination.

Much of the misery of air travel occurs at the airport, and some airports rank far higher on the misery index than others. As airport congestion increases, selection of a metropolitan airport becomes more and more important. In some cities, such as Denver or Milan, you have only one choice (Stapleton in the former, Malpensa in the latter), and it's not a good one. If you are headed directly for these cities you're stuck, but you can certainly avoid going *through* them if you are connecting onward to another destination. In a growing number of locations, selection of a different airport (which is often smaller and newer than the major field serving the city) yields great dividends to the executive traveler.

Oakland International Airport is probably the best-kept secret in the Bay Area surrounding San Francisco. It has one of the best batting averages for on-time flights in the United States. Moreover, not only is it a faster and easier drive from Oakland International into downtown San Francisco than from SFO, you can also get into the city by taking an airport shuttle that hooks up with BART, the area's mass transit system. The airport layout is attractively and efficiently designed. You can get from the gate and into a rental car in fewer steps than it takes to change planes at O'Hare in Chicago.

Because delays at O'Hare are frequent, many executive travelers are rediscovering Midway Airport, which is closer to the Loop. In Los Angeles, Burbank is a better choice than LAX. Unfortunately, Burbank, Midway, and Oakland are pretty much limited to domestic flights. Passengers traveling internationally are generally stuck with the biggest, most overloaded airport. That's not necessarily the case in New York. Although most transatlantic carriers use JFK, Virgin Atlantic and SAS fly into Newark, where airspace is less congested and Customs lines are shorter. And then there's San Jose. American flies a nonstop into San Jose from Tokyo. Since it's the only international flight landing at that time, Customs is a breeze.

European airport congestion can be even more serious than the same problem in the United States, particularly at overloaded fields like Heathrow, Frankfurt, and Milan's Malpensa. However, there are new and upgraded airports—generally speaking, well-connected to mass transit—which simplify making connections. The new Munich-Strauss Airport is far more efficient than Munich-Reim. International service to Chicago, New York, and Tokyo is available.

When I have the choice, I prefer going through Schiphol in Amsterdam or Kastrup in Copenhagen to dealing with Frankfurt. Kastrup is the domain of the very capable and business-oriented SAS, with thirty check-in counters, free baggage carts, and a squadron of little scooters. Officially the scooters are for the use of airport personnel, but more than once I've observed a latecomer borrow one to zip to the gate on time.

In addition to alternate airports mentioned above, keep in mind that **your best alternate airport in some cities might be the train station.** This will be discussed in more detail in Chapter IX.

Aisle vs. Window: The Benefits of Contemplation

It's fine to leave the actual process of making reservations to staff, if they know your preferences. It's your job to make your preferences known. I know many traveling executives prefer aisle seats, especially in coach. It's easier to get up and move around, and you can sprint for the exit and be the first one off the plane.

Nevertheless, I always ask for a window seat. It's a lot more private. No one is leaping over you during the flight. You can get yourself settled and stay there. There are no ringing phones or other interruptions. I sleep on planes a lot. It's a habit worth developing. I couldn't maintain my schedule if I didn't. For me, it's better to lean against the window than to start to fall asleep and end up on the shoulder of the person seated next to you or falling over into the aisle.

I think the window seat also promotes clear thinking. Some business travelers think that if you've seen one cloud, you've seen 'em all. But for me, looking out over the clouds can create a mood of contemplation that channels creative ideas to the forefront. I've had some of my best thinking sessions on planes. Jim Biggar, Chairman and CEO of Nestlé Corporation, says the same thing. "I find that I do a lot of my most creative work when I'm just up there in the sky with nothing around but daylight. My mind is more open somehow."

Sir Christopher Lewinton, Chairman and CEO of TI Group Plc, says, "I like being in that calm environment up there. Telephones can't reach me. It is a time when you are detached but your brain is engaged. Very rarely do I talk to the chap next to me, and I don't want him to talk to me, either." David Frost concurs. "I don't use the telephones on board. I don't find that a particularly great idea because I actually think in terms of working and *thinking*. The one thing I tend to do, which can momentarily alarm the passenger in the next seat, if there is one, is ask for two or three air-sickness bags and then quickly move to reassure the person next to me that it's for torn-up paper and not for other purposes. I find that a plane is a perfect place to be alone with your work and alone with your thoughts. I therefore find flying to be a positive refreshment."

Getting a Good Fare

Everyone is ready to negotiate today. If you and others in your firm travel a lot, you are in a great position to negotiate with airlines for blocks of tickets at a discount. Our headquarters in Cleveland generates 500 trips a year to New York. We can strike a deal with Continental or USAir to buy tickets in bulk for use by our staff at maybe half the going rate.

Buying tickets in bulk also gives you a relationship with an airline that helps put you in contact with its Special Services personnel, who can be enormously helpful. Remember those long Immigration lines at Heathrow Airport in London? Not everyone has to wait in them. Some arriving passengers are more equal than others. If you have a relationship with British Airways, one of their Special Services representatives can arrange to meet you at the gate and escort you through a VIP Immigration line.

You don't think your business is big enough? You never know until you ask. People are trying desperately to get business these days, especially business that can grow. Airlines and others in the travel industry are willing to negotiate and they are willing to make accommodations with you in anticipation of future revenues.

Having a block of tickets in hand is also the best defense pricewise against the possibility of a last-minute trip. Airlines structure their fares by proximity to date of departure. The closer to leaving you get, the more expensive your seat becomes. Buying a ticket the night before for the first flight out almost always means paying a premium for your seat. However, if you've already got a prenegotiated ticket in hand, all you need is a reservation. I'll talk more about ticket prices and special fares in Chapter VII.

Booking a Hotel

If you ask a travel agent or a company travel representative to book you a room, that may be exactly what you'll get—a room and nothing more. And it will be *your* fault, not theirs. How do you get a good room at a good rate? A great deal of that is up to you.

You Are Still *Your Own Best Travel Agent*

If you want to get a good room at a good rate, before you talk to a travel agent or your inhouse travel service, put in a call to your own private travel agency, the one with the clientele of one. My first rule about hotels is **do the initial research yourself.** If you are going to stay at a hotel for the first time, it will pay great dividends for you to make a personal call and find out something about it. Most guidebooks will give you the bare minimum facts about a hotel. A few will go into greater detail, but it's often surprising that much information useful to the executive traveler is omitted. How firm are the mattresses? Are there blackout drapes? Is there soundproofing between rooms? Does the hotel serve brewed decaffeinated coffee rather than those vile crystals? (Brewed decaf is almost universal now in the United States, but is less common in Europe. However, even there it's easier to find now than it was five years ago. In Asia and Latin America, however, brewed decaf is still a relative rarity.) Are there complimentary terrycloth robes in the room? If so, are they generously sized? (All too many of them are skimpy.) Is there a health and fitness facility? If so, where is it, and what's in it? (This last may be a letdown. In some hotels a small corner of the basement has been outfitted with a tread-mill, a stationary bicycle, two barbells, and an old Jane Fonda video—voila! the fitness center.)

Is there twenty-four-hour room service? Is there a concierge? Is there limousine service available for guests? If so, how many cars does the hotel maintain? (One car for a 600-room hotel is a joke.) Is there voicemail? What facilities are there for receiving faxes? What newspapers can be delivered to the room? Where are the outlets? Is it possible to comfortably use a laptop computer with modem in the bed? (Hotels vary widely in their capacity to accommodate modern portable business equipment.)

How Many Telephone Lines Does It Take to Plug in a Phone Call?

Only you know which amenities are frills and which are essential to you. For me the most important questions of all have to do with the telephones. I do a lot of business from my hotel room by phone. It's important for me to know where the phone is in relation to the bed. I prefer to have the phone to the left. I'm right-handed, and that way I can cradle the phone and still take notes without having to deal with a jumble of wires. I hate phones with short cords and phones on desks in hotel rooms. Rarely do you really find yourself sitting at the desk in the hotel room. The phone on the desk looks nice and "professional," and I am sure some decorator thought it was convenient, but to my knowledge few business travelers ever use them very much.

I also need to know how many lines (not extensions—lines, with distinct telephone numbers) are in the room. It's important for me to have at least two lines. Frequently my wife is traveling with me, and with two lines we both can make calls. I'm still pretty much of a "yellow pad" executive, but a growing number of business travelers are carrying not only laptop computers but their own portable fax machines as well. If computers are part of your business life on the road, that second line is crucial, not just for voice communications but for data traveling along the "information superhighway."

Even when I'm traveling alone I want two lines, not as a convenience to me, but for others trying to reach me. It's often difficult to make contact with a traveling executive. Even when you know the hotel and the room number, the truth is that for most of the day, that person is not going to be in the room. You have just a couple of windows of opportunity. There is one in the morning, from whatever time you dare call them until about 9:00 A.M., when they leave for the day. The second window is in the evening at cocktail time, before they go out to dinner. In both those instances that's exactly when the person you are trying to get in touch with is going to be making outgoing calls, phoning home, checking in at the office, making dinner reservations. Without a second line, you are going to get a busy signal, putting you at the mercy of the hotel telephone operators, dependent on them to get your message through to the room.

The Hotel Has a lot in Common With a Quart of Milk

Some hotel information, like the milk you buy at the supermarket, has a "shelf life." The success of your visit may depend on what I call "perishable information"—things that are true on one visit that may not be true the next. Call ahead to make sure that your hotel will be what you expect it to be. Has it been renovated? This can be great news, but not if they have removed the oak paneling from your favorite hideaway lobby bar and turned it into a cabaret. Is renovation still ongoing—is your room going to be subjected to construction noise at all hours? Is there a big convention booked into the hotel at the same time you plan to be there, so that hotel facilities will be hard-pressed to keep up with demands by a large number of guests?

To find out this information, call the hotel directly. Waste no time with any toll-free centralized reservations numbers. The people who answer those phones are not physically located at the hotel where you will be staying. It's an even money bet that they've never *seen* the hotel you're asking about. It's much better in any event to establish a personal rapport with the manager or other high-level hotel staff representative and to develop a reputation as a demanding repeat customer.

Be Demanding

That, indeed, is my second rule: **Be demanding.** This is not the same as being a pain in the behind, but you have every right to expect a hotel stay to be a positive experience. Remember your status as an executive traveler. Good hotels keep records on the preferences of their best patrons, so they can meet your demands, but they can't do that if they don't know what you like. Unfortunately, many business travelers are reticent about making their preferences known. I assure you that even the very top hotels have less desirable rooms that are next to the elevator, over the loading dock, or over the discotheque. Someone may stay in them, but it doesn't have to be you.

When you call a hotel that you are unfamiliar with, find out how extensive the room choice is. Ask what kinds of rooms are available. Get rather elaborate descriptions of the rooms and what floor they're on. Are all the floors the same? Has one been refurbished and the others not? Is one quieter than the other? (Is there work going on next door to the hotel?) Is there a balcony? Is there a view? Are there some corner rooms available with two views?

Create Your Way to a Good Rate

How do you get a good room at a good rate? There are many ways to do it, and I'll go into detail in Chapter VII, but here are a few ideas. You must think creatively. Consider the possibilities for tradeout or barter agreements between your company and the hotel.

At IMG, we've made all kinds of barter arrangements for travel. We named the Claremont Hotel in Oakland as the official hotel of the Bank of the West Tennis Classic, and we made a similar arrangement with a limousine company. These kinds of barter arrangements aren't limited to the sports and entertainment business. Anything from computer hardware and software to medical and legal services can be negotiated.

I know—if you manufacture ball bearings or jet engines, you probably don't have much to trade, but you can still get a great room. If I were the CEO of the Wichita Widget Company and I were planning a trip, it would not be stretching the truth too far to have my secretary contact the hotel's convention manager and say, "Look, I'm making a reservation for my boss, the CEO of the Wichita Widget Company. He will be staying at your hotel on business now, but he is also thinking about doing a sales conference sometime next spring. He's looking for a venue to do it. We've heard you have a nice spa and tennis facilities."

That call places you on a whole different level in the view of that hotel. Suddenly you could mean extra business for them. You're going to end up getting a better room, possibly a better rate, certainly better service, and more attention from the staff, but a secretary or a travel agent will generally not think that way.

I also make a habit of booking a longer stay than I think I will ultimately need. Once I've checked in, it's more convenient for me to say I'm leaving early than to try to extend a stay in a hotel that might be booked. On some international flights it's worth it to me to book the room the night before I arrive as well. An unsophisticated traveler arrives on an overnight flight with a Tuesday reservation and assumes he will be able to walk into his room at 8 A.M. when the prior guests haven't checked out yet. In many hotel lobbies, particularly smaller ones in Europe, it's common to see weary travelers and their baggage strewn all over the lobby, waiting for their room to clear. If I know I'm going to want a nap as soon as I arrive, I'll take the room for the prior night in order to make sure that my room is ready when I arrive. Often I don't even have to pay for it unless the hotel is completely booked up.

Booking Restaurants

Do you eat meals in the same restaurants every time you travel? You shouldn't. People who are insecure about traveling often opt for "safe" choices. Because they try to make the experience as much like being at home—or as much like their last trip—as possible, their trips take on a depressing sameness and familiarity. They get into a routine instead of discovering what's unique about the city they're in. To enjoy travel, you've got to make the experience a little fresh for yourself each time. You've got to have something to look forward to. You have to be adventurous.

Meals are a great place to start getting out of the rut. If you need a security blanket for a particular lunch or dinner, fine. Go where you are known and the service and ambience are reliable. Otherwise, experiment. Unlike staying in an unknown hotel, it's a small adventure which, if unsuccessful, won't ruin your trip. If you travel at this level, you are already a successful executive. You didn't get to your position without taking risks. You learned how to gather information, listen to advice from peers and colleagues, and take the calculated risk when it was called for. Travel is the same. Most of the time, informed risk-taking pays off in enhanced enjoyment.

Restaurant knowledge, even more so than data about hotels, is highly perishable information. The newest guy on the block is often the best, but star chefs can be highly mobile. Many restaurant kitchens nosedive when their superstar moves on. On the other hand, some celebrity chefs like Wolfgang Puck have become restaurant entrepreneurs. When they open new eateries, they are likely to be not merely branches of the original but innovative new restaurants in their own right. The restaurant scene in our major cities changes quickly. If you took the hundred most cosmopolitan New Yorkers of twenty-five years ago and had them list their favorite restaurants of the time, today more than half of them would no longer be in business. Of the half that remain, half of those would have deteriorated or gone to other management. Even a five-year-old listing of favorites would be dated and would leave out the trendiest places in cities like New York and Los Angeles.

Guidebooks tend to be a little behind the times on restaurants. Magazines and newsletters are more helpful. Better yet, use your personal contacts in town to find out the names of the new interesting restaurants. If you have chosen a restaurant to make your client happy and he is well known there but you are not, ask his help in getting a good table.

People Who Live There Will
Always Know More Than You Do

Sometimes, not using your personal and business contacts to select a restaurant can be bad for business, especially if it reveals your ignorance about the city you are visiting. Investment banker Marvin Bush describes the problem well. "People like to show off their cities. When I travel, I rely a great deal on the people I'm dealing with to select a suitable restaurant. They know why we're meeting. They know what the tone of the meeting should be, that there ought to be a quiet and serious environment where we can sit down and talk. I've always felt it was rather strange when people came to Washington to see me and said, 'I'll be in Washington next week and I want to meet you at The Palm.'

"My first reaction is, 'Who the hell is this yahoo?' He wants to go to the busiest restaurant in Washington, with waiters who won't leave you alone, where you can't talk without screaming at each other. It's completely inappropriate for a business meeting."

How to Get a Great Table at "21"

For years "21" has been one of the classic power restaurants of New York, where titans of finance, industry, and show business can dine well, with the confidence that they will always be recognized, shown to their favorite table, and coddled by a familiar staff. For regulars, "21" is a private dining club that happens to serve the general public, too. Although I have dined there many times, I would be flattering myself if I suggested I was a regular. I'm not. But my friend Herb Siegel, the Chairman of Cris-Craft, is definitely one of their great customers. If Herb Siegel and I are planning to meet for lunch, I often ask him to take me to "21"—because he gets the best table, the best service, and by extension so do I.

In fact, if I wanted to dine at "21" *without* Herb Siegel, I would still ask him to make the reservation—in the hope that he would introduce me as his friend and suggest that I be well taken care of. This isn't an imposition. It's a winning tactic in three ways: It's not unflattering to Herb Siegel, who surely must derive some tiny but distinct pleasure in demonstrating his power on behalf of a friend. He also gets credit—in the form of the restaurant's continuing gratitude and goodwill—for bringing in a new customer. And I get treated royally at an establishment where I am not that well known. I'm a visitor in Siegel's power base, but I don't hear anyone complaining.

If a friend has more clout than you do at a tough-to-book restaurant, let him or her make the arrangements. You are doing yourself and your friend a favor.

The Man Who Didn't Come to Dinner

When I book a table, I always make a reservation for three people, even if there are only going to be two of us. I don't like tables where everyone is too close together, and often tables for two are lined up so that diners are elbow-to-elbow. The people seated at the next table are actually physically nearer to me than my companion seated across from me. This is especially true in densely developed urban areas (like New York, Boston, and Paris) where many buildings are older, and space is at a premium. If I want to say something over dinner that is moderately confidential, I don't want people from the next table to be in on our conversation. A table for three gives more personal space. I prefer corner tables for the same reason. With walls on two sides, the setting is far more private.

When you book the table for three, you must be sure to maintain the fiction with the waiter or waitress that the third member of your party is expected and is surely on the way. It's always a good idea, however, to clue in your companion about your charade, lest he or she inadvertently blow your cover. If your associate blurts out, "Who's joining us? I thought we were going to work out the details between the two of us before the meeting!" you'll find yourself with a great deal of explaining to do, both publicly and privately. Remember to officially "give up" on the missing phantom member of your party if you want your food to appear. Many restaurants will wait to take your order till the third person arrives.

Make Contact With Management

If you are going to a restaurant on the recommendation of a good friend or business associate and that person is not accompanying you, be sure to mention his or her name to the owner or maitre d'. You will get better service as the "friend of a friend" and your business contact will get better treatment on the next visit as well. For example, one of my favorite restaurants is La Marée in Paris, and I frequently recommend it to others. Eric Trompier, owner of La Marée, told me, "I can't know how to help someone if I don't know who they are. I'm always grateful if a customer introduces himself to me. I'm especially anxious to help them if I know that they are coming from another friend that I know. I pay special attention to them because I know that here is someone who is likely to become a good customer. I also know that here is someone who is going to go back to the person who referred him here and tell him about his experience at La Marée."

To get a better table on your own, tell them you're scouting a location for a function in the near future when you book your table. Ask to see their private facilities. It gives a restaurant a little more incentive to do their best on your behalf.

Use a Fancy Suite for Lunch—Without Paying for It

If you are making plans for a larger group at lunch, be creative. The fatal error that most people make is that they don't think very far in advance and they think in very limited ways. A business lunch doesn't have to be in a dining room or restaurant. Use the full range of services your hotel has to offer. A business meeting with lunch served in an otherwise unoccupied suite is potentially much more impressive than one held in the hotel restaurant. Since the room isn't booked, often the hotel will not charge you for the use of it. The suite is likely to be far more

ˉious than any of those "banquet" rooms, which tend to be devoid of both charm and windows.

For groups of six or more, consider preordering the meal. Very little business at a standard business lunch gets conducted until the coffee arrives. If there are eight people around a table, the first time the waiter comes by, I guarantee you that some of the group won't be ready to order. By the time he returns and starts explaining the specials to each person as he goes around, you've wasted over a half hour. Preordering shows that you are efficient, that you think ahead and can anticipate what people's desires might be.

Planning Yourself Out the Door

Check and Double Check

Even the most careful pretravel arrangements need some follow-up on the day you leave and the day you arrive. It helps for the executive traveler to have some standard travel-day procedures that staff members perform automatically. Establish a regular routine with your support staff for your travel days.

Among the routine departure day procedures should be the following:

- Set a "standard" time when you will check in with your office for messages.
- Establish a "window" when other people will be able to reach you at your hotel.
- Have your secretary call your hotel to confirm your arrival and booking arrangements. If possible, do this even before your plane leaves the ground.
- Make sure she gets the name of the desk clerk she speaks with.
- Make certain you are carrying a fax transmittal with your confirmation number on it *in your carry-on baggage.*
- If you are going to arrive after 6 P.M., be sure to contact your hotel prior to that time, so that they will hold your room.

- If you're still in transit at that hour, make sure that someone else is assigned to place that call.

What is the one single piece of advice that almost always pays off? **Call your airline before you leave for the airport to make sure your flight is on time.**

Even though airlines always ask for a local phone number so they can call you in case there's a problem with your flight, don't depend on airlines to let you know there will be a delay. I can't tell you how many times I've been on flights that have been delayed or canceled. I *can* tell you how many times the airline has called me in advance to give me this information. I remember these occasions very clearly—both of them.

What Goes Up Must Come Down— and It Must Come Down Before It Can Go Up

Although many seasoned travel veterans know they should make this call, most of them don't ask the airline the right question. If you call and ask your airline if your flight is on time, the person looking at the computer screen will be checking a Departures board—and generally the information they have at their disposal will show the flight leaving on time. However, in order for your plane to be on time, it most probably had to come from somewhere else, and somewhere else before that.

The question you need to ask involves a little research with your *Skyguide*. What you need to know about is arrivals, not departures. Find out what had to happen for your flight to be on time. Does your flight originate in the city you're leaving from? If so, did your aircraft overnight there previously? Is this the first plane out in the morning? If so, if it didn't make it in last night, it's not going out this morning.

If yours is a continuation flight, ask when your flight is arriving from its prior destination. There were a number of travelers headed for Los Angeles who got stuck in Cleveland during the big blizzard of '93 that hit New York and the entire east coast. Their airline, Continental, kept assuring them that they would be subject to only minor delays, despite the fact that their leg of the trip was the continuation of a flight originating in New York—and all airports in the New York metropolitan area were completely shut down.

The Joy of Packing

Are your personal belongings organized for travel or do you have to put yourself together anew each time you leave? Do you have a toiletries kit and some standard business attire packed and ready to go? Do you have an onboard care package— bottled water, eyeshades if you use them, a personal pillow— that's already assembled?

I try to really think through every night that I am going to be gone, what I'll wear every day. Obviously, you try to match your shirts and ties and socks and all that with your coats and suits, but if I'm going to have to be wearing a coat for a few days, I'm going to pack the one that isn't going to wrinkle as much as that one I know will look awful after I've worn it for a day. If I know I'm going to be doing some shopping, I'll pack a soft empty suitcase inside a larger one to be able to bring other things back. If I know I'm going to take a small side trip from a longer trip, I'll take a small suitcase inside a big suitcase then as well. This time, however, it won't be empty. I'll throw in a toilet kit, a shirt, and whatever else I'll need so it's prepacked before I leave. In Chapter VI, "The Traveling Office," I'll talk more about what to bring and what to leave at home.

Carry-On, Business Traveler

Baggage snafus are among the worst problems of air travel. The three main problems with baggage are misrouting, damage, and theft. To deal with the first difficulty, carry anything that really matters with you in the cabin—jewelry, furs, important papers, anything electronic. Frequent flyer Jay Leno jokes that it's better just to throw your bags away rather than to check them in. On a short trip, almost every seasoned business traveler will try to fit all of his or her needs into carry-on pieces. It's tried and true advice.

Luggage Appearance and the Appearance of Luggage

Nevertheless, taking the carry-on rule to extremes isn't useful. I used to try to get on the plane with a hanging bag and two or three briefcases, but that got me into trouble with the airlines because I was over my carry-on limit. Airlines are getting more and more stringent about enforcing carry-on limits. It was also bad for my back.

Sooner or later, the executive traveler has to deal with the need to check baggage. Some travel experts give you a great deal of advice about what brand of luggage to carry, but my ego is not tied up in the appearance of my luggage. My main concern is that the luggage *appear* on the baggage carousel.

Leather luggage is stylish and durable, but it's also extremely heavy. If you're an international traveler carrying leather bags, you're most of the way toward being over the excess baggage limit before you've even packed your underwear.

Serviceable softsided baggage made out of some lightweight space-age synthetic fiber is a reasonable alternative, but the most popular brands of this kind of luggage look pretty much the same. It's a good idea to make your luggage look different or distinctive so it's harder for other people to pick your bag off the carousel by mistake. Mike Baverstock, a Special Services agent with British Airways, recommends adding a colorful ribbon or baggage tag to suitcases to make them easier to spot. "It's so easy to misidentify a suitcase. So many people have baggage that looks similar, but the chance of you putting the same ribbon or color around the handle as another passenger is remote."

Junk the Trunk

Designer luggage, although it looks chic when new, often can't stand up to the abuse that airlines dish out. From many years of watching that carousel go round and round, I can assure you that baggage handlers do not heave Vuitton luggage any more gently than they do the flimsiest cardboard suitcase belonging to the person holding the cheapest ticket in coach. Vuitton and other expensive designer bags are great for crossing on the *QE2*, but if you fly, abandon the steamer trunk mentality and opt for practicality.

Don't Worry About the Wrong Thing

People who are afraid someone will steal their luggage from the baggage claim area (as opposed to someone picking up their bag by an honest mistake) are by and large worried about the wrong thing. Most passenger baggage items stolen at airports are not stolen off the baggage carousel. They are stolen *before* your bags ever get there, by people you can't even see. As often as not, thieves are people who have infiltrated the ranks of behind-the-scenes baggage handlers at the gate.

To would-be thieves, designer luggage like Vuitton and the aluminum-sided Halliburton stuff all but screams out, "I'm valuable. My contents are valuable. Steal me." Most of the time thieves don't steal the bags themselves. They steal items *from* bags.

Baggage locks are no real help. Basically they are a fraud that does little more than announce that you are worried about the contents of your luggage. Thieves will either pop the flimsy locks or "accidentally" rip soft-sided luggage to get at the contents.

It's a relatively risk-free occupation. Why? Because when you're at the carousel and your bags come off the plane, you never open them to see if anything's missing. On the contrary, you are so happy and relieved to see that they have arrived that you jump into your car and get on with your trip. When you get to your hotel and discover that something is missing, it's too late.

Bad Luggage Is Good Luggage

The best way to foil behind-the-scenes baggage thieves is to lead them to believe that you have nothing worth stealing. Travel with the most unassuming luggage that you or the person who picks out your clothing and cares about your appearance will permit you to be seen carrying.

For some hardcore travelers, modest luggage is not enough. They choose not unpretentious luggage, not undistinguished luggage, but disgusting and hideous luggage—luggage that looks like it escaped from a fire sale in the bargain basement of Moscow's GUM department store.

A few years ago an associate of mine was landing at LaGuardia Airport one night on a flight from Chicago. Standing next to her at the baggage claim was Italian fashion designer Emilio Pucci, wearing an impeccably tailored suit. While waiting for the bags, she found herself speculating on what kind of luggage Pucci traveled with. She was expecting perhaps Vuitton, possibly Gucci, or maybe something custom made, sporting one of his trademark prints.

She was shocked when he retrieved what must surely have been the homeliest suitcase in the world. How homely was it? Vivid yellow naugahyde. It might not have been chic, but he'd never lost it. On the other hand, someone as stylish as the late Mr. Pucci gave his yellow naugahyde a cachet all its own. It was his version of the Personal Touch in travel. I'll talk about personalizing your travel experience in the next chapter.

Chapter III
The Personal Touch

A major component of enjoyable executive business travel is doing it with a Personal Touch. That touch is manifested in two ways. One aspect is bringing some of your own personal creature comforts along with you (or making sure they are waiting when you arrive). Just as rental car agencies track the make and model preference of recurring customers, better hotels keep records of the preferences of frequent guests. The business traveler knows how to make travel arrangements that optimize both comfort and operating efficiency, and how to make support personnel aware of his or her likes and dislikes.

The other facet of the Personal Touch is getting the most out of airline, hotel, and other travel personnel by providing them with the positive stimulus they need to make them put their best foot forward on your behalf. Sometimes this stimulus is financial, but even more often it is the dynamic personal style of the executive traveler. The business traveler knows how to motivate and empower someone to provide an extra level of service, above and beyond the call of duty. With this empowerment, airline ground personnel cheerfully try to solve your booking problem; without trepidation a waitress asks the chef to prepare something special that is off the menu.

The Personal Touch on Board

Life Support on Your Flying Island

A good hotel should be able to supply all the comforts of home. On an airplane, however, these creature comforts may be harder to come by. Think of an aircraft as a small desert island flying through the atmosphere. What's there is available to be utilized for your comfort, efficiency, and enjoyment. If it's not on the plane, however, that item is not available at any price. What the executive traveler wants on board the flying island is the same thing he or she wants on the ground—control of the environment.

Bring Your Own Creature Comforts

The executive traveler maintains this control by packing his or her own collection of personal traveling paraphernalia, the small things that make you comfortable while in the air. Most business travelers keep this airborne care package stocked and ready to go. All that has to be done is to grab the bag and go.

Everyone's assortment is different. Pioneering travel writer Temple Fielding used to bring three jars of his favorite mustard to augment (or perhaps to mask) the flavor of airline food. My wife brings along her own pillow. It is a lot more substantial than the little flimsy ones provided by the airline, which have a tendency to slip down between the seats or get wedged between the seat and the window. She's covered it with a bright pillowcase so she doesn't forget it.

Others bring earplugs, eye masks, and inflatable neck braces. Neck braces support and cushion the head upright as you sleep, so that it doesn't flop over as you nap, creating a particularly painful stiff neck. (You also avoid the embarrassment of sleeping on the shoulder of the passenger next to you.)

One publishing executive brings a Walkman, with his own selection of music or audiobooks. One entertainment executive has an understandable aversion to airline headphones. Sometimes you get recycled ones. Oftentimes they don't work or don't fit properly. He always carries his own with him. They are a lot more comfortable than the ones that airlines offer, and the plugs are universal—they work on any airline.

The Importance of Water

More and more business travelers have chosen to bring their own bottled water on board, such as Evian, Perrier, San Pellegrino, or Calistoga. It's a truly smart move. Frequent flyers know that it's important to drink as much water as possible while traveling. It's your body's best defense against dehydration, and also helps to reduce the effects of jet lag.

The water on board your flying island, however, may have come from a multitude of sources. If you're traveling on an international flight from Los Angeles to Paris that stops in Chicago, the plane's holding tank is not drained in Chicago and refilled. It's topped off with Chicago water. This is not in and of itself bad. However, this procedure is likely to be repeated when that same flight continues on from Paris to Hong Kong, stopping in Cairo, Calcutta, and Kuala Lumpur, where water quality can range from unpalatable to unhealthy, and bacteria counts are likely to be far higher than in Europe or North America.

Airlines that test their water will add chlorine if the count is too high. This may kill off the bacteria, but the water will then have a taste resembling household bleach. From a health standpoint, too much chlorine can be as bad as too little. Water that is overly chlorinated may also destroy healthy naturally occurring organisms in your own system, causing gastric distress.

Even water that started out as good-quality drinking water can develop a high bacteria count if it has stayed in the holding tank long enough. You have no way of knowing how long your flying island's water has been in that holding tank, where it came from originally, or when the tank was last cleaned. The safest advice for the business traveler is to bring your own water or drink only name-brand bottled water served by the flight attendants. Don't be fooled by the frosted silver pitcher. If you don't see the bottle, don't drink the water, at least not cold. Hot beverages like coffee and tea are safe to drink because the water has been boiled. Ice is safe to consume, since it was made with purified water, not water from the holding tank, and was recently delivered to the aircraft.

Eating on Board

Many executive travelers preorder special meals. Most airlines now have a wide variety of such meals available. Selections include vegetarian, kosher, low fat, salt-free, and diabetic, but you have to give the airline fair warning, usually at least twenty-four hours. To make sure you get what you want, book the meal when you book your seat, but don't stop there. Remind the ground crew of your special meal when you check in at the gate; make sure your meal is shown in their computer log for your ticket. In addition, remind the flight attendants when you board the plane.

With regard to business and first-class meals, you should be aware that the elaborate meal service that most airlines offer, especially on transcontinental or overseas flights, tempts you to indulge in something that most health experts advise you not to do—which is to eat heavily and consume alcohol on a plane. It's easy enough not to eat the unidentified flying omelet or other cruel and unusual nourishment on a two-hour hop from New York to Cleveland. It's a lot harder to just say no to a glass of Grgich Hills chardonnay, grilled swordfish with macadamia nuts and mango chutney, followed by chocolate raspberry torte and a brandy, between Los Angeles and Honolulu. Nevertheless, the overwhelming advice from doctors and other business travelers is to eat lightly on board, and to avoid alcohol, including wine.

Some executive travelers control their diet by bringing their own food on board, sometimes from home, more often from a preferred restaurant. Anne Rosensweig, chef and owner of Arcadia, one of my favorite restaurants in New York, caters her onboard meal from her own restaurant kitchen. She has a wonderful meal, of course, but she also has to fight off the envious glances of other passengers.

Pack a Picnic for Your Flight

You don't have to be Anne Rosensweig to do this. It's easy enough, if you plan to do it in advance. A day or so before you leave, call the restaurant or deli and ask them to pack you a meal to go. When you get your car or cab to take you to the airport, allow a little extra time and ask them to make a stop on the way. (Of course, meals packed for early morning flights should be picked up the night before.) It's not that unusual a request. Any restaurant that can pack food to go, whether it's for lunches at a board meeting or a picnic at the Hollywood Bowl, can equip you with food for a plane trip. Balducci's and Dean & DeLuca in New York, Il Fornaio in Los Angeles and San Francisco, and other restaurants and gourmet food emporiums across the country pack inflight care packages for their customers all the time. Many better hotels, such as the Ma Maison Sofitel in Los Angeles, are also beginning to provide the same service for their guests. Guests at many airport Hyatt hotels can order takeout meals for the plane. Known as AirFare, the food is ordered through room service, packaged in a special bag or box, and delivered to your room or left for pickup at the front desk. Getting a special meal from your hotel also eliminates the need for a special stop on the way to the airport.

What should you eat on the plane? I'm not that much of a stickler about following any kind of formal anti-jet lag diet. I generally eat lightly. Often all I eat is the first course of the meal. However, my advice is to do what works for you. One of my associates makes a point of visiting Coesnon, one of the best *charcuteries* in Paris, before returning to Los Angeles. Coesnon packs him an inflight feast of *foie gras* and an assortment of pâtés and terrines, accompanied by a baguette of bread from Poîlane. Because these foods are not canned or processed, they can't be brought into the United States. However, it's never a problem because they are always consumed before landing, often with a good bottle of French wine, frequently with the eager assistance of other passengers. Does this violate almost all of the advice about what to consume on a flight? Absolutely. Does it make his jet lag worse? Perhaps, perhaps not. Does he have an enjoyable travel experience? You bet.

The Personal Touch at Your Hotel

Training Your Hotel to Serve You

When you stay at your regular hotel in a city you visit often, do the "welcome" flowers in your room make you wheeze and sneeze? Is the phone cord always too short? Does room service invariably bring regular coffee when you drink only herbal tea? If so, you need to revise your hotel's dossier on you. Many business travelers visit the same cities over and over. Better hotels monitor the preferences of their frequent guests, and strive to have everything in order for their arrival. At a good hotel on your first visit, you should be able to get almost anything you ask for. On your second visit, it should already be there waiting.

For this to happen, however, the hotel has to know what your preferences are. For some reason, many executives who have no difficulty making their wishes known in the office are reticent about making requests when on the road. It's a tendency which innkeepers worldwide deplore.

Michael Gray, general manager of the Hyatt Carlton Tower in London, says, "Give us as much information about your visit as possible. Arrival times are important, so we can plan which rooms to allocate to avoid having people waiting in the lobby. Give us information about the number of people in your party. If we suddenly find that a party of two has turned into a party of three and we're not prepared, you may not get nearly as spacious a room as you would have if we had known in advance.

"Our front office manager noticed that many American guests arriving early on Monday morning were football fans. During the fall season he now gets the scores late on Sunday night and has them available for new arrivals, who are tickled to be able to follow the San Francisco 49ers or the Dallas Cowboys even in London.

"This is the kind of service we are delighted to provide. Hotels *love* to be able to do something extra, personal, thoughtful. If we can find out things like what particular food or drink you might like, or dislikes about anything—soft pillows, hard pillows, bedboards—or whatever preferences or idiosyncrasies you might have, please tell us, or get your secretary to tell us. It makes us feel good. We're constantly seeking out ways we can really make the visit a personal one, to make the guest feel they're not just another number."

The Hotel de Crillon in Paris Will Keep Your Cigars in Stock

Hervé Houdre, manager of the Crillon in Paris, concurs. "When you are new to the hotel, we keep track of your requests. The next time you visit, we will know what kind of cigar you smoke, which newspaper you want to read, so you don't have to call us and ask. However, a good traveler needs to convey what he needs. Before being upset with anything which doesn't suit you in the room, call reception and speak with the reception manager as soon as possible. Always go to the number-one person if you can. We can't assist you if you don't make us aware of what your needs are."

What can you have waiting for you? Two phone lines. A fax machine or a portable computer to use in your room. Fax machine and computer modem capability for you to hook your own equipment into. Restaurant reservations for the duration of your visit. Theatre tickets. A secretary. Voicemail. A treadmill, exercise bicycle, or Stairmaster in your room. Your favorite newspaper. Your favorite scotch in the minibar. Your choice of flowers, or no flowers at all.

You can even have your own clothes waiting for you. If you regularly travel to a city with a climate markedly different from your own, it may well be simpler just to keep some clothing there, rather than pack it anew each time you travel. Michael Viner, President and CEO of Dove Audio, Inc., is a southern California executive who travels frequently to London. He stores a suitcase full of wool and tweed at his favorite hotel. When he has an upcoming trip, all he has to do is call the hotel and tell them to unpack his bag and hang his clothes in his room. (Of course, they press items, if necessary.) After he leaves, the clothes are repacked until the next visit. Is this an imposition? Hardly. "The hotel is delighted to do it because I'm a regular guest," says Viner. "To them it means that I'm a captive in their hotel and I'm not going to desert them for another."

It also means that Michael Viner can fly from Los Angeles to London with only carry-on luggage, get off the plane, and head straight into the city for a round of meetings. Getting your bags to your hotel if you are going to do business before settling in at your hotel is a difficulty business travelers encounter all over the world. No one wants to haul their luggage all over town before checking in. At Chicago's O'Hare Airport, American and United have offered a service whereby for $7 a bag your luggage is delivered straight to your hotel.

Although this service is currently suspended, travel expert Peter Greenberg solves this problem in another manner. A number of cities, among them Orlando and Miami, have airport hotels that are not just nearby, but that are actually physically part of the airport complex itself. When Greenberg is arriving in Orlando, one of his top hotel choices is the Hyatt Regency at the airport. "As the plane is on final approach," he explains, "I call the hotel from the airphone and ask for a bellman to meet the plane. He walks forty feet. I get off the plane and give him my baggage tags. He claims my luggage and takes it to the hotel. I go straight downtown for my dinner meeting. I give him a $10 tip for his trouble. I also know exactly which staff member is going to be responsible for my bags. You can't do this everywhere, but where it's possible, it works great. If you're going to be staying at an airport hotel, use that location to your advantage."

The Crillon and the Carlton Tower pride themselves on taking excellent care of their clientele and anticipating their needs, but extraordinary service happens not just there but at better hotels all over the world. Most American hotel chains keep similar if less comprehensive records. Even if they don't, you should keep a list of preferences (and sometimes more important—aversions) on file with your travel agent, inhouse travel service, or secretary. When they book your room, they can tick off the listings as they make the reservation. The important concept is advance planning—**give the hotel time to do what you want them to do.**

Getting Others to Give You Personal Service

How does the executive traveler get others to extend themselves to the utmost on his or her behalf? By using the Personal Touch. The Personal Touch is an extension of my business philosophy. Many executives have already learned to utilize it within their own corporate structure and in their business dealings, but it can be extended into your traveling relationships as well.

What Personal Service Is Not

In defining what I mean by personal service, it would perhaps help to give an example of what personal service is not. Personal service is not being carried in a sedan chair from airport to hotel to meeting in a state perilously close to unconsciousness. You must maintain control over your own schedule and your own environment. The only good kind of personal service is the kind that enables you to do that and get on with your business. Everything else is simply debilitating.

There's definitely such a thing as being too helpful. "There's a big difference between having people around who can help you and having people around who are always thrusting themselves down your throat," says tennis star Virginia Wade. "Some hotels have started to make too much of a production out of service. It can become intrusive."

Jay Leno, one of the most frequent flyers in the entertainment business, knows the difference. Because he is a celebrity, he gets the red carpet treatment wherever he goes. Intelligently, however, he is able to distinguish between service that really helps and service that provides a substitute for real thinking and independence. "Traveling when you're in show business can be a little like being retarded. People are always telling you what's going to happen," he says with his trademark grin. "'Wait here, Mr. Leno.' 'I have your briefcase, Mr. Leno.' 'Someone will bring the car around, Mr. Leno.... This is the car, Mr. Leno,'" he drones in an obsequious, fawning falsetto. "I don't need that. I *know* what a car looks like! In far too many places there's someone to meet you and they talk to you like that. You've got to work hard to prevent becoming their prisoner." Because he's a star, Leno may have more trouble than most travelers, but his point is well taken. **Don't sit back and be "served" to the extent that you lose control over your life and decisions.**

Make Yourself Known

The Personal Touch is not something you can delegate. When you see the same faces over and over, make a point of learning the names that go with them. Build your own relationship with them. Ask about their health and family—let them know you are interested in them as human beings. As you develop these sorts of personal relationships with various people, even having little things you kid around about with them, somebody will end up getting you more service or extra help.

It doesn't take much, in part because surprisingly few people do it. If you've developed a friendly rapport with the elevator operator in your building, the next time you're taking stuff from your apartment and he's got two other people in the elevator waiting, he's going to be more inclined to make them wait for you and your stuff than to make you wait till he's taken them downstairs and come back up for you.

Get to know the secretaries of your business associates—a secretary will control access to her boss more often than not.

When you phone, it may make the difference between "He's not in. I'll take a message," and "He's not in, but you can catch him in the car on the car phone, and here's the number."

The key is empowerment—giving people in offices or at the airlines, at the hotel, or in a restaurant the belief that they can really be of service to you, and making them want to put themselves out on your behalf.

How do you do this? The basis for the success of the Personal Touch is that everyone likes to feel important, and everyone likes to show their authority. A great deal of it is public relations and establishing a genuine rapport with the people you meet.

It works with your travel agent. It works with the airline's reservation agent at the boarding gate. It works with the desk clerk and concierge at the hotel. It works with waiters and waitresses in restaurants.

How to Become a VIP at Your Favorite Restaurant

You have to be a power broker to become a big deal at "21" or The Four Seasons in New York, the kind of VIP who can stroll in at a moment's notice and be confident that your favorite table will be waiting for you. However, it doesn't take a lot to become a big deal in your favorite local restaurant, with your own favorite table.

What's important to a restaurant is not how big your company is, not how big your title is within the firm, but how often they see your face for lunch or dinner. **Plant your flag.** Make yourself known to the owner and the maitre d'. If you have a favorite waiter who gives you excellent service, ask for him by name.

How many visits to a restaurant does it take to make yourself known and become a "regular" customer? It may not take as many as you think. You don't have to be a weekly habitué of a restaurant to be a "regular"; however, this kind of loyalty should certainly get you special treatment in almost any restaurant I know. I am a "regular" at La Marée in Paris, even though I only get the chance to eat there about three or four times a year. I made myself known and developed a special relationship with Eric Trompier, the owner. Because I've been treated extremely well there, I also make a point of sending a lot of my friends to his restaurant.

You'll find that most restaurants will hold visiting out-of-town business patrons to a much gentler standard than local residents in order to qualify as "regulars." An owner or maitre d' can't help but be flattered knowing that you patronize his or her establishment each time you're in town, but he won't know to be flattered unless you tell him.

A Lesson in Diplomacy for Jack Nicholson

If you remember Jack Nicholson's classic restaurant scene in *Five Easy Pieces*, it never would have happened if he'd used a little diplomacy and the Personal Touch. Let me give you my version: The luncheon special in a nothing-special restaurant says "Soup, salad, sandwich of the day—ham & Swiss, $6.50. No Substitutions." Fine, except you want turkey & Swiss instead of ham.

If you tell the waitress, "I'd like the luncheon special but I would like turkey & Swiss instead of ham & Swiss," you're going to get a hard time. The standard "Sorry, we can't do that" response is probably the best you can hope for. If, on the other hand, you befriend the waitress and ask her, "Do you have enough influence with the chef to get him to agree to substitute turkey for the ham?" the answer may be quite different. The request is not unreasonable—it's not as if there isn't any turkey in the kitchen back there. What you are doing is acknowledging her importance and empowering her to utilize her authority to act on your behalf. Likely as not the response will be a smile and "I'll see what I can do."

It's the same when you get on a lunch flight on a plane. You know that depending on where you're seated, by the time they get to you, one of the meal choices is likely to be gone. If you greet the flight attendant warmly as you board and ask what the lunch choices are, she may tell you there's a Cobb salad and lasagna. It's easy enough to ask her if she'll save you a Cobb salad. If you are even moderately civilized in making the request, she will do it.

It helps to do it with a smile and a sense of humor. I have made it clear to the doormen in my New York apartment building *never* to ring my bell when a hired car comes to pick me up. I'll know the car is there if I've asked for it. Half the time a car I've requested at 8:00 A.M. is there at 7:40, at which time I'm in the bathtub. No one likes to get out of the tub to answer the bell. I tell all our doormen on the different shifts so they know not to ring me when the car comes. It's just a small thing, but I make a point of not being officious about it. It's just a matter of explaining to them, "Hey—I'm in the bathtub," something any human being can relate to.

The Personal Touch—Japanese Style

The Personal Touch works on me, too. When the 1972 Winter Olympics were held in Sapporo, I was in Japan traveling with Arnold Palmer and Jean-Claude Killy. I had the chance to meet and become acquainted with Yoshiaki Tsutsumi, who owns the Prince Hotel chain. Some years later, he invited me to dine with him at the Tokyo Prince Hotel, in one of their private teppan grill rooms. For the hotel staff, this was the equivalent of Lee Iacocca spending the afternoon at a Chrysler dealership in Des Moines. It was a huge deal for them. The hotel called my office three separate times asking for the license number of the car that would take me to the hotel. I couldn't figure out why until my car pulled up at the curb and the doorman opened my door saying, "Good evening and welcome to the Tokyo Prince, Mr. McCormack." I was a guest of their CEO and the hotel staff wanted to be able to greet me personally and by name. I was impressed.

My dinner with Mr. Tsutsumi was another manifestation of the Personal Touch. Although he was at the top of a large organization, he knew how to gather data. Toward the end of the meal he asked me through an interpreter, "You travel all the time, Mr. McCormack. What one thing about our Japanese hotels should we improve? What could we do differently?"

First of all I was flattered that he asked me, and it was clear that his question was sincere. I told him, "You should serve brewed decaffeinated coffee. If you order decaf in a Japanese hotel, you will get a little bowl of instant coffee crystals, a teapot full of boiling water, a cup, and a spoon. It's not as good as brewed coffee."

He turned to his assistant and told her, "This is the kind of information that I need. Nobody tells me this kind of stuff." Shortly thereafter, brewed decaf began appearing in Mr. Tsutsumi's hotels.

The Fine Art of Tipping

Tipping is perhaps the most obvious manifestation of the Personal Touch. Many business people handle tipping awkwardly, but the business traveler knows how, when, and who to tip to achieve the desired results. Never lose sight of what you are trying to achieve by tipping.

There are three main objectives:

- Are you tipping for something you want to make happen immediately?
- Are you tipping to show gratitude for something that's already occurred?
- Are you tipping to set up a smoother visit or a better table the next time you come?

Tipping is a custom that varies widely from one country to the next, and even from one region to another. In the United States, tips are bigger and more frequent on the coasts (the East Coast in particular) than they are in the heartland. In Japan, tipping is not generally expected. On the other hand, small gifts are appropriate for people who serve you frequently. In Eastern Europe, a tip in a hard currency, such as dollars or deutschmarks, is appreciated far more than a gratuity in the local coin of the realm. In Europe, most restaurants include a service charge in the bill, but a modest additional tip is considered in order for service above and beyond the ordinary. How do you know what's appropriate? Ask around. Ask your local business contacts for advice. A good concierge will know what cabbies and waiters expect in his town. Many of the better guidebooks will also provide guidelines for tipping.

Tips in Advance—"To Insure Promptness"

Keep in mind that the term "tip" was originally an acronym for To Insure Promptness, and it is in this context that tips are often the most useful. At the airport, I always give the skycap a good tip—*before* he checks my bags. Let's say a baggage handler at the curb figures he's going to get a dollar for checking some luggage. The executive traveler knows only too well what happens, of course. The skycap is hailed by other passengers, and now there's yet another pile on the curb. But if you're going to give the skycap a big tip, let's say $5, hand him the money with the ticket and he'll be very happy. He's really going to pay more attention to your baggage. More often than not he'll load your bags directly before he takes luggage from anyone else. I always wait until he actually puts the destination tag on the luggage, and loads it either on the cart or onto something that looks like a conveyor belt. I never enter the terminal if my bags are still piled up at the curb.

One of the smartest tipping techniques in the world is to tip the telephone operators in hotels before you get there. Nobody tips them because they are forgotten people, in the background. People tip concierges, bellboys, captains, waiters, etc., but for the business traveler, tipping hotel operators is unbelievable. They will find you and do things for you if you want to be found. They won't "find" you if you don't want to be found. You can explain stuff to them and they will kill themselves for you.

One executive traveler I know frequented an "establishment" restaurant in New York about twice a month. It was a place where seating was hierarchical and no one wanted to be in "Siberia." He always got a great table, but even though he was there every two weeks or so, he would tip the maitre d' only twice a year. When he did, he'd give him $50. His theory was that everyone gives the guy $5 or $10, so he kind of expects it. It doesn't make much of an impression. By giving him $50, he made himself stand out. He also created a level of uncertainty that worked to his benefit—the maitre d' never knew when that next $50 was coming.

People Who Can *Really* Help

The Personal Touch taps into a universal human need to be needed. It even works with small children by making them want to do what you want them to do. Within the travel industry, however, some people are in the business of responding to the Personal Touch, and can be incredibly helpful to you when you most need it.

Airline Special Services

The best resource an executive traveler can have at the airport is a Special Services representative from the airline. Special Services reps are the SWAT teams of the air travel business— solving problems ordinary agents fear to tackle and are not equipped to deal with. Employees of long standing, they've earned their stripes with their companies for good reason, and they have the authority to accomplish what most other airline personnel will tell you simply cannot be done.

They handle celebrities and VIPs, but you don't have to be rich or famous to use their services. What can they do? They can rewrite your ticket, break a sold-out flight, or rebook you with another airline if your flight has been delayed or canceled. They can walk you through Customs and Immigration, or make sure that your missing luggage with all your conference presentation materials is delivered to your hotel in time for the big meeting.

If you're a frequent executive traveler, airline Special Services personnel are available to you, but as with hotels and restaurants, the airline needs to know that you need them. Mike Baverstock is a veteran Special Services agent with British Airways. "There are some people who travel really regularly and never call on our services. Others depend on them. The bottom line is that we would like everybody to understand that we exist. Should they have a problem, they should know they can ask for our assistance. People prefer airlines where they feel comfortable, where they feel recognized. This recognition and courtesy cost us nothing. The personalization of the travel experience is the important thing. It builds passenger loyalty; it rewards passenger loyalty."

How do you meet them? If you do a lot of business with an airline, your travel agent or inhouse travel department can find out who the Special Services people are. You can also ask at the counter or the gate in the airport if the airline has a Special Services representative. (Only American, Delta, and United among U.S.-based carriers have them. Some airlines have representatives only in larger cities or in hubs.)

However you learn the name, you will want to make personal contact yourself. Ask to meet him or her. Make it a point to get to know them. The best time is before you need them. Introduce yourself and trade business cards. When you return to your office, write a letter confirming the contact. Keep the name handy. You never know when you'll need it. Don't abuse the relationship, however.

When they've worked wonders, it helps, of course, if you can show your appreciation, even in a small way. I'm fortunate in being able to give out tickets to concerts and sporting events, but remembering people during the holiday season who have helped you all year long is always a good idea. It's something that can pay big dividends not just for you, but for your company as well. If you get some of these Special Services people on your side by doing a lot of nice things for them, they will treat you, your clients, your employees, and your friends very well.

Your Hotel's Inhouse Magician

Many hotels have a magician on staff who can do things on short notice, but there's often no limit to what they can do given sufficient warning. This wizard is the concierge, and getting to know a good one is among the most valuable personal connections you can make at a hotel. For starters, a trained concierge will have the best connections in the city. I've known native New Yorkers whose out-of-town guests got them "impossible" Broadway tickets through their hotel concierge.

The concierge concept crossed the Atlantic from fine European hotels. Perhaps for this reason, many executive travelers are intimidated by them. There is also the problem that at some American hotels, the concept lost a little during the voyage. A kid in a hat at an information desk filled with flyers for local tours and attractions is not a concierge desk, despite a hotel's claim to offer "concierge service." A bell captain is not the same as a concierge either, no matter how much gold braid bedecks his epaulets. Even within a hotel concierge staff, there may be variations in competence. If one concierge in the French Quarter of New Orleans has to look up the phone number for Antoine's or the Commander's Palace, wait for the shift to change before you ask for anything else.

The function of a concierge is to do things for you outside the hotel. Don't complain to them about your bill or ask them to arrange a special function in the private dining room. The domain of the concierge begins just outside the hotel walls. Dinner reservations, and theatre and concert tickets are the most common requests, but if you need a place to play golf or tennis, a ten-speed bicycle, a behind-the-scenes tour of the local brewery, an expert who specializes in antique watch repair, or a helicopter to get you quickly to a remote construction site, use the Personal Touch with your concierge. The concierge is also trained to solve last-minute emergencies. When you discover while dressing for a black-tie dinner that your home town cleaners returned your tuxedo without the pants, when you've lost your airline tickets or when you've forgotten your anniversary, get help from the concierge.

A good concierge knows not only his or her own city, but is connected to a concierge network whose branches reach all over the world. They can make things happen for you anywhere. Many hotels encourage their frequent guests to utilize the services of their concierge—whether they're staying there that night or not. If you're a good client of the Four Seasons Hotel in Washington, D.C., and you have a problem, the hotel will encourage you to call them from New York or Paris and take advantage of their concierge services.

How to Complain

What happens when things don't work out? I can envision many of you saying, "Oh yeah? Well I did all that stuff McCormack told me to do and I still got treated badly." It helps to know how to complain. When used properly, it's part of the Personal Touch. When something goes awry at the airport, at the hotel, or at a restaurant, if you find yourself dashing off a torrid complaint letter on the plane returning home, you've lost the battle. The best and most effective time to complain is at the time and spot of the infraction.

Complain as Soon as You Can

At a hotel, a desk clerk facing an irate guest may call for backup and summon another member of the hotel staff to intercede. Do not deal with him or her until you know what their title is. Is this person the head of public relations—in other words, someone who can make soothing noises but can't really help? Is this the reservations manager, much better, or best of all, the hotel manager himself?

Above all, don't let the problem fester. Michael Gray, general manager of the Hyatt Carlton Tower hotel in London, says, "There's nothing worse than receiving a letter after the guest is gone, because it leaves me powerless to do anything about it. If there's a problem, tell the hotel at the time. Don't hold back. A good hotel and good management will want to hear a problem. I genuinely thank guests who complain to me. I may not like what I'm hearing, but I'm grateful that someone is letting me know. We're human; we make mistakes. But this way we have a chance to put things right during the visit. It will also make us a better hotel for you in the future."

Air Your Dirty Linen in Public

When you are negotiating a business deal, it is best to do so discreetly and in private. When you are negotiating a solution to an airline or hotel booking snafu, however, often the best place to do it is in public. The one exception is at a restaurant. There, any disagreement that cannot be resolved with the waiter can usually be settled by a discreet chat with the owner of the restaurant or the maitre d'.

If you have a reservation but the room you are shown to is hopeless, don't stay there even for a minute. Return to the reception desk immediately. Don't call the desk from the undesirable room. Keep your belongings with you. Don't leave your bags in the room when you return to the lobby to complain. Leaving the bags in the room is an indication to the hotel that they may yet talk you into staying put. Plant yourself, bag, and baggage at the reception desk.

When there is a problem, junior-level airline and hotel personnel may try very hard to shunt you aside into an office or even a quiet corner—anywhere out of the public eye. Don't go. The business traveler stays put. A public and potentially embarrassing complaint at the reception desk or boarding gate that holds up a lengthening line of other guests or passengers waiting to check in will be resolved a lot faster—and generally more favorably to you—than a dispute behind closed doors.

Find Your Target: Aim High

Sometimes the most difficult part of complaining is aiming your protest where it will do the most good. At the airport, use your connections to the Special Services representatives to deal with your problem. Failing that, the magic words usually are, "May I speak with your supervisor?"

If I've really been mistreated, it's usually a middle-level employee who is responsible. Because that person reports to a supervisor who's probably going to protect him, I go one step above that to the chief supervisor, since that's where the problem is going to end up anyway.

The first objective is to represent yourself as part of the solution, not part of the problem. I let them know at the earliest point in the conversation my credentials as a frequent flyer and a loyal fan of the airline.

From the minute our discussions begin, I'm a cheerleader on the side of the angels. My conversation follows something along these lines—"This airline has always been great for me, but I wanted to let you know about a problem *we* have, and I really hope you can help." I'm not calling to start the battle, but to report the outbreak of a minor skirmish in which I might have been a participant. The situation thus becomes not me vs. the airline, but me and the supervisor defending the integrity of *our* airline vs. the intransigent idiot in the middle who's causing all the trouble.

Know What You Want

Decide in advance what you want to have happen. Distill your anger and exasperation into a simple but specific request, such as:

- "I want to be booked on your flight #334 leaving in half an hour."
- "I'm holding a reservation on Another Airlines flight #123 leaving in half an hour, and I need you to endorse my ticket for your delayed flight over to Another Airlines."
- "Here's my confirmation number—I want Room #679, the corner suite I booked three weeks ago."
- "You should have told me the place was all torn up with construction. I want you to book me an equivalent suite at Another Hotel at the same rate, and I want you to transfer me and my luggage there immediately."

Complain Toward the Building of a Better Relationship

Remember the Personal Touch. Once you've found someone with the authority to solve the problem, give them a chance to demonstrate their clout. Most of the time you'll get the situation resolved in your favor if you remain calm but firm. Don't be vindictive. Don't gloat publicly when you "win."

Winning one battle is not the objective. The war goes on, and will continue as long as you travel. You'll be in the air again next week, and the same faces show up all the time. If you create an adversary by pushing someone to the wall over one incident, they may be truly disinclined to do anything on your behalf the next time you need them.

Chapter IV
A Month on the Road
With Mark McCormack

The month of February was a heavy travel month for me. It was also one in which I was confronted with a number of travel fiascos. How I used the weapons at my disposal to deal with them provides a real-life illustration of the principles put forth in the last chapter. In this chapter you'll spend a month on the road with me and see how I travel. You'll also get a view of how and where I realize time savings, and how I invest them to enhance my travel experience.

February 1st – February 4th: Tokyo

On February 1st I was in Tokyo. I arrived there on January 31st, on a Delta flight from my home in Orlando, Florida. My trip is proof that Orlando International Airport is becoming more and more global. I flew from Orlando to Tokyo direct, staying on the same plane with one stop at Los Angeles. It was a sixteen-and-a-half-hour flight—five hours to Los Angeles, one and a half hours on the ground, and ten hours in the air to Tokyo. The flight to Los Angeles was very crowded and first-class was full of sports celebrities, including Don Shula and Dan Marino of the Miami Dolphins.

I sleep a great deal on planes—it's a good habit for the frequent flyer to cultivate. On this flight I slept a total of eight hours. I slept a solid four hours from Orlando to Los Angeles, dozing off shortly after takeoff and waking up somewhere over Arizona.

I also slept four of the ten hours on the way to Japan. The rest of the time I was doing paperwork. I didn't have any leisure reading at all with me. I was working on my advance yellow pads, trying to get everything lined up and thought out for the week of meetings ahead.

The service on Delta was good, but the flight did prove the adage about flying the national flag of the home country. When we landed we were left well out on the field and bussed into the terminal. Everything else about the flight, however, was first-rate. When I reached my hotel, I went to bed that night around ten o'clock and woke up at 3 A.M.

That may strike you as an odd time to get up, but it was part of my plan for dealing with jet lag. On this trip I really dealt successfully with the time change. Every day was very full. The pattern I developed was to get up very early in the morning, anywhere from 2 to 4 A.M. At that time I would make my international phone calls, and do three or four hours of work. Then I would have my coffee and begin breakfast meetings at 7:30 or 8:00 A.M., followed by morning meetings, followed by a business lunch. By the end of the lunch hour I was usually very tired, and I scheduled no meetings after lunch on any of the days of my trip.

I instructed my staff to block off the hours between 1:30 and 4:00 P.M. for a nap. Of that time I'd end up with about two hours of solid sleep. When I awoke I'd have meetings, mostly business dinners, then sleep about five or six more hours at night. Although it was broken into two segments, I really was getting about seven and a half or eight hours sleep a day.

That was my daily pattern in Tokyo. When I got up at 2 or 3 A.M., I'm sure there were a lot of nightspots in Tokyo that were still open, and a lot of people who hadn't gone to bed yet. It may have been the wee small hours in Tokyo, but it was like getting up in New York at 1 in the afternoon or Los Angeles at 10 A.M. It was almost like staying on American time.

February 5th: Tokyo – New York

I was scheduled to leave Tokyo on a United Airlines nonstop flight to New York that was due to leave at 5 P.M. and land at 3:30 P.M. at JFK. A few months before, IMG had acquired control of Millrose Games, an indoor track meet held annually at Madison Square Garden, and the oldest track meet in the United States. The grand finale and the signature event of the Millrose Games is the Wanamaker Mile. I was to present the award to the winner of the Wanamaker Mile that night at about 10 P.M.

With six and a half hours between my arrival at Kennedy and the presentation of the trophy, I was sure that I had left myself more than enough time to clear Customs, get home, shower, get dressed, and get myself to Madison Square Garden. I planned to arrive there at about 7:00 P.M., and have a buffet supper with executives from Chemical Bank, which was the sponsor of the event. Other dignitaries would be there as well, including the Irish ambassador to the United States.

As I do routinely, on the morning of my departure I asked my office to call the airline to make sure everything was in order with the flight, and to reconfirm my seat. After my Tokyo office made the call to United, however, they gave me the appalling news that my flight was going to be six hours late. An incoming United flight to Tokyo was delayed, and that was the aircraft we were to be leaving on. We didn't have an airplane.

This was absolutely horrendous news. It meant that I was going to miss everything at Madison Square Garden, which wasn't very satisfactory. I was the host of the event. This experience demonstrated one rule that many business travelers have learned the hard way: **Don't rely on the airlines to let you know when things go wrong**—even though they always ask you for a contact telephone number where they can reach you in case there's a problem. They hardly ever call. In the normal course of events, I'd have just gone to the airport and been told the bad news when I arrived.

When I got the news, I called my senior personal assistant, Laurie Roggenburk, in Cleveland, who handles most of my travel arrangements. We both thought she had done what she normally does, which is double- or triple-book me, so that I might have some alternative nonstop flights. There was one other nonstop flight, but it was full, and I hadn't booked myself on it. Normally I will make multiple reservations, just in case something like this happens, but this time I hadn't done it.

I was moderately depressed and a bit angry with myself because I hadn't followed my own advice. At least now, however, I had the chance to work on an alternative. I consulted my *Skyguide* and discovered a Northwest Airlines flight to Chicago, connecting to an American Airlines flight to LaGuardia.

Every time I've flown Northwest in Asia in the last couple of years, I have been immensely impressed with the airline. In the old days Northwest was just awful, and even today you don't hear a lot about them. Everyone talks about Singapore Airlines and Japan Airlines, but Northwest was super. When we got to Chicago, they bused us into the Customs area and an unusual and impressive thing happened. They had a special bus for the first-class passengers. Northwest does this all the time, apparently. They whisked us in and got the first-class luggage off first, which is something foreign carriers do but very few American carriers do. Because we were an early arrival, the Customs area was a piece of cake. There was no other flight there.

From Chicago I could have flown either United or American to New York, but I chose American because in O'Hare they have the nearest terminal to Northwest, and I knew that I had to get my luggage from one terminal to another. I went to American, boarded my flight, and got into LaGuardia at just a little after 6:00 P.M., compared with my planned arrival time of 3:30 on the delayed United flight.

Mary Wenzel, my New York secretary, met my flight and took me directly to my New York pied-à-terre. I worked with her for about half an hour, then freshened up and got changed before heading over to Madison Square Garden and my dinner with the Chemical Bank people, the Irish ambassador, and our client, Irish runner Eammon Coughlin, who won the Masters'

Mile. At the end of the evening I presented the Wanamaker Mile trophy in front of a sellout crowd.

February 6th: New York

I had slept seven hours on the flight from Tokyo to Chicago. I had absolutely no time change problem at all coming back, which I attribute to a combination of the naps and getting up at 2 or 3 A.M. while in Tokyo. Starting at about 6 A.M., I worked with Mary, going over stuff that had accumulated while I'd been in Tokyo. In the evening I worked with my senior personal assistant, Laurie, who had come in from our Cleveland headquarters.

February 7th: New York – Orlando

During the night New York was hit by a blizzard. Although the city looked beautiful, it was not very cheerful news for me, since I was due to fly south to Orlando. We started calling the airports, and of course everything was delayed. LaGuardia was snowed in.

I was scheduled on an 11:00 A.M. Delta flight, but when I got out to the terminal at LaGuardia they said it wasn't going to leave until 12:40 P.M. Given the conditions, this was not so terrible. However, I was dubious that they could actually get off the ground at that time, since I quickly determined that my aircraft was coming in from Cincinnati and it hadn't left Cincinnati yet. This demonstrates yet another maxim for the executive traveler: **Don't believe the times posted on the Arrivals and Departures boards.**

I consulted my *Skyguide* and I saw that there was a 10 A.M. flight on USAir. Even though it was now 10:30, I figured that since everything was delayed, maybe the ten o'clock flight was still there and was leaving at 11:30 or 12:00. I called USAir from the car while it was sitting out on the curb in front of Delta. In circumstances like these, **don't dismiss your limousine or car until you are positive you no longer need it.**

When weather problems scramble flight schedules, airport phones—whether they are pay phones or phones in VIP lounges—are in short supply. When you are in your car or limo, you have instant access to a phone of your very own.

Sure enough, the USAir 10 A.M. flight was leaving at 11:30. The best news was that although the plane was not yet physically at LaGuardia, it was already in the air from Buffalo. The driver took me to the USAir terminal, LaGuardia's newest, and a state-of-the-art facility that is very efficient and comfortable. Even though the flight was delayed a little further, it did ultimately leave. I got a bit more work done in the USAir VIP lounge and arrived in Orlando in time for a meeting I was scheduled to have late that afternoon.

That night I had dinner with Gary Player.

February 8th: Orlando – Chicago

The next morning I flew from Orlando to Chicago. I had no baggage, only carry-ons. My wife Betsy had left before me on Sunday and had taken my luggage with her. She was there to play in the Virginia Slims tennis tournament.

My flight landed at 11:15 A.M. Since I had a lunch date at 12:15 P.M. downtown with Bill Smithburg, the chairman of Quaker Oats, I was cutting it a little close. I had a limousine meet me at the airport, but at O'Hare they no longer permit limousines to pull up to the curb and wait. They must park in a garage, which is most inconvenient. Nevertheless, the driver met me at the gate and I got to Nick's Fishmarket right on time.

That night I had dinner with my friend Phil Stefani, who owns Tuscany restaurant, which is one of the all-time great Italian restaurants, and with Ivo and Denise Cozzini.

February 9th: Chicago

After making phone calls early in the morning, I had breakfast with Billie Jean King at the Mayfair Regent, followed by a late lunch in Schaumburg, about fifty miles outside the city. Betsy was scheduled to play both her matches, singles and doubles, that day. She lost her singles match 7–6 in the second set, but won her doubles that night with her partner, Monica Seles.

The match ended very late, but after the victory Betsy and I went out with Christie Hefner and her companion, Illinois State Senator Bill Meirovitz. We went to Un Grand Cafe (the local wags pronounce its name as the Ungrand Cafe), which is one of twenty-eight owned by Chicago restaurateur Rich Melman.

February 10th: Chicago – New York

The next day I had lunch with Rich Melman at a place called Maggiano's. It has a bakery at the front which produces outstanding bread. There is a little cafe in the bakery, plus a substantial main dining room. It was so good that Betsy and I returned there again that night with my son Todd and Monica Seles. It was a terrific dinner. After dinner I flew to New York on the last flight out, which got in at 1 A.M.

February 11th: New York – Chicago

In the morning I had a meeting with executives from American Express, and lunch with legendary editor-in-chief John Mack Carter of *Good Housekeeping*. John used to work for my Dad, and he's been a friend for more than twenty years. We had lunch at "21."

That afternoon I met with some businessmen from Argentina to talk about a new tennis tournament in Buenos Aires. Then I took a flight back to Chicago, where Betsy and Monica were playing doubles in the quarter-finals that evening.

February 12th: Chicago – Norfolk – Williamsburg, Virginia

The doubles match (which they won) ended very late, about 2 A.M., which made it a very short night, since I was leaving on a 6:39 A.M. flight to Norfolk, Virginia. It was a sleety, snowy morning. Five or ten years ago the weather would have canceled everything for 100 miles around, but because of all the new electronics and technology, it was no problem at all. We just took off.

The flight landed at about noon. From the airport I went to Williamsburg, home of the College of William & Mary, one of the oldest institutions of higher learning in the United States, and my alma mater. For the last three years I've been the national co-chairman of a $150 million capital fundraising campaign.

I was there to help the college celebrate its tricentennial Charter Day. I'd also donated some money for the construction of a tennis center, and had lunch with the tennis coach and the women's athletic director. I was in meetings at the school in the afternoon, followed by a gala evening Charter Day celebration.

February 13th: Williamsburg, Virginia

Following breakfast, I arrived for the Charter Day Ceremony at 9:30 A.M. The college had invited HRH Prince Charles to help commemorate the anniversary. The students welcomed him with great acclaim, which was very gratifying for him. He gave a stirring address in honor of the 300th anniversary of William & Mary, after which I joined him (and a hundred or so others) for lunch.

February 14th: Williamsburg – Washington – Paris

The next morning, after brunch with the president of William & Mary, I hired a car from Williamsburg to Washington, D.C., where I was to catch an Air France flight to Paris. The three-hour drive allowed me to get in some reading and paperwork. I arrived at Dulles Airport at 4:30 for a nonstop flight that was due to leave at 6:05.

In the smallish but pleasant Air France VIP lounge at Dulles, I went over some more paperwork. Twenty minutes before boarding, Air France announced that the aircraft had *un petit* mechanical difficulty—the flight was going to be delayed for seven hours.

This was a catastrophe of the first magnitude. The following day at noon I was scheduled to have a crucial meeting in Paris with the head of Canal Plus, one of the major private television stations in France. The meeting had been set up for a long time. I absolutely had to get to Paris. There was no way I would wait for the flight.

Be there or be square. My staff and I immediately began scrambling. The only alternative seemed to be to catch a United flight to London, and then connect on the Air France hop from London to Paris. This would get me into Charles DeGaulle at around 10:15 A.M., as opposed to 7:30 A.M. with the original flight. Getting to a noon lunch date in the heart of Paris would be tight, but it was doable.

My main concern about the switch to United was that I wanted to make sure my baggage got off the Air France plane. It had to be transferred from an Air France flight to Paris to a United flight to London, then back onto an Air France flight from London to Paris. It was all too easy to envision a baggage handler second-guessing me and leaving the bags on the original flight. After all, either way the luggage was going to end up on Air France in Paris.

I was very insistent that Air France retrieve and give me the luggage, which they eventually did. This demonstrates another rule for the smart business traveler: **When you have to make**

emergency revisions to your flight plans, never get separated from your luggage. Demand that it physically be delivered to you from the delayed or canceled flight.

I rushed over to United Airlines and personally re-checked my luggage onto the new flight, rather than rely on someone who promised to take care of it. Then I called my secretary in London to make sure that someone met me at Heathrow.

On the United flight to London, I was very impressed with the quality of their food, but very unimpressed with the length of time it took them to put the meal in front of me. It took them literally an hour and a half from the time we pushed back from the gate till I had the first course in front of me—on a six-hour flight. United inherited this route from Pan Am, and I think it has something to do with the age of the plane and the fact that the galley has to come up on an elevator.

I mentioned it to the flight attendant who was serving me. I told her, "Everyone on a transatlantic flight is trying to get to sleep. British Airways would have had the meal two-thirds served by the time you put the first course down." The flight attendant told me that many of her passengers complained about it, but there was nothing she could do. I made a note to avoid United on this route until the situation improved.

February 15th: London – Paris

We landed at Heathrow. I knew the United Airlines Special Services people, who used to be Pan Am's Special Services representatives when Pan Am was flying this route. They expedited my way through Customs.

My London personal assistant Sarah Wooldridge came out to the airport in the limo with Peter Herst, our driver. They drove me over to the Air France terminal. Since we had a little time before the short flight to Paris was due to leave, Sarah and I decided to get some work done while we were waiting. In the meantime I sent Peter down to the counter to make sure that the flight was on time. Peter returned with startling news that the baggage handlers at DeGaulle were on strike and that the flight was delayed for an hour.

While we waited in the coffee shop at Heathrow, Sarah and I did get some work accomplished. The flight ultimately landed in Paris at 11:15, but the luggage did come out quickly. I had arranged for a driver from the Hotel de Crillon to meet me. The car took me directly to the hotel. I quickly shaved, washed my hands and face, changed my shirt, and drove over to Canal Plus for the meeting. I wasn't there on the dot of twelve, but I was close. In Paris I was reunited with Betsy, who was playing in a tennis tournament, both singles and doubles. She was again paired with Monica Seles. That night we had dinner at La Marée, my favorite restaurant in France, with Jean-Claude Killy and his partner.

February 16th: Paris

Betsy played her singles match and lost. Unfortunately, she and Monica played their doubles match very late on Tuesday and lost that as well.

February 17th: Paris

I had meetings all day. That evening Betsy and I dined at Duquesnoy (another Parisian personal favorite) with Monica Seles, her father, and her coach. We were joined by my daughter Leslie, who works in our Paris office, and her beau.

February 18th: Paris – London

Betsy and I flew to London. That night we had dinner with Sir Christopher Lewinton and his wife at the newly refurbished Ivy restaurant, which was great in the old days and has now made a terrific resurgence.

February 19th: London

I was in meetings pretty much all day, but had a wonderful lunch in the Rib Room at the Carlton Tower.

February 20th: London – Gleneagles, Scotland

The bulk of the day was devoted to a business meeting with the chairman of Wimbledon at his home in the suburbs. In the late afternoon I flew to Gleneagles, Scotland, where we would be having two days of internal meetings with executives of our television division. I had sent Sarah up earlier with my luggage, so all I had with me were my two briefcases. That evening Sarah and I had a dinner in my suite to go over the arrangements for the meetings.

February 21st: Gleneagles – St. Andrews – Gleneagles

In the morning I drove to St. Andrews to meet Michael Bonallack, the head of the Royal & Ancient Golf Club. The discussion continued into lunch, which was served in a private dining room at the top of the Old Course Hotel. I drove back to Gleneagles late that afternoon, where I had a dinner meeting with three senior executives in my suite.

I heartily endorse dinner meetings in your room, particularly if you have serious business to discuss and don't want the distractions and interruptions of a public dining room. However, it helps to think it through.

When you dine in your suite at a hotel, particularly a first-class establishment, you are generally assigned a head waiter for the evening. He serves you and stands at your beck and call. If you are discussing confidential or sensitive matters, you might let the waiter go, but then when you finish the first course, you have to call room service to get him back. It's a needless complication, which I have solved by giving the waiter specific instructions about when and how fast I would like each course served. He knows when he's needed; I don't have to keep calling.

February 22nd – February 23rd: Gleneagles

I headed up two days of intensive meetings, lasting from 7 A.M. to 10 P.M.

February 24th: Gleneagles – London

I returned to London for an all-day meeting with Michael Sohlman, the executive director of the Nobel Foundation, who had flown in from Stockholm, for a report on our various activities on behalf of the Nobel Foundation.

February 25th: London

I hosted a press conference at the Royal Palace at Hampton Court to announce the inaugural season of a major ten-day festival to be presented by our classical-music division, IMG Artists, in June.

That evening I was the guest of Sol Kerzner, the developer of South Africa's famous Lost City resort, for dinner at the marvelous private dining room at Annabel's.

February 26th: London – Los Angeles – Palm Springs

After an early morning haircut and an interview with a magazine reporter, I flew from London to Los Angeles. Then I drove from LAX to Palm Springs, where we were running the Matrix Essentials/Evert Cup tennis tournament. In Palm Springs I rejoined Betsy, who was playing doubles in the tournament and also was providing television commentary on the matches for ESPN.

February 27th: Palm Springs

This was a leisurely day for me. After internal meetings with our tennis executives in the morning, I watched the matches while Betsy attended to her broadcasting duties.

February 28th: Palm Springs – Los Angeles – Vail

After the national telecast was finished, Betsy and I returned to Los Angeles and flew to Vail, Colorado, for a brief vacation.

Chapter V
Sometimes It's Worth It

Time is money, but money is money, too, and the recent economic climate has forced many firms to cut back on some of the "frills" of business travel. From either a personal or professional perspective, there's absolutely no point in being a frequent but miserable traveler. It makes you far less able to make the deal or participate in the negotiation, which is why you made the trip in the first place. Over the long run, if you travel unhappily often enough, even the most dynamic executive gets used up and worn down. The purpose of this chapter is to illustrate where spending the extra dollars pays off, and where savings can be realized.

There is no denying the fact that comfortable and efficient executive travel is, on the average, about twenty percent more expensive than standard business travel. For me, however, the premium pays extra dividends to both the smart business traveler and his or her corporation. The additional outlay, properly expended, produces a refreshed, invigorated executive and a business person who looks forward to traveling on business.

This is not to say that spending more always gets you more. Many executives incur extra charges needlessly, often without being aware of it. By trimming these costs, which frequently do not affect comfort or efficiency, the executive traveler can either allocate those resources toward travel expenditures which make the trip far more enjoyable, or have them accrue at the Bottom Line.

You Gotta Ask, Part I

No Charge for Tickets by Overnight Delivery

With a last-minute trip, often one of the big problems to be solved is getting the ticket and boarding pass in hand before departing for the airport. For this reason many executive travelers, even those who have made their own reservations, go to their travel agency to purchase their ticket. This should not be necessary. If you are a volume traveler, your travel agency should be delivering those tickets to your office, even to your home. All you have to do is ask.

What if you need to be ticketed after normal business hours? Using a travel agent isn't the only way to get tickets on short notice. Many airlines will send you your ticket by Federal Express or other overnight delivery service.

Will you get hit for the cost of delivery? Not necessarily. This is not a service that the airlines advertise. It's not even a service they will offer you over the telephone. However, if you need the ticket right away, all you have to do is ask them to send it overnight. When you consider it, it makes great economic sense for them. The airline would pay a ten percent commission to a travel agency to write up the ticket. It would cost them $100 on a $1,000 ticket. If they pay $8.75 for a Fedex delivery, they can save themselves $91 *and* demonstrate to a frequent passenger that they are providing extraordinary personal service.

It gets to be even more of a bargain when you remember that these people are in the transportation business. It's highly likely that they have special arrangements with one or more overnight express delivery services. It probably costs them virtually nothing to put your ticket in your hands overnight. However, it won't happen unless you ask.

You Gotta Ask, Part II

You and Your Travel Agent

One of the first opportunities an executive traveler has to save money is with his or her travel agent. Ten percent is the standard commission travel agents earn on airline tickets. Because times are hard in the travel business, many agents are now rebating—splitting their commissions with their best clients.

Some agencies rebate on any airfare. Others require a minimum ticket price, usually anywhere from $100 to $500. If you do a significant volume business, ask your travel agent for a rebate. You'll most likely get the discount if you request it, but most people don't ask. If you are a good volume client but the agency refuses, call around. It shouldn't be too difficult to find an agency willing to give you a break.

Traveling executives should know, however, that at some point the rebating policy will impinge upon the agency's ability to provide service. Often this means that they will do little more for you than write up your ticket. "If an agency is rebating," says Anastasia Mann of Corniche Travel in Los Angeles, "they have less money to pay staff. If you're dealing with a really sophisticated travel management company, they should be saving you so much money you don't want the rebate on an individual ticket." Corniche, which has a prestigious corporate and entertainment industry clientele, does not provide rebates to its clients, and Mann believes that clients who demand them are being penny-wise and pound-foolish. "It's like cutting off your nose to spite your face," she says. "You're getting a kickback that's not big enough to pay someone in the mailroom, and you're sacrificing the proper handling of the key people who can make or break your company."

Despite declining service, many hard-pressed companies are forging new arrangements with their travel service providers. Hewlett-Packard doesn't pay any commission to the travel agencies it uses. Instead, it actually takes that commission from the airlines and pays a flat fee to those who book their flights and hotels. HP executives believe that this eliminates the divided loyalty that is built into the commission arrangement—agents earn more from selling higher-priced fares than they do from selling cheaper ones.

A consortium of major corporations is gearing for battle with the airlines. Seventeen companies, including General Motors and Merck pharmaceuticals, are banding together to try to negotiate with the airlines for lower fares. In exchange, they are offering to abandon frequent flyer miles and eliminate commissions to travel agents. In theory, these corporations believe the agreement will both cut their costs and boost airline revenues. This attempt may or may not be successful, and depends in part on anti-trust clearance from the Justice Department.

Other companies are taking travel matters into their own hands. With some of the most computer-literate employees anywhere, Apple Computers has established a network that gives its workers direct computer access to fare information as they plan their trips. This information includes data on potential savings from discounts which the company has arranged with various airlines. The program is paying off—in the beginning of 1994, the firm paid 25 percent less on travel than it did in 1993, even though its employees took 14 percent more trips.

It pays any executive traveler to keep track of the fluctuating relationships between airlines and travel agencies. If your travel agent is suddenly urging you to fly TWA, perhaps it's because that airline has been offering an 18 percent commission to travel agents for booking full coach, business, or first-class tickets on transcontinental round-trips, such as those between New York and Los Angeles.

Does this TWA offer constitute a "bribe" by the airline that compromises your travel agent's "independence"? Certainly it does. However, if you find out about it and you are willing to fly TWA, there's no reason why your travel agent shouldn't split it with you and give you a nine percent rebate on the cost of your flight. These inducements from airlines to travel agents are not uncommon. A recent survey in the trade journal *Travel Weekly* found that more than half of all travel agents chose a carrier for a client in order to obtain that added commission at least some of the time.

You Are How You Fly

The Class Struggle: First-Class vs. Coach

Nothing clarifies the pecking order in a corporate hierarchy as plainly as who flies first-class, who flies business-class, and who flies coach when traveling on company matters. From an outsider's perspective there are two impressions made by a firm that flies its upper management personnel first-class:

- They treat their executives extravagantly well;
- They don't keep a careful eye on their expenditures.

Image and Status

Within a firm, however, the tug-of-war over first-class travel usually boils down to a question of status. Traveling first-class validates an executive's perceived sense of personal worth to the company. Noses get out of joint when those who believe themselves "entitled" to first-class travel find themselves in steerage in the back of the plane. At such times someone in my position is likely to hear a great deal about how important it is for the "image of the company" for an executive to be in the front cabin. I've had executives in my own firm ask for permission to fly first-class because a client was going to be on the same flight in first-class, and they didn't want to be seen in coach. The reason they gave me was that they didn't want to be seen flying economy because it put our company in a bad light.

I actually believe it puts our company in a good light because it demonstrates that we are being responsible about costs. I am far less swayed by these kinds of "image" arguments in favor of flying first-class than those which are rooted in personal physical limitations, practicality, and efficiency. The "need" to fly first-class because a client is flying with you and you have to be perceived as his or her peer is far less persuasive with me than common sense reasons such as these:

- That time together on the plane is the only opportunity you will have to talk something over with him
- You suffer from a bad back
- You need to sleep on a long intercontinental flight in order to be rested and effective during a full day of appointments and meetings immediately upon arrival

Frequent Flyer Benefits

Since their inception, airline frequent flyer programs have been considered the perk of the business traveler making the trip, not of the company that paid for the ticket. Airlines have thus far sided with the individual passenger, believing in that fashion that they can guarantee themselves more customer loyalty. Even though frequent flyer programs have made "mileage junkies" out of many executive travelers, there are now strong pressures to change this situation. Corporations realize the value that these miles represent, and many of them are seeking in a variety of ways to capitalize on them. Several firms have offered to abandon frequent flyer miles entirely in an attempt to negotiate for a deeper discount on tickets.

To date, airlines have resisted these efforts, but frequent flyer miles are increasingly viewed as a bargaining chip by companies trying to cut their travel expenses. Boeing, among other companies, retains for itself the frequent flyer miles its traveling executives pile up. This might sound a bit Scrooge-like to some road warriors who have logged a lot of uncomfortable hours squeezed into a coach-class seat. Dr. Pepper/Seven-Up has taken a softer approach. It has started compensating its executive travelers who use their frequent flyer mileage for business trips. As an inducement, they offer a $300 incentive payment to their traveling business executives to use their frequent flyer miles for a trip that otherwise would have cost the company over $600.

It's not my place to judge the travel policies of corporations other than my own. There is a sizable publishing industry that counsels travelers on how to make the best use of frequent flyer programs. (See especially *Inside Flyer* and *Frequent Flyer* magazines, both of which are published monthly.) My watchword to the traveling business executive is to **be aware that frequent flyer mileage has become a sensitive issue.** It might be ill-advised to take off for Bora Bora for three weeks on a free ticket using mileage you racked up chasing a contract that never materialized, or a job that lost the company a lot of money.

Integrity

I am assuming a high degree of integrity on the part of my readers. The last thing I would want my book to be used for is to chisel a company for the cost of luxury travel when it is not warranted, or when everyone else in the firm is going through a round of close-to-the-bone budget-cutting.

I applaud the business travelers who use their own upgrade stickers garnered through their frequent flyer programs to boost themselves out of coach in order to have a more pleasant travel experience. From a management perspective it demonstrates a team-player attitude toward company travel. At International Management Group, we've had all kinds of policies on first-class travel at various times, depending on fares and the deals we've been able to negotiate with the airlines. There have been occasions when we have said to an executive that if he flies first-class the company will pay part of the difference, but he's got to pay part of it as well. If someone is truly sincere about the "need" to fly first-class, he should be willing to put up part of the cost out of his own pocket. We might split the cost fifty-fifty, or if the case is truly compelling, we'd pick up two-thirds and the employee would pay one-third.

Doing Business in First-Class

I've been able to do a lot of paperwork on the plane, but flying first-class has never led to new business opportunities for me, perhaps because I really try to sleep on my flights. Other business travelers, particularly in the entertainment field, however, have been able to use first-class to enhance corporate profits. Henry Rogers, founder of the Los Angeles-based public relations firm Rogers & Cowan, tells the story of one of his account executives who violated the company's "economy-class only" policy. On his own authority, without telling anyone about it, the executive had been flying first-class between Los Angeles and New York.

It was a major offense, a significant breach of company policy, made without consultation. Rogers called the offender into his office, confronted him with his malfeasance, and was somewhat taken aback by his executive's levity in what he considered a very serious situation.

"I was wondering how long it would take you to catch on," he told Rogers, laughing. "In fact, I've kept a record of the results of my first-class travel in the past year." The executive produced a notebook and read Rogers the log of his eight transcontinental flights, including the difference in cost between coach and first-class travel, and the names of people he had met and talked with on each flight.

Then he played his trump card. "The contacts I made on those flights brought four new high-paying clients to Rogers & Cowan. However, here is my personal check for the difference between coach and first-class fare." With that, he placed the check on Henry Rogers's desk. Rogers took the check and tore it up without looking at it. Although he did not revise the company policy, Rogers did issue a special dispensation for his intrepid account executive, with the proviso that it was only in effect as long as first-class travel continued to pay benefits to Rogers & Cowan.

Business-Class

Business-class on many airlines can be a viable and affordable alternative to first-class. It is usually head and shoulders above coach travel—but not always. On lengthy flights, the amenities offered in business-class generally approach those of first-class, with roomier seats, better cuisine, and free entertainment. However, on shorter hops, especially within Europe, business-class can be only a marginal improvement on coach travel. Business-class is surely not worth a premium if the food is better and the alcohol is gratis but the seat is the same cramped size as that in coach.

In general, international business-class service is far superior to domestic business-class service. On carriers based in the United States, this is true even on the same airline. I was on one American Airlines flight from Los Angeles to Paris that stopped in Chicago for a change of aircraft. Booked as a first-class passenger for the L.A.–Chicago leg, I was "just" a business-class passenger for the Chicago–Paris portion of the trip.

Domestic first-class service was indifferent at best. The flight attendants seemed to be sleepwalking through their duties. However, the business-class international service was superior, far better than the American domestic first-class service, and indeed better than many international first-class flights I'd experienced. I came to the conclusion that the flight attendants closed the privacy curtain between first-class and business-class not to keep business-class passengers from seeing what the first-class passengers were getting, but to prevent the first-class passengers from realizing that business-class service was virtually indistinguishable from their own.

Many airlines have recently upgraded their business-class service. The most innovative business-class may well be on Richard Branson's upstart Virgin Atlantic Airlines, whose "Upper Class" service is available between New York and London, and Los Angeles and London. Virgin's business-class amenities include fully reclining seats of first-class proportions, stand-up bars and lounges (reminiscent of those on the first generation of 747s more than twenty years ago), an inflight entertainment system giving each passenger his or her choice of movies, and free limousine pick-up on departure and delivery on arrival. On some flights an airborne masseuse and manicurist are also on board. What more do Virgin's first-class passengers get? Nothing. There is no first-class, only Upper Class. (Virgin has also pioneered a "midclass" service, an "enhanced" economy service with coach-class meals, more legroom, and wider seats.)

Airlines with augmented business-class service have forced other carriers to upgrade their own service just to retain market share. Virgin has certainly spurred British Airways to further refinements and improvements in their already generally excellent service. This is by no means uncommon—a general rule of thumb to bear in mind is that the more hotly contested a route is, the better business-class will be (and for that matter first-class and coach as well). You can expect the very best service on heavily traveled transcontinental and intercontinental business routes, such as L.A.–New York, L.A.–Tokyo, New York–London, and New York–Paris, where competition among the various carriers is keen.

On travel to more remote or more vacation-oriented destinations, it pays to be cautious. On these kinds of routes, there is a much higher probability that business-class may not be worth the money. If you are not familiar with the airline or the aircraft in service on this particular run, question the reservation agent closely when booking. Make sure you know how big the seat is, how much legroom there is between rows, and whether business-class has its own cabin. This last is crucial—on some airlines, business-class is like an accordion, stretching if bookings in coach are light, but crumpling down to just a few rows if coach reservations are heavy. I find this unacceptable. Business-class service should not be subject to the vagaries of coach reservations. If an airline is able to turn business into coach at will and vice versa, there isn't enough difference between the two classes of service to justify the added expense. Either find another airline or save the money and fly coach.

Indeed, if the flight is a short one, let's say two hours or less, the benefits of either business or first-class travel may be marginal. I can sleep on a plane under almost any circumstances, and for two hours anyone can survive the indignities of coach. The business traveler needs to decide whether the money spent by flying business or first-class might be better spent by flying coach and allocating the difference to a more desirable hotel room, or other amenities which will make your travel more enjoyable. After all, you'll spend a lot more time in your hotel room than you will on the plane for a short flight. **Put your money where it will do you and your company the most good.**

Some corporations have made this company policy. I know of companies who have started to offer senior executives a personal financial incentive *not* to fly first-class. Some authorize a generous hotel-room upgrade for the duration of the stay. Others pay half the difference between coach and first-class fare directly to the executive as a bonus.

Of course, the best solution by far is the one where you pay for a coach ticket but fly business-class. This can be accomplished on an individual basis by use of frequent flyer upgrades, or special deals that airlines make with other travel service providers. Members of the Sheraton hotel club program pay a $25 fee for membership—with that membership they also receive a round-trip upgrade on United Airlines. To me that's $25 very well spent.

Other executive travelers end up in business-class through negotiation at the corporate level. Some firms who arrange purchase of tickets in bulk from a particular airline (see Barter and Volume Discounts in Chapter VII) are able to get free upgrades as part of their agreement. One entertainment firm was able to strike a bargain with TWA which provided everyone traveling for the company a Gold Card. Company representatives traveling on corporate business purchase coach-class seats, but are automatically upgraded to business-class immediately. If space is available, they are bumped up into first-class.

How Good a Bed Do You Need?

On a long transcontinental or intercontinental flight, what do you do? If you're like most executive travelers, you eat a little, drink a little, and work a little—but mostly you sleep. That means that despite the fact that all airlines try to win your loyalty with inflight food and service, that is not what the business traveler is really paying for. What you are actually buying is not a seat, but a bed.

How good a bed do you need? It depends on how long your flight is and whether you are a good sleeper on flights. You certainly pay a premium for a seat that allows you a fighting chance at sleep. According to a recent *Condé Nast Traveler* magazine study of service between New York and various destinations in Europe, business-class and first-class passengers pay a great deal more for a few inches of comfort. The average economy-class ticket was $442 round-trip, with a seat width of eighteen inches and a pitch (distance between your seatback and the upright seatback in front of you) of thirty-one inches.

In business-class, the average ticket price jumped to $3,367 with a seat width of twenty-one inches and a pitch of forty inches. In first-class, the average ticket price was $5,709, with a seat width of twenty-two inches and a pitch of sixty inches.

The Price Per Inch

In dollar terms, a business-class passenger on a transatlantic-round-trip flight was paying $325 an inch for extra legroom, and $975 per inch for more rump room. The first-class passenger was paying $182 per inch for more legroom than a coach traveler, and $117 per inch for the space gained over business-class. He or she paid $1,316 per inch for more room for his or her posterior than was available in coach. That extra inch in first-class seat width (as compared with business-class) cost $2,342.

If you can sleep on the plane and arrive rested, the cost may well be worth it. However, if try as you might you can't sleep on the plane and experience terrible jet lag no matter what, you'd be better off surviving the flight as best you can in coach and putting the money into a good hotel suite.

British television host Michael Parkinson suffers no matter how he flies: "I've never been able to beat jet lag at all. I have a metabolism which requires at least seven days to recuperate if I go to Australia. It's a full seven days before I stop falling asleep with my head in the soup. A man named MacGregor once told me, 'There's no such thing as jet lag. All you have to do is don't eat, don't drink, wrap your feet in brown paper and lie on the floor of the airplane.' I actually tried it once. I didn't eat, didn't drink, wrapped my feet in paper bags and just lay there. It still took me seven days to recover."

Saturday Night Fever, or
Doing the Frequent-Flyer Two-Step

I recognize that by company policy, many business travelers, especially in recent difficult economic times, have no choice but to fly coach, no matter whether it's a weekly trip from

Washington to Chicago or a monthly jaunt from Dallas to Madrid. However, all too often business travelers get nicked for full coach, or "Y" class fare. Considerable discounts can be achieved by buying tickets a week or two before the date of departure, but most of these seven- or fourteen-day advance purchase tickets have a Saturday-night stay proviso appended to them. Coach-class business travelers, the vast majority of whom want to be in their own home on a Saturday night, are the intended victims of this stipulation.

For a trip between Los Angeles and New York, the difference is not insignificant. Depending on what airline you fly, round-trip unrestricted coach fare is approximately $1,300, vs. less than $400 for a ticket purchased a week or two in advance with a Saturday-night stay. It's irritating, to say the least. There are few inflight experiences more galling than spending five hours wedged into a middle seat in coach, squeezed between two fellow passengers who paid less for their two tickets combined than you paid for yours.

Unless you stay over a Saturday, it may seem that there's no way around the problem. Let's say a business traveler wants to fly from Los Angeles to New York and back again next week. He wants to leave on a Monday and return on Wednesday. He's not staying over a Saturday so he's out of luck, right?

Wrong.

It may sound counterintuitive, but the answer for the clever business commuter who is a repeat traveler between the same two cities is to book two flights rather than one. In our Los Angeles–New York example, the first flight would be a round-trip LAX–JFK–LAX, leaving Los Angeles on Monday and returning, well, let's say seven weeks from now. The second flight is a round-trip originating in your destination city, in this example New York. The JFK–LAX–JFK round-trip would leave New York on Wednesday and return, again, seven weeks from now. (The exact dates of the return flight segments on both tickets are relatively unimportant. It could be two weeks from now, or six weeks from now. However, if you can pinpoint the date and schedule of your second trip, you're that much further ahead.)

The important thing is that both round-trips are long enough to include a Saturday-night stay. For the first trip, use the LAX–JFK flight coupon from the first ticket, and the JFK–LAX flight coupon from the second ticket. The remaining flight coupons are used for the second trip.

What have you done? You've booked two trips for less than the price of one, and in the process saved over $1,800, without giving up anything. By my evaluation, someone clever enough to have pulled this off is entitled to a limo and a couple of very nice meals on the expense report.

Cabs, Limos, and the Bottom Line

When you travel on business, unless you are an individual entrepreneur, never lose sight of the fact that **when you are on the road, you are spending someone else's money.** I own my own company. When I travel, I can measure for myself whether to spend an extra $200 on a limousine because it makes me a happier camper, or whether I want the extra $200 in the profit line of the company. I hold myself accountable for my expenditures. I'm not trying to impress anyone; it has nothing to do with my "image."

Although I can make a decision to get a limo or not on my own authority, the questions I ask myself are the same as the ones any business traveler should be able to answer, even if they came from the chief financial officer of GM or an auditor from the IRS: "Can I get $200 worth of work done in the car? Is the added convenience worth $200 in time saved vs. the hassle of getting a series of cabs or the struggle and expense of parking a rental car?"

A limousine to me is almost always worth it. I work in cars a great deal, dictating in them or going over paperwork. In cities where we have offices, I will often ask one of my secretaries to accompany the driver in the limo coming to the airport to pick me up, so I can work with her on the way back into town. I also utilize the phone in the car a great deal. If my home office hasn't already done so, I can determine the latest on-time status of the flight, confirm hotel reservations in my destination city, and verify meeting dates, times, and agendas.

A limousine doesn't have to be thirty-five feet long and seat seven people for it to be functional. Many limousine services offer sedans with car phones. If you are traveling alone, there's plenty of room in them to spread out. In fact, I prefer cars that are not ostentatious. There's no point in having everyone point at your limo wondering which rock star or politician you might be. In London I have my own car and driver. The car is an estate car, or station wagon. It holds a lot of gear, which is great if I'm having a business meeting on the way to or from the airport. I can eliminate clutter and put my briefcase behind the seat, but I have access to papers and documents if I need them.

Sometimes what you need is not a car, but a driver. In Los Angeles, you can get a uniformed driver to chauffeur your own car (or, presumably, a rented car) for as little as $16 an hour. In a city where destinations are spread out, limos are expensive, and cabs are scarce, this expense may be a highly cost-effective solution to your transportation problems. You can make calls or complete paperwork in your own vehicle while someone else deals with the unpleasantness of rush-hour traffic. If you are based in Los Angeles and accomplishing some last-minute meetings before going on a lengthy business trip, the chauffeur may turn out to be a real bargain, since you won't have to pay for airport parking.

You and Your Expense Account

Guard Your Image

Even if your expenditures are justifiable, it's a good idea to **be sensitive to how your travel expenditures will be perceived by others within your firm.** The ill will you engender by flamboyant high-end travel, even if it ultimately is financially beneficial to the company, may poison your inhouse relationships. From this perspective, it is far preferable for an executive traveler to select a hotel with as many useful but conspicuous "frills" included in the basic cost of the room. This is especially true if the company is facing a round of budget or personnel cuts. Itemized costs for health clubs and limousines may look a bit too much like "let 'em eat cake." If you remember the story earlier in this chapter about the guy at Rogers & Cowan who always flew first-class to New York, he may have brought in a bundle of new contracts, but I'll bet he didn't endear himself to his coworkers who were still stuck in coach.

Flag Your Eyebrow-Raisers

He probably wouldn't have endeared himself to me, either. Although I would, of course, have been delighted that he had brought in so much new business through his new contacts in first-class, I would not have been pleased by his catch-me-if-you-can attitude. Henry Rogers tore up his check, but I'm not so sure I would have. I may well have permitted him to fly first-class in the future, but I also might have accepted the check to teach him to clear that stuff ahead of time. **Call attention to your own unusual expenditures.** If you have an eyebrow-raiser—an egregious expense that's way out of line but justifiable—it's far better to call attention to it upon submittal than wait for it to be challenged.

If you have the perfect, bulletproof answer to the "Why did you fly first-class?" question, short-circuit the interrogation process and save everyone (including your superior) a lot of time. It doesn't take much to annotate your expense account, saying, "Joe Blow was on my flight. I upgraded myself, and closed a $50,000 sale."

It happens in my company as well. There is a very trendy restaurant in Miami called Joe's Stone Crab, which doesn't take reservations. One of my executives submitted a $140 expense account for a meal there—$100 for the dinner, plus a $40 tip. Because of the outlandish size of the tip, it got bounced up to me. The executive explained that Jim Courier was with him. Although Courier is a superstar in the tennis world, his face is not necessarily one a maitre d' would recognize. The line at Joe's Stone Crab was huge, so my exec tipped the maitre d' $20 to get a table. The other $20 was the waiter's tip on a $100 meal, which was quite reasonable. I thought he handled it very expeditiously, and the extra $20 was money very well spent in service to a valuable client. However, if he had annotated his request for reimbursement when he handed it in, he would have showed a whole lot more responsibility than he did by submitting it and waiting for someone to catch it and refer it to me.

If you don't call attention to the discrepancy, it may appear as if you were trying to put a fast one over on your company. Once you have been challenged even on a justifiable outlay, your subsequent expense submittals are likely to receive far more scrutiny. If you're supposed to stay at a hotel for $150 a night and you spent $200, rather than trying to slip it by, hoping nobody catches it, highlight it yourself. Call attention to it, but explain why you did it.

The Little Hotel Bill and How It Grew

On the other hand, $150 hotel rooms turn into $200 hotel rooms every night, all over the world. As a business traveler staying at a hotel, you are an easy target for surcharges and hidden fees imposed by hoteliers who all too often seem to have their hand buried in your back pocket. Any business traveler who has ever awakened thirsty in the middle of the night has confronted the $10 bottle of mineral water and the $8 bottle of orange juice in the mini-refrigerator.

Sometimes you succumb. Sometimes you don't. One wise and wily associate of mine, who always brings her own water on planes (see Chapter III), packs some extra bottles of Perrier for her hotel room for just such occasions. The only times she runs into difficulty are when she has to remove some bottles from the refrigerator in order to make room for her own water. Often the bottles removed turn up as charges on her statement, even though they were not consumed and were placed prominently on the dresser.

Then there is the long arm of government. Room occupancy taxes levied by governments large and small cannot be avoided. Nevertheless, they can be shocking. Business travelers pay a 12.5 percent hotel tax in Los Angeles, a 13 percent tax in Atlanta, and a 14.9 percent tax in Chicago. In New York City, hotel guests pay a whopping 19.25 percent in taxes, plus a $2 per night surcharge, over and above the cost of their room. That makes the $150 hotel room a $181 hotel room, even before you pick up the phone.

Hotel Phone Charges:
Just Think of Your Hotel Telephone as a Pay Toilet

The most maddening charges are associated with costs which I believe ought to be part of the service, including phone calls and receipt of faxes. It is quite understandable to charge guests for sending faxes, but to charge them anywhere from $.50 to $2.50 per page for incoming faxes strikes me as nothing but gougery.

Most travelers do not find out about these unconscionable rates until the end of their stay when they are handed a bill that is two or three times what they anticipated for the entire cost of their visit. Then, it is too late. (However, hotels have been known to negotiate telephone bills with angry travelers who defend themselves.)

At the otherwise wonderful Stanhope Hotel in New York, an associate made only local calls, credit card calls, and (800) calls to the airlines to firm up his outbound flight plans. For a three-day stay, there were over $60 in phone charges on his bill. He was not only charged $1.00 for each (800) call and an "access fee" for each credit card call, he was also charged for each local call. Some calls were $0.80; others were $2.00. What was the difference? It wasn't the time of day. When he examined the bill carefully, he found that the "cheap" calls were calls which did not even go through—when he had run into a busy signal or someone was not in. The expensive ones were those when he had actually talked to someone. The only times when it didn't cost money to pick up the receiver were when someone called in or when he asked for a wake-up call.

I have heard hotel managers try to maintain that these exorbitant charges are justified because hotels have to spend millions of dollars to provide updated telephone equipment. OK. Hotels spend millions of dollars on plumbing, too. Why don't they charge $5 every time you flush? The same is true for health facilities. In most hotels, use of the health club is included in the cost of the room.

You can save yourself unpleasant surprises and aggravation if you **ask hotels in your destination cities to inform you of their telephone policies and surcharge price structures before you arrive.** Some of the flagrant abusers in this area may make you consider staying at another hotel. (While you are at it, request their charges for sending *and receiving* faxes.) Inquire, also, if your hotel blocks calls to the AT&T, MCI, or Sprint access lines. This practice has become common in several cities, especially in Europe. If you plan to stay in a hotel that heaps draconian surcharges on your telephone use, you may want to borrow a desk at a colleague's office for some phone time each day or investigate the availability of nearby pay telephone facilities. (Frankly, both choices would so negate any other pleasures of a hotel for me that I would go elsewhere.)

Compared with the other costs of doing business on the road, hotel phone charges may not seem like a lot of money, but they can really add up if you use your phone a lot. Hotel telephone surcharges are often between fifteen and thirty percent above what the phone company charges. You may also find that many hotels have a minimum three-minute charge for an operator-assisted call (i.e., any call that is not local), even if you only talk for thirty seconds. Others charge AT&T long distance rates, even if they subscribe to cheaper competitors like MCI and Sprint.

When you check in, ask how calls will be shown on your statement. I like to be assured that when my bill arrives, all the calls are logged as to time, duration, and phone number called. Although most newer hotel billing systems in the United States do itemize calls in this manner, this is not always the case in Europe and Asia. It's not very enlightening to receive a bill with a long list of telephone charges, with no more description than "local call" or "long distance."

Hotel phone charges have received a lot of negative publicity in the travel press, and many chains have been stung by how irate and indignant the business traveler is over these practices.

Stouffer hotels recently revised their phone rates downward dramatically. Others may follow suit. If these hotels want to raise basic room rates a bit so as not to nickel-and-dime guests for telephone usage, it's fine by me. I'd much prefer to pay more for the room itself and have all local phone charges be included. As it is, I often get hotel bills that are fifteen pages long because I use the phones a lot and each call is listed separately. It's wise to keep a log of phone calls you make while in your hotel room, so that you are prepared to dispute any questionable charges. Many executives do this as a matter of course, just for their own records.

Reach Out and Fleece Someone: Beating the High Cost of International Hotel Phone Charges

Many foreign hotels (especially in Europe) are quite shameless about extorting a pound of flesh from the business traveler to make an overseas call. Hotel surcharges of up to 300 percent on the cost of an international call are unfortunately not uncommon—nor are they prominently displayed or announced. All too often, travelers get the highly unpleasant bad news only when they are checking out. By that time, of course, it's too late. When you're rushing for the airport, you're in a very bad bargaining position to dispute an $80 charge for a ten-minute call from Frankfurt to New York.

As with a domestic hotel, I always ask for a statement of telephone charges when I check in, particularly in a new hotel or one where I have not recently been a guest. I also ask how the calls will be shown on my bill. If the calls are not itemized, I make a point of keeping a very careful record of my outgoing calls.

Travelers unwilling to pay hotel surcharges know they can make overseas calls from international telephone booths, or from government post offices with international telecommunications facilities. If your objective is to contact your family to let them know you've arrived safely, this arrangement is inconvenient but workable. However, for important business phone calls in which you need to sound professional and have access to documents or statistics spread out around you, it is entirely unacceptable—only Superman should do business in a phone booth.

When you call international long distance from your hotel room, the point at which you incur the charge is right at the switchboard, when the hotel operator places your call. Therefore the way to beat the system is to go around it and place the call yourself. In doing so you have an unlikely ally—your American long distance telephone company. The situation abroad became so notorious among business travelers that American long distance services such as AT&T, Sprint, and MCI instituted "home-direct" service. By dialing a local number from your hotel room in a foreign city, you are connected with an English-speaking U.S. operator who places your call. A charge for a local call appears on your hotel bill abroad; the charge for the international call appears on your phone bill at home.

The system isn't limited to calls between the United States and other countries. It also works between foreign countries. AT&T WorldConnect Service and MCI WorldReach provide this service in most of the world's business destinations.

The "home-direct" system is by no means a secret, and hoteliers in many parts of the world have tried to fight back by obstructing calls to the "home-direct" local access numbers. If you try to call a "home-direct" local access number and can't get a connection, chances are there's nothing wrong with your hotel phone—the hotel has blocked access to the number.

To overcome this problem, AT&T has tried to market its "Teleplan Plus" program to a number of hotel chains, especially in Ireland, Israel, Portugal, Germany, Austria, and in the Far East. Participating hotels agree to offer guests a variety of methods to call the United States; most importantly they also agree to place "reasonable" limits (currently about $10) on phone call surcharges.

Executive TeleCard is another system that bypasses hotel switchboards. It tries to keep an open local number in each city where its service is available. In this system, dialers enter their PIN number (Personal Identification Number) on a touch-tone phone (it won't work with a rotary) to connect to a computer-ized switching system. The switching system is inhabited by a voicemail-type voice that leads you through the international calling process by offering a series of dialing choices. Calls are billed to your credit card.

Hotel Phone Charges That Are Worth It

For a hotel with a state-of-the-art phone system, however, I don't mind paying a premium. The Hilton in Lake Buena Vista, Florida, has a telecommunications system that controls far more than your incoming and outgoing calls. Buttons on the phone can turn on the heat or the air conditioning. Other but-tons control the TV. The room phone also serves a security function—it lights up if the room door is not locked and bolted.

Each phone unit provides access to two separate phone lines, a hold button, and word- and data-processing capabilities. If you don't want to be disturbed, you can press a button which will block your line and forward your calls to the front desk where the staff will take messages.

The system even works when you're not there. Housekeep-ing staff uses the phone to key in a code when they enter your room, and another code when they leave. As an energy saver, the system also adjusts the temperature when guests leave their rooms, and then readjusts it to "occupied" status when guests key back in.

The Rihga Royal in New York will give you a cellular phone to use during your stay. The cellular phone is tied into your room phone. If you don't pick up the phone in your room within four rings, it automatically forwards the call to your cel-lular phone—anywhere in the city. If you don't pick up on the cellular within three rings, it bounces back to the hotel and takes a message on your voicemail. How much for this super service? $15 per day in a standard room, no charge if you are staying in a suite. (Rihga suites are also equipped with fax machines.)

This is a bargain. Isn't it inconsistent to complain about be-ing nicked for a few bucks for local calls but happily spend $15 a day for a cellular? Nope. I live by the phone. Our business is dependent on maintaining communication with cities from To-kyo to Cleveland to London to Paris. For me, this kind of telephone service is a bargain. Unlike the hotel charges for gar-den-variety phone service that I grumble about, I'll happily spend the extra money for extraordinary service like this be-cause it makes my trip so much smoother. And that's a very different thing from spending it when I get the feeling that I have no choice and I'm being ripped off.

Pay More if It's Worth It

In other words, pay more if it's worth it. Sometimes, it's *always* worth it. There are some expenditures which pay for themselves almost immediately, and are, from a corporate standpoint, "No Brainers" in terms of expenditure. An Ameri-can Express Platinum card carries a hefty $400 fee. For that $400, however, they are now offering two international tickets for the price of one. Is that $400 fee higher than most prestige credit cards? Yup. Is it worth it to get that second international ticket? If you do a lot of international travel, of course it is.

There is a new restaurant credit card now being offered called the Transmedia card. With the card you save 25 percent on your meals at selected restaurants—including not just en-trees but wine and other beverages as well. The restaurants involved are by no means bush league—Los Angeles eateries include top establishments like Citrus, Locanda Veneta, Kate Mantilini, and Chaya Venice. Use the card like any other credit card to pay for the meal. When you receive your monthly state-ment, it will reflect a 25 percent discount.

The benefits of this card to any business traveler are direct and immediate. The cost of the card is $50 a year, which will pay for itself in just a few weeks. To make the deal even more desirable, many executives are now being offered the card with the first year's fee waived. What's wrong with this picture? Not a thing.

Sometimes, of course, it's not so clear. Let me give you an example of the mental gyrations I go through to decide when something is actually "worth it."

In November of 1992, I locked myself into a difficult week of travel and business appearances. I had to be in Frankfurt on Sunday. That night I was due to fly to Milan to deliver a speech on Monday to Italian sports executives. On Tuesday morning my schedule sent me from Milan to London, stopping there briefly on my way to Edmonton, Alberta, Canada, where on Wednesday afternoon I was scheduled to give the first of two speeches. I also planned to attend a hockey game on Wednesday night. On Thursday morning I was to fly to Calgary to give another speech, after which I was planning to fly on to Maui, Hawaii, where my wife was hosting the tenth annual Betsy Nagelsen Kapalua Pro-Am Invitational Tennis Tournament.

My wife's tournament was a holiday for me and the sort of bonus that made the five intense days preceding it seem worthy of my best effort. After my speech in Calgary, my fondest wish was to arrive in Maui as early as possible. I knew that I could get there at 8:30 on Thursday night if I flew Canadian Pacific from Calgary to Honolulu and then changed planes. The only kicker was that the Canadian Pacific flight didn't have first-class service, and the people who were sponsoring my speech were going to reimburse me for a first-class ticket. If I wanted first-class service from Calgary to Hawaii, my alternative was to go from Calgary to Denver and then on to Hawaii, but then I wouldn't get in until midnight.

In the end I decided that arriving early was more important than flying first-class. But I didn't intend to fly in misery. Instead, I booked two business-class seats side-by-side, which cost $250 more than the single first-class seat I was contractually entitled to. The $250 would come out of my pocket, but it would really be worth it if I could put my briefcase next to me and work, or really stretch out and recuperate.

The thought process is simple: Once I make up my mind that a trip is a worthwhile exercise, I want to make that worthwhile exercise as comfortable for myself as possible.

As it turned out, when I showed up at the Canadian Pacific counter at Calgary to check in for my two seats, the ticketing agent informed me, "The flight is only half full, Mr. McCormack. You won't really need this second seat, since no one will be seated next to you anyway. Why don't you save the extra ticket for another time?"

It is this sort of little thrill that makes business travel such an interesting adventure. Despite all the efforts to make sure that everything goes my way, sometimes things work out even better.

Chapter VI
The Traveling Office

When you mention "traveling office" today, most people think of laptop computers, mobile telephones, beepers, fax machines, and other technology. These electronic marvels (which we will discuss later in this chapter) can be of valuable assistance, but they are not my primary definition of "traveling office."

For me, the traveling office is both a state of mind and a system of organization for continuing to do business effectively while on the road. Since I am on the road many more days of the year than I am in any one office building, I am constantly "in" my traveling office—whether I am in a hotel room, sitting on an airplane, or in one of my actual offices at a branch of International Management Group.

Yes, I have several rooms in different cities with walnut paneling, impressive plaques on the walls, bookcases full of important-looking volumes, large desks, filing cabinets, and so forth. But that is not where the work gets done. The work gets done in my head. That is also the truth for people who primarily operate in an office environment. For all of us, the best "office" is one in which we have immediate access to necessary decision-making information, comfortable surroundings in which to think, and communications facilities to discuss our thoughts with associates.

Do You Need to Bring That Plaque on the Wall?

In an earlier chapter, I discussed the need for "attitude adjustment" in order to be more efficient and positive about business travel. Part of that adjustment is rethinking what an "office" means to you and how you bring it on the road. For example, be honest with yourself: Are the architectural surroundings and decorations of your physical office important to you and—more important—to your clients? If your answer is "Yes," that tells you that you may need to spend the money for fairly luxurious accommodations when you travel. If the answer is "No," then let's discuss what aspects of your office you do need to bring with you when you travel.

In my experience, there are real advantages to conducting business while traveling. You can cut down on your paperwork, make better use of your secretary, focus on the most essential aspects of your work, and see your job and your company in a new perspective. Your traveling office can truly be a more efficient version of that room in your office building if you plan to make it that way.

Being "Out-Of-Town" Has Its Advantages

No doubt you have read the management studies about the high percentage of telephone calls, memos, and letters dealing with various problems received in an office on Monday which—if unanswered—resolve themselves by Friday. You can get the same effect by being "out-of-town." Callers who insist on the urgent need to speak to you in the office suddenly lose their urgency when they have to pay for a long distance call to reach you in London. Employees who would have involved you in a decision-making meeting find that they can summarize their recommendations in a memo for your approval when you are not in the office. Almost everyone tends to cut down on the conversational chit-chat when they are talking to you on a long distance line to Sydney, Australia.

In other words, when you are traveling, your business associates will extend to you a level of courtesy and thoughtfulness about your time that they should be giving you every day. When you are not easily accessible, your associates will do a little bit more of the work themselves. But—and this is a major BUT—be sure that they are reporting to you on what they are doing. The best part of a traveling office is that you can be selectively inaccessible while staying in close touch with your business. How close depends on the lines of communication you establish, and we will discuss that in a moment.

The Time Zone Advantage

In an international business such as mine, traveling through time zones can offer you opportunities to extend your business day that many travelers do not consider. For example, I always get the jump on my business day by rising early. If I am on the West Coast of the United States, at five or six o'clock in the morning I talk to associates in Europe (in the afternoon), and catch New York business people in their offices at 7 A.M. my time before I have an eight o'clock breakfast meeting in the hotel. After my business day in Los Angeles or San Francisco is over, I make calls to Asia before dinner and have the advantage of reaching people there at the beginning of the next day. I always schedule my telephone call list with one of those convenient little world time zone maps at hand to calculate the most efficient times.

This is another simple area in which too many business people feel "victimized." They complain to me that wherever they are in the world, they are never near a telephone when they need to talk to their home offices. With a little planning, their "problem" can be an opportunity. If time changes make communications with your office difficult during normal business hours, arrange telephone appointments with your secretaries or associates at home. Most of them will be impressed that you are making the effort to talk to them after their dinner time—when, in fact, this may be a convenient early morning hour for you.

Just as your associates will be more considerate of your time when they call you long distance, they will also be more likely to take your calls when you call long distance. I am a strong believer in setting up specific times for telephone appointments and placing the calls myself when I am on the road, so generally my calls are expected. But, when I have to call someone unexpectedly, the news that "Mr. Mark McCormack is calling from Bangkok" will often inspire a secretary to put someone else on hold who is calling locally.

What to Bring—and Equally Important—What *Not* to Bring

I do not presume to know the diverse business requirements of my readers or the specific materials each of you may need to carry on a trip. But I do know that most business people head towards the airport woefully disorganized, usually without many timesaving and useful tools, and often carrying materials that they don't need on the road. To know how to pack your "traveling office," you need to plan three ways of bringing materials:

*   Materials and equipment you will need en route to the airport, at the airport, on the airplane, and en route to the hotel. This will usually be in your carry-on bags;
*   Materials and equipment you will need to take in your checked luggage to work efficiently in your hotel room;
*   Materials and equipment that can be shipped to the hotel or rented in the city you are visiting.

Mark McCormack's Travel Itinerary Checklist

Let's start with your travel itinerary. Most busy executives are satisfied with the computer printout provided by a travel agency, which contains the bare bones of airline, hotel, and sometimes rental-car arrangements. This is not adequate. Here is a checklist for the information a thorough business traveler's itinerary packet should incorporate:

1. The name and telephone number of the car service picking you up.
2. The car number, license plate number, and name of the driver for your pickup.
3. The name of the person who confirmed your pickup and the time of the last reconfirmation by your office.
4. The names and telephone numbers for two or three other car services. (Especially necessary if you are not leaving from your office.)
5. Your flight number, departure time, gate number, seat number, and the most exclusive telephone number for flight information from that airline. (That is, if you are a Gold Card Frequent Flyer, make sure you have the Gold Card information number instead of the general number. Be certain your itinerary also includes your Gold Card number.)
6. Directions to your departure area and the airline club lounge (especially important if you are departing from an unfamiliar airport).
7. The times and flight numbers of alternative flights that you have booked with telephone numbers for those airlines.
8. The names and telephone numbers of Special Services personnel at the airline. (Or, if you have particular contacts at the airline club lounge, include those names.)
9. The name and telephone number of the car service picking you up at your destination.
10. The car number, license plate number, and name of driver for your pickup at your destination.
11. The name of the person who confirmed your pickup and the time of the last reconfirmation by your office.
12. Specific information about the best transportation alternatives at the airport if your car does not arrive on schedule.
13. Name, address, telephone number, and confirmation code number for your hotel.

14. Specifics of your arrangements with the hotel, including rates, room location, special requests. The name of the person with whom these arrangements were confirmed—or, better yet, a copy of the confirmation fax from the hotel.
15. Name of the hotel manager and concierge.
16. Names, addresses, and telephone numbers of two alternative hotels.
17. Name and telephone of your travel agent. Get the home telephone number, too. (Just requesting this will guarantee you a more careful quality of service.)
18. Home telephone number for your secretary. (She is an important lifeline—more about that below.)
19. The address of one or more banks or other locations where you can use your ATM card, and their hours of operation.
20. Pocket *Skyguide*, for making emergency alternate travel plans.

This checklist sounds as though it might be a lot of work. But, truthfully, it simply requires you or your secretary to ask just a few more questions while you are setting up an itinerary. Much of the information can be recycled trip after trip. And the first time you need that information, the extra effort will have been repaid.

The next group of travel documents that you should carry with you is quite valuable in an emergency. These are photocopies of your most essential personal documents:

- Passport
- Visas
- Driver's license
- Other relevant ID
- Medical prescriptions
- Insurance cards
- Airline tickets

Always carry them in a place *separate* from the originals.
At home and/or with your secretary, you should also have photocopies of your credit cards. When you are going to a

foreign country, you should also have the address and telephone number of the American embassy or consulate, as well
as the name of a contact there. If you purchase travelers'
checks, here is the place to note down the serial numbers, in
the event of theft. Again, this procedure may sound too cautious, but you will be very happy to have the information in the
unpleasant event that you need it.

In addition to those fundamental travel documents mentioned above, I always bring my most valuable business
documents in two large briefcases that I carry on. From the
time that I depart on a trip to the time that I set them down in
a secure hotel room, they never leave my sight. They are under
the airline seat in front of me, next to me in the limo, and in my
hands during most transfers. Normally I take only the materials I need for two weeks, although sometimes I have to carry a
month's worth of documents. The contracts and memos I need
for my business undoubtedly will be different than the papers
you carry for your business. But if you need them for your business, put them together in one carry-on bag (or, in my case,
two), and treat that bag almost as though you were a bank
courier who has it handcuffed to you.

In those briefcases, I carry dozens of yellow pads, which are
what my computer-literate friends might call my "data bases."
For example, for a city such as Chicago, I have a pad with lists
of restaurants that often contain pages of specific information.
Some restaurants I have tried and some are recommendations
from associates—or suggestions from newspapers, magazines,
or travel newsletters which I may have clipped. After I have
gone to a new place, I will usually add some notations on my
yellow pad to remind me of particular strengths of a restaurant
or a maitre d's name or a dish that I liked. On another pad, I
have the names of shops, art galleries, plays, concerts, or other
experiences to which I can look forward. On yet another
Chicago pad, I have lists of friends, with addresses and telephone numbers. These personalized guidebooks—they could
be notebooks or computer files, too—can be part of adding the
Personal Touch to your travel experiences.

Regarding business documents, I avoid grabbing the entire
file for a project unless I need to read it. I prepare a folder for

each appointment that I have made, and in that folder I include copies—not originals—of the relevant papers. (The only time I carry original documents on a trip is when they need to be presented to a client or are contracts for signing.) My secretary keeps a duplicate of each folder so that she knows which documents I have and can refer to them quickly. I keep the folders in the chronological order of my appointments.

What *Not* to Bring on a Business Trip

Too Many Clothes

Most travelers, business people or not, overpack on the theory that they "might" need that cardigan sweater (that they haven't worn at home in three years) for an early golf game—or whatever. Part of the problem for many men (and I am not being sexist about this) is that they ask their wives to pack for them. Unless your wife has made business trips to Stockholm—dressed as a man, presumably!—how would she know how to pack for that trip? For fear of not preparing you for every contingency, she overpacks. The *Hit the Ground Running* traveler takes responsibility for his or her own packing.

When I pack I have my itineraries at hand, and I envision how I will be dressed and what materials I will need for each phase of the day. If I have planned to use the health club at a hotel, I will bring exercise clothes, but I don't throw my sweats in a bag just because I might need them. If you are going to be seeing the same clients or business associates several times on a trip, you will need more changes of clothes. If you like to change shirts for the evening, as I do, calculate the need for laundering some of them with the overnight valet service at the hotel. With a few contingency exceptions—a raincoat or a folding umbrella—there should be a place on the schedule for every item in your bags.

Plan your packing the way you plan your trip. It's one way of making yourself really think through your days on the road. If you're not sure what to pack, it may be a sign that you

need to firm up your plans a bit more. The next time yo
late between packing a "nice to have" item on a b
trip—say, a fourth business suit for a four-day trip, tr
member what I think is a Nobel laureate packing job. L
sports columnist Ian Wooldridge went on an assignment that
took him away from home for fifty-five days. He traveled
32,400 miles, made twenty-three takeoffs and landings, and
was subjected to temperatures that varied from sub-zero in
St. Moritz and Aspen to 109 degrees in Melbourne, Australia.
Despite these temperature extremes and the wide range of
events he was covering, he was able to fit all of his clothing
needs into a single suitcase. Here's his lean but quite sufficient
packing list:

1	Navy lightweight suit
1	Navy blazer
1	White cotton trousers
1	Tan chino trousers
1	Grey wool trousers
1	Ski pants
1	Parka
1	V-neck lambswool sweater
1	Wool ski hat
1	Sun hat (for fishing)
1	Pair black formal shoes
1	Pair deck shoes
3	Dress shirts
3	Silk ties
4	Casual golf shirts
4	Boxer shorts
4	Pair of socks
4	White handkerchiefs
1	Medicine bag, containing anti-diarrhea pills, painkillers, cold relievers, vitamins, sunblock, bug repellent, and antiseptic ointment (none of which was ever needed)

I must confess that life is still unfair to women traveling on
business, and it's unlikely that a woman could get away with
packing as lightly as Ian Wooldridge did for as long a journey.

There is a good rule of thumb for any trip, however, and it applies to both men and women. **Pack as if you have to carry it yourself.** If you travel long enough, you may have to. If you arrive at the airport and find that the skycaps are on strike, or discover that you have to carry your own bags when you make a change of planes between airlines, you'll be very thankful that you're self-sufficient.

Too Much Paper

Not unlike throwing the entire closet into a bag, some business people throw the entire filing cabinet into their briefcases on the "just in case" theory. The smart business traveler plans more carefully. If you sincerely intend to sort through your mail and browse all those trade magazines on the plane, then, by all means, put them in your carry-on bags. But there is no point hauling pounds of paper onto the airplane if it could be in your checked luggage or—even better—overnighted to your hotel. Decide what you will have time to do on your trip and plan when to do it. Schedule the packing or shipping of materials accordingly.

Readers of my previous books on business know that I do not believe in elaborate presentations for clients. (I think that these dog-and-pony shows can divert discussion from the *deal* to the *show*.) But I recognize that demonstration equipment is essential in some businesses. What is *not* essential is to require each sales person or speaker to bring inordinate amounts of equipment, boxes of catalogs, or company supplies as excess baggage. When I see men and women in the baggage claim areas struggling with large containers, I wonder if their companies never heard of air freight. This is poor planning in the extreme. Piano movers are not generally the most exhilarating speakers, and no one can be expected to give an energetic after-dinner presentation if he or she has been wrestling with heavy packages all day. Businesses that need demonstration equipment should plan to ship ahead.

The Magic Bag of Travel Tricks
That Turns Into a Life Raft

In addition to your most valuable papers that must stay with you and the materials you intend to read or work with in transit, every smart business traveler should **pack a survival kit**—enough barebones essentials for a day or two—in his or her carry-on luggage. This small bag of "travel insurance" might include:

- Fresh shirt
- Prescription medicines
- Personal toiletries, including a toothbrush, deodorant, makeup, razor, comb, hairbrush, shampoo, and compact hairdryer
- Tissues
- Aspirin
- Spare contact lenses or eyeglasses
- Change of socks (or pantyhose)
- Change of underwear

Of course, you may wish to add or substitute other indispensable items to your own personal survival kit. On long flights, this kit is a pleasant personal convenience. However, when (not if) you are separated from your luggage—as a frequent flyer, this will happen to you eventually—this little bag is a joyous security. Far more baggage is misplaced than is permanently lost or stolen. Having interim clothing and supplies minimizes potential inconvenience if your luggage arrives after you do. If you are on a short trip, it can make the difference between being able to continue your trip and accomplish what you set out to do, and having to either extend your stay or turn around and come home. Moreover, if you are stranded at an airport or at an any-port-in-a-storm hotel by weather, labor problems, or other travel difficulties, that bag will look a lot like your personal life raft.

What Can You Accomplish
En Route to the Airport?

One of the most foolishly wasted time opportunities for business travelers is the trip to the airport. If you ask most travelers what they do while they are being driven for a half hour to an hour across familiar terrain, they will usually reply that they doze off, look out the window, or talk to the driver. Here's a chance to make time that the smart traveler doesn't miss. Frequently I ask my assistant to make the trip with me so that I can go through mail with her or dictate some memos. Sometimes I will schedule a business meeting with an associate. He or she rides with me to the airport and occasionally will continue our discussion in the airline lounge until my flight is called. Some executives regularly schedule business meetings in these lounges to save themselves the trip into town when they are visiting a branch office for the day.

There are many other ways you can use your time going to the airport, even if you don't have a limo and a secretary. One economical variation might be to drive your secretary to the airport—you can dictate en route—and let her drive the car back to your office. (Repeat the procedure when she picks you up from your return flight.) Or make a similar arrangement with an office colleague: If he or she wants to have a good hour meeting with your full attention, here's the chance.

I have a friend who prefers to drive to the airport and enjoys listening to audiotapes of books en route. As he was leaving for a recent trip, one of his junior executives handed him a tape.

"What's this?" he asked, hoping for a new bestseller.

"It's the report I've been trying to get you to read for two weeks," answered the ambitious associate. He was rewarded with a phone call from the airport to congratulate him for a good report and for his innovative presentation.

Sometimes, depending upon the time of day, I will schedule a series of telephone calls from the car. In that case, I try to alert the car service of my intentions to make sure that there is a phone in the car and to have my assistant set up telephone appointments. You can accomplish the same good use of time with a cellular telephone. At the very least, I periodically use the car travel time to sort through mail, although the movement of a car makes that less efficient than doing it on the airplane.

Your Secretarial Lifeline

Periodically I will be visiting the offices of a colleague and notice a secretary reading a book or magazine in the mid-afternoon. Invariably, when I ask why she is not busy, she answers: "Oh, my boss is out of town and I have nothing to do." I shake my head in amazement. My secretaries work harder when I am out of town—and I am *always* out of town. I am blessed with some exceptionally dedicated and hard-working personal assistants. And I have trained them to give me maximum support as I travel. They keep my home office running and they keep my traveling office connected to events that occur while I am away. How does my secretary function as the prime connection to my traveling office? Let me count the ways:

1. Pre-Trip Planning
She assists in all of the pre-trip planning, so that she is aware of my travel logistics, the documents I am carrying, the places I will be visiting, the people I will be seeing, and the hour-by-hour specifics of my itinerary.

2. Communications
She talks with me several times a day at prearranged times to keep me informed of phone calls, memos, minor or major crises, and general office functioning. She knows where to reach me at any time of the day if there is an emergency. She also knows not to bother me with anything less than an emergency when I am having important business conferences, in transit, or relaxing. Usually I call her at the appointed times and I try to stick to a fairly rigid schedule. But when I make an unscheduled call, I expect that either she will be there or she will have left detailed instructions about where she can be reached.

Nothing can be more frustrating than to call your assistant or one of your business associates for a piece of vital information and be sitting there listening to a bland voicemail message. There is no time for "telephone tag" when you are on the road, and the efficient business person plans his or her telephone appointments with the same care given to personal appointments. Your secretary must be available for your calls at all times. Depending upon my time zone, I call her at her home when necessary.

3. Confirmations and Revisions

She reconfirms all travel arrangements, and she confirms both my "in person" and telephone appointments. As the schedule shifts (as it inevitably does), she prepares a new itinerary with detailed instructions for me each day, including lists of phone calls which must be returned.

4. Keeping in Touch with the Office

At the end of each day, in addition to the revised daily itinerary, my secretary provides me with what I call a "Headline Fax." This is simply an overnight report on the highlights of the previous business day. Results of meetings, important phone calls, reports from branch offices, significant pieces of mail, a reminder of my anniversary—almost anything I should know about or that might need my attention is noted briefly on this fax. Ideally, it is the first piece of paper waiting for me in the morning, having been slipped quietly under the door without knocking, without phoning in the middle of the night, without setting off the blinking red light on my nightstand telephone. If I need more information about any item on the Headline Fax, my secretary can send it to me.

5. Crisis Management

When things go wrong, your secretary must be Crisis Central— because you are in no position to handle crisis details at a distance, even in the most efficient hotel room. She should be well-versed in how to provide information to you, how to offer brief (usually non-committal) assurance to your clients, and how to convey your orders to associates if you are not able to give them directly. Sometimes you are the cause of the crisis. If you are sick or stuck in a holding pattern over Pittsburgh or diverted from your schedule by a sudden emergency—guess who must tactfully handle the apologies and the postponements?

The Telephone: Your Most Important Business Travel Tool

By now it must be obvious that I regard the telephone as the most important tool that the business traveler uses. Airlines and hotels feel this way, too, which is why they are trying to outdo each other with telephone services. In order to maximize your traveling efficiency, you need access to the best telephone service almost continuously. Some hotel chains are making more effort to cater to the business traveler than others—and the business-hospitable hostelries offer impressive traveling offices. The Four Seasons hotels, for example, all provide two telephone lines in every room and will bring a fax if needed. Westin has introduced a "Westin Business Package," which consists of a fax machine, extra business phone, portable cellular phone, personal computer, and printer. All that can be waiting for you in your room for a minimal cost.

At the most rudimentary level, every traveler—business or otherwise—should have one of the telephone charge cards issued by AT&T, MCI, or Sprint. These are free of charge and will save you money calling from most hotels. There is also a list of tie-line numbers for use by these carriers in different countries, which help you to beat the escalating cost of long distance calls. New companies are entering the long distance telephone competition every day. A North Carolina firm called Metromedia offers a calling card for travelers ($15 annual fee) which claims to be less expensive to use than the three big carriers. It also provides a Help Connection for access to translation, medical, legal, and other services wherever you are in the United States and thirty-two foreign countries. You can obtain information about Metromedia at (800) 275-0200.

Specific telephone services are changing rapidly, but you should know about a few of the most useful currently available. AT&T offers "Easyreach" service, with numbers having a 700 area code, which allows you to carry a single telephone number, unique to you alone, with you wherever you go. You are not tied down to any particular phone, and people who need to get through to you have one number where you can always be reached. By dialing your personal 700 number, clients and associates can reach you through hotel room phones, car phones, portable cellular phones, pay phones, or just about anywhere there is a telephone with a number. They must, however, place their call through AT&T rather than another long distance company. Special, designated callers can even call you for no charge if they have access to your PIN (personal identification number). An Easyreach 700 number also allows you to dial the U.S. direct from overseas, paying only for the actual cost of the call, bypassing costly international telephone surcharges. For information about AT&T Easyreach, call (800) 982-8480.

The newest wrinkle on the horizon is the coming of 500 numbers, marketed by AT&T under the name "True Connections." True Connections expands the universal telephone number concept one step further. Like the Easyreach program, with True Connections you will be able to pick up the charges for some callers who have access to your PIN, whereas others will be billed for their calls. As with a 700 number, clients and staff can call you on your 500 number anywhere there is AT&T service. One big advancement, however, is that callers can place the call using not just AT&T but any long distance company including Sprint, MCI, and a myriad of foreign carriers. True Connections 500 numbers are also "follow me" numbers, and can be programmed to seek you out at a number of possible locations. For example, it can be set up to ring first at your office, then your home, then your cellular phone, and if it doesn't find you at any of these locations (or if you don't want to be found), it will finally switch into your voicemail.

The business pages of every newspaper are inundated with advertisements for mobile telephones, car telephones, and cellular phones. If you don't own one, you will want to consider hiring a car service or a taxicab with a mobile telephone when you are en route to the airport. When you need it, you will be glad to have it, and the additional cost, if any, is modest. All of the major car rental organizations have cars with mobile telephones that can be activated by credit cards. Currently, the most aggressive company is Hertz, with both installed phones and portables available in seventy American cities.

U.S. cellular telephone owners will have little or no trouble using their phones anywhere in the United States and Canada. Beyond those borders many variables apply. The AMPS (Advanced Mobile Phone Service) system that is standard in the U.S. is technically usable in fifty other countries with compatible systems, but billing arrangements may be difficult. All of Europe works on the GSM standard, so renting a phone is your best option. U.S. travelers can obtain information for most foreign cellular rentals from TravelPhone at (800) 872-8746.

A pager is another option. Paging companies within the United States are legion, but Skypage is the most prominent system offering international connections via satellite. They don't offer truly worldwide service, but they are in major business cities like Hong Kong and Tokyo. Once you become part of their network, you get access to their entire system; you don't have to buy into additional cities if your travel pattern changes. Moreover, the person wearing the pager must activate the system by punching in a PIN and a contact telephone number. When your beeper goes off in Tokyo saying, "Call the office," you still have to decide whether the call is frivolous, important, urgent, or life-and-death. Many smart beeper wearers have developed code systems with their secretarial and support staffs to indicate levels of priority. "Call the office/55" may indicate a need to soothe some ruffled feathers, but "Call the office/99" might mean that an office coup d'etat is in progress.

Although the charges for cellular telephone use are still high, some travelers have found to their astonishment that those charges are less than the telephone surcharges some hotels are adding to your bill. One simple way to rent a compatible cellular is to contact the local carrier in your destination. Often your hotel will be able to arrange a rental. Book and audio publishing executive Michael Viner has come up with an innovative way to circumvent these charges. "I always carry a mobile phone with a car plug," he says. "When the car picks me up in New York or in any other city, rather than pay the $2.50 a minute that the limousine charges, I just plug my phone into their lighter and pay about 25 percent of their rate."

Because hotels know that the telephone is the second most important piece of equipment they provide (after a bed), some of them have decided to gouge business travelers with outrageous rates and surcharges on calls that literally cost the hotel nothing. Assuming that you can endure the telephone rates, make it a point to stay in hotels that provide the sort of telephone service a good business traveler requires for his or her traveling office. Personally, I need a room with at least two lines and at least three phones—one by the bedside, one in the bathroom, and one on the desk. In a larger suite, I need more phones. I don't use computer modems or fax equipment, but if you do, be sure that your hotel is updated to provide the necessary connections. Despite all of my best efforts, occasionally I still end up in a room with the phone on the wrong side of the bed for me or, worse yet, on the desk with a four-foot cord. Most hotels utilize universal jacks. One solution for the resourceful traveler is to **carry your own 25-foot telephone extension cord.** Just plug it in and put the phone where you want to use it. One entertainment industry executive found his own extension cord invaluable when he spent a lengthy stay in Zagreb on location for a movie shoot.

Making the Executive Club
in Your Hotel a Posh Office

A relatively new innovation in hotel service that is truly making the traveling office concept a reality is the "club," "concierge," or "executive" floor. These can make the larger hotels where they are normally found far more pleasant for the business traveler. The idea is that a large lounge area, usually on one of the top floors of the hotel, provides privacy and luxury for small business meetings that would be awkward in a room. In addition to amenities such as computer terminals, stock ticker tapes, Xerox machines, fax, phone, and VCR, some of the clubs incorporate small business libraries about local businesses. Depending upon the style of business entertaining you need or the number of meetings you will be hosting, the club floor can be an important added value.

Free hors d'oeuvres, coffee, and drinks in a prestigious atmosphere can make your business clients feel more comfortable than in a restaurant. Most of these clubs are also staffed with hotel employees prepared to do anything from changing your airline reservations to taking dictation.

The most elaborate hotel clubs right now are found in Asia. The Regency Club on top of the Grand Hyatt in Hong Kong has a spectacular view of Victoria Harbor and a staff of eleven to tend to your every need. The Shangri-La chain throughout Asia features Horizon Floors with twenty-four-hour business services. The Orient knows how to provide service: At the Hotel Seiyo Ginza in Tokyo, you are assigned a personal "secretary" and "room assistant" when you arrive.

For business travelers on a tight budget, these club floors can be a particular bargain. Often your membership in a frequent flyer or hotel frequent-guest program is enough to get you an upgrade onto these floors. But a serious business person who offers the potential of return business can usually negotiate an upgrade to the club floor if the hotel is not full—and few are full in these recessionary times. Even if you are not able to obtain a free upgrade, the $20–30 per night additional cost for most of the clubs may be worth it to you in comfort and convenience.

Your Choice: Yellow Pads and Pencils or Laptops

In order to have a true traveling office, some business people need to bring along business equipment. The technology of microelectronics, along with modern telecommunications linkage, is providing us with more efficient and economical equipment every month. Although I am still perfectly happy writing my notes and memos on a yellow pad with a pencil, I have been impressed by colleagues who can crunch numbers on a laptop with Lotus 1-2-3 spreadsheets or zap the latest revised version of a color advertising campaign to a client via modem. These electronic "toys" can be expensive and cumbersome, but they make work more efficient for some travelers.

Today you can purchase 486 laptop computers with large hard disks which will give you the computing power of the desktop models back in your office. You can transfer files and programs between desktops and laptops easily. Traveling representatives of data-intensive companies will benefit from these powerful units. Even with readable backlit color LED screens, however, it will be worth investing in programs which enlarge the typography on the screen or make the cursor more visible. One other modest investment that I recommend to laptop computer owners is a password entry program that prohibits access by unauthorized persons. These protection programs are fairly standard now in offices, but business travelers often forget to put one on their portable unit.

If you decide to carry a laptop computer, inevitably you will need a modem, which will allow you to communicate to other computers anywhere there is a telephone line. Large quantities of data—including words, numbers, and even pictures—can be transmitted through a computer more quickly and more accurately than via a fax machine. A modem can also connect your laptop computer to electronic networks all around the world which can place at your fingertips databanks of current stock and bond information, medical or legal data, news wire services, and library services.

If you travel with a computer, one way to avoid the excessive telephone charges in hotel rooms is to **take advantage of E-mail or electronic data delivery systems** which will hold letters, messages, or reports for you from anywhere in the world and allow you to download them into the laptop in your hotel room.

Electronic road warriors are sometimes so focused on the wizardry of their machines that they neglect one of the least expensive aspects of bringing computers and other equipment along: the carrying case. If you are trying to avoid checked luggage, as you should be, some of these well-designed bags can hold clothes and provide protection for your electronic gear at the same time. Targus sells a diverse line of cases, all with lifetime replacement guarantees [(714)-523-5429]. The Calise Valise Executive Attaché, which includes plenty of well-organized briefcase space, is another good option [(800)-942-8916]. But if you are seeking the fully equipped hi-tech look for the 1990s, you must see the MicroCase from Galizia. This all-in-one electronic briefcase holds and displays a laptop computer, a slimline printer, a portable fax, a cellular phone, extra batteries, connection cables, and other peripherals. I don't know how you could make use of all this at one time, but the guy in the seat next to you is certainly going to be amazed. For more information about Galizia, call (800) 833-2273.

The most annoying problem still facing laptop computer users is battery life. Despite manufacturer promises, most mobile batteries will only hold up for two to three hours of normal use, which is far too short a time to make use of on a flight from New York to Los Angeles. Laptop manufacturers have begun to replace the conventional nickel cadmium (NiCad) batteries with nickel-metal hydride (NiMH) batteries, but faster color machines have been eating up the increase in power. The serious road warrior simply carries extra batteries (make sure that they are easily replaced in your brand of laptop). The expensive alternative is the recently marketed zinc-air 12-volt battery that can power both your laptop and your cellular phone for twenty hours. For further information contact AER Energy Corporation at (800) 769-3720.

Details about portable computers, printers, fax machines, and cellular phones are changing constantly. You can obtain the most up-to-date information from a monthly publication called *Mobile Office*. For more information call (800) 627-5234.

I Have Seen the Future, and It Computes

I am fascinated by what the near future holds for telecommunications in the traveling office. The world I travel in today is markedly different from the world I traveled in as a boy. Just as the three-hour Concorde hop across the Atlantic would have been unimaginable to my father, there are changes coming in the world of travel that we cannot yet envision. Although you can now take any number of transpacific flights and sleep not in a reclining seat but in an actual bed, it will be interesting to see how soon the need for these airborne dormitories will be diminished by higher speed aircraft.

Acceleration on the information superhighway will be even more dramatic. Despite my own preference for working with old-fashioned paper-and-pencil when I am on the road, I know that generations of business travelers to come will be far more dependent on computers and modems than I am.

What kinds of innovations can we see coming? Earlier I mentioned the AT&T EasyReach 700 and True Connections 500 numbers that stay with you wherever you travel. We are also fast approaching the end of the era when traveling on a plane meant being incommunicado for the duration of the flight. Airphones have been around for a while, but now people will be able to call you in the air.

A passenger who wants to be reached on board swipes his or her credit card through an activator and punches in an ID number. People on the ground can reach you by dialing a general access number and giving your ID. They don't even need to know what flight you're on, only that you're "in the air somewhere." As soon as the ID numbers match, the phone at your seat lights up and you're in contact with the world. Of course, it's still the passenger's decision whether to be reached or not.

A new age of airborne data communications is upon us as well. The situation is evolving rapidly, and at present equipment varies not just from one airline to another, but from one aircraft to another within a given fleet. Budget-minded Southwest Airlines has installed digital air-to-ground systems which include a jack in the receiver for plugging in a modem to send faxes, get into your electronic mailbox, or boot up on the information superhighway via a service like Prodigy or America Online. Northwest, American, United, Delta, USAir, and America West are following suit with similar systems. It may not be long before voice and data communications on airlines are as common as carphones.

In a few years, the next step in personal communications services (PCS) will be the satellite cellular. Instead of being chained to the local radio broadcast for your calls and counting on the development of international "roaming" agreements, cellular telephone owners will be able to bounce their calls directly to and from communications satellites which will provide rapid access and better (lower noise) sound quality. Obviously, satellite fax and satellite computer modem connections will be available at about the same time. As we solve the problems of data compression, eventually individuals will have the same wireless PCS that television stations enjoy right now.

I have no doubt that Marshall McLuhan's notion of "the global village" will be a reality early in the 21st century. I also have no doubt that some business travelers will be better equipped to take advantage of it than others. Which business travelers will they be? By and large they will be the ones who have already learned to use technology (and common sense) to overcome difficulties in travel today. I'll talk about some of the strategies they use in the next two chapters.

Chapter VII
Insider Techniques in the Trenches

Travel as Murphy's Law

Moreso now than ever before, it's a jungle out there in the world of business travel. Because so many more people are on the road and in the air, congestion and delays have become far more common—and more difficult to deal with. The biggest and most important insider technique of all is to **expect the unexpected, and plan for it in advance.** Always have a backup plan. Always line up your alternatives in the event that your plane is late or canceled, your luggage is lost or damaged, or if you discover that your hotel is under new management.

In general, the travel industry has done a mediocre job of planning for the travel explosion, and airline deregulation has surely not helped. From airlines to hotels to rental cars, the age of computerized reservations, which was to have simplified everything, appears to have succeeded only in making everything more complicated. Computers have above all facilitated a far more complex pricing structure than was ever possible in the good old days. And if you sometimes get the feeling that they're making up prices on the spot, you're not far wrong.

Although some part of successfully dealing with these situations is attitude adjustment—treating these difficulties not as debacles to be endured but rather as interesting challenges to your ingenuity and your intellect—there are techniques which help level the playing field between you and your hotel and airline. This chapter deals with how to cope with the lumps and bumps of airline and hotel pricing structures and airport snafus, the maddening delays and disasters large and small that rob so many executives of any joy whatsoever in the travel experience.

When Your Flight Is Delayed or Canceled

"When the going gets tough, the tough get going," as the old saying goes, but when the going gets tough at the airport, often it's *only* the tough who understand how to get going. Knowing what to do when your flight is delayed or canceled is one of the things that distinguishes *Hit the Ground Running* executive travelers from novices on the road. The first thing to understand is what rights you have when negotiating with your airline.

These rights vary with the situation. If your flight is canceled because of weather, air traffic delays, a labor dispute, or a mechanical malfunction of the aircraft, the airline staff will generally try their best to assist you in making other arrangements, but you are not "entitled" to a free meal, immediate booking on the next flight out, or a free hotel room if you're going to be stuck overnight. Airline schedules are not considered guarantees, and your recourse in case of these kinds of commonplace difficulties, which are entirely beyond the control of the airline, is very limited.

What the Airlines Are Supposed to Offer You

In the United States, the airline doesn't owe you anything—except a refund in the event that you don't make the trip at all. Airline policies in the event of delay or cancellation are wildly disparate. It also appears that there may be little internal consistency within a particular airline on what passenger inducements and mollifications are offered when a flight is late. It was formerly commonplace for the pilot to announce complimentary alcoholic beverages on an inbound flight that was stacked up for over an hour in a holding pattern waiting for landing clearance at JFK—the airborne equivalent of "breaking out the grog" on a rough sea voyage in days of yore. As the New York skies have become more congested, however, delays have multiplied and free drinks have gone by the board.

On one recent United Airlines flight that was delayed for an hour due to a minor mechanical malfunction, flight attendants distributed vouchers good for a $25 discount on a future United trip. I've often received far less remuneration for far greater inconvenience—there are airlines that make little more than an apology, even for a flight delayed for several days. It is worth noting that United's generosity occurred on the Chicago–Los Angeles route, where competition among airlines is intense.

In Europe, passenger logistics problems due to delayed and canceled flights tend to get solved in a distinctly hierarchical order. First and business (or club) class passengers almost always have priority with airlines in getting staff assistance with making alternate travel arrangements or with getting a hotel for the night. Holders of discount economy class tickets generally get far less support. The stranded travelers you see holed up at Gatwick, sleeping amidst their piles of luggage while waiting for the weather to clear, are not first or business-class travelers. When things go wrong at the airport in Europe, you truly get the service you've paid for.

Keep Cool and Negotiate

No matter what kind of ticket you are holding, however, if you choose to try for a different flight rather than wait it out, you are at the mercy of the gate agent or supervisor. Your job as an executive traveler is to **become your own best negotiator** with airline personnel. Getting angry is not only nonproductive but counterproductive. There is no sense alienating the only people who can remedy your problem.

If a last-minute delay is announced or you are seated on a plane which pushes back from the gate but then does not take off and instead returns to the airport, your first move should be to grab your *Skyguide*. If you have planned ahead, you should already be aware of some alternative flight arrangements that are open to you. If you've really planned ahead, you may still be holding reservations on a later flight. Even if you have not done those things, however, if you have the *Skyguide* with you, half your battle is won.

Know Your Alternatives

In this situation, **information is power.** Even if you are still stuck on the tarmac on an aircraft with a mechanical failure, at least you can find out who else has a flight going that you can make. Once you find the alternative flight (or flights) and get off the plane, it is at this stage that your skills as a negotiator *and* your good relationship with an airline's Special Services representatives may come into play.

You're Still *Your Own Best Travel Agent*

When you hit a last-minute snafu at the airport, no travel agent can help you nearly as efficiently as you can help yourself. No matter how useful the airline staff may be, remember that **you are still your own best travel agent.** This not only helps you, it helps the airline as well. Mike Baverstock, Special Services representative of British Airways, describes what it's like to deal with the madhouse that ensues due to delayed and canceled flights from his side of the counter. "Keep in mind that we at Special Services or at the gate might be surrounded by as many as forty or fifty people whose lives and schedules, to them, are as important as yours is to you.

"You can save me about five minutes by telling me specifically the airline name and number of the flight that you want to get on—that five minutes could be your saving grace. It takes no time at all for me to verify that the flight you have chosen does exist; it's certainly a lot faster than having me start from scratch and hunt through the entire schedule for you. If an executive traveler is able to present me with a concrete option, he or she is fifty percent ahead of everyone else. From an efficiency perspective, I'll probably deal with them first, since their situations can be resolved rather quickly. I can get them on their way and concentrate on the rest of the problems that require more attention. The faster we can deal with the cases that are easy to solve, the faster everyone is going to get where they're going."

Consider the Indirect Route

As was the case with my delayed flight from Washington, D.C., to Paris that I talked about in Chapter IV, it helps a great deal to be flexible and inventive about your alternative arrangements. Peter Kuhn, an executive in my London office, has studied my methods well. "If you are stuck in a city, don't necessarily insist on another flight going straight to your destination. It may be more important to get a flight going somewhere—anywhere," he says. "I got stuck in Milan one evening when my London flight was canceled. I didn't want to spend another night there, since hotels are expensive and the airline was not offering to put us up. I found an Air France flight heading for Paris rather than London. I flew into Paris, hopped a shuttle within a half hour, and was back home rather efficiently. You've got to keep thinking about where you can go that might get you to where you need to be."

Losing Ground Is Not Necessarily Losing Time

Kuhn's advice is even more valid if you are faced with the prospect of being stranded in a small city, where flight options are limited. **Maximize your alternatives.** When you are trying to solve a delay or cancellation problem, the more choices you have, the better shape you're in. For example, there are about ten times more ways to fly to Phoenix from Chicago than from Omaha. If it looks like you might get stuck in Omaha and a flight to Chicago opens up, grab it. Going to Chicago is technically going "backwards," since it takes you geographically farther away from Phoenix. However, in situations like that, head for the hub that gives you the widest range of flight alternatives. Remember that your objective is not to fly the fewest possible miles, but to get where you're going in the shortest possible time. Of course, if you can catch a flight to a hub that's closer to your destination, that is by far the best option.

Above All, Get Your Flight Coupon

If you do change flights *and* airlines, you must **retrieve the value portion of your ticket coupon and get the gate agent to endorse the ticket over to another carrier.** This may be more difficult in some cases than in others. Special Services representative Mike Baverstock has a relatively enlightened view of the problem. "It's important to be honest and keep people informed," he says. "However bad the flight situation may be, it's better to be honest and up-front about it. If you have a delay, the worst thing you can do is hang on to a passenger if there's an option by which he or she can get to their destination quickly. I always send them off to another airline with my blessing. I believe that sooner or later the loyalty factor will come into play because you were genuinely interested in helping them."

Not every agent at every airline is so broadminded. There will be times when gate agents will be reluctant to surrender your flight coupon and see you "defect" to a competitor. If you are holding a restricted ticket, the airline is not required to hand you over to another carrier; worse, the second airline is not required to accept the ticket if its value is less than their own fare for a ticket without advance purchase. Nevertheless, these switches are often made, but money still talks. If you hold a first-class, business-class, or full-fare coach ticket, you are in a much better bargaining position.

If your ticket is one of a block of tickets bought under a special arrangement between your company and the airline, your "Personal Touch" skills getting the ticket endorsed over to another carrier will be exercised to the fullest. There's no harm in taking your best shot with the gate agent, but it's quite possible that your choices will be limited to other flights within the route system of the deal-making carrier. If you *really* have to get to your destination and your airline can't provide a viable timely alternative, **retrieve the value portion of your flight coupon anyway.** It's unused and is available for use by you or another member of your company on a future trip. Make your own reservations with another airline, with the understanding that it's going to be more expensive and you may have some explaining to do when you file your expense report.

Use the Agents at the Lounges

When flights are canceled or delayed, if a Special Services agent is not available (or your airline does not maintain them at this particular city), chances are that the gate agent will be swamped. If you still have the value portion of your ticket, you may be better off retreating to the airline's executive lounge (Admiral's Club, Red Carpet Club, Crown Room) to complete your alternative travel arrangements. The agents who staff these lounges have been given these status duty positions because of their competence and ability to deal with the needs of business travelers. When a particular flight has a problem, they are also going to be far less busy than the gate agent. They may be able to solve your problem much faster.

Know When to Hold 'Em and Know When to Fold 'Em

How do you know when to stick with your original carrier and when to bolt? It's not easy. A lot of times it depends on your prior experiences with the airline, what you know of their reputation for honesty when there is a delay, *and* whether you've checked your luggage.

Sir Christopher Lewinton, Chairman and CEO of TI Group Plc, says, "I try not to fly with marginal airlines because they haven't got the backup. I fly with mainstream airlines. You have greater flexibility within the airline's own route system in case things go awry. There is a much better likelihood that they will be able to fix a minor problem quickly or produce a second aircraft if something is really wrong."

Bob Anderson, former CEO of Rockwell International, says it helps to set a limit for yourself and to know when you have reached a crossroads. "If I find when I get to the airport that the flight is delayed forty-five minutes, I usually figure that's the point I really have to make a decision. You ought to make up your mind. Either decide to sit there and ride it out, because of some feeling you have about the situation, or decide to jump ship.

"If you put off making the decision, you might be there three hours or you might be there all night, waiting to see what happens next. Airlines don't always level with you, or else they are giving you a definite time for departure when the truth is that they really don't know. I know they think they have to say something—I suppose they can't just put a big question mark up there on the Departures board—but forty-five minutes usually doesn't mean forty-five minutes. It's almost always more.

"For me, forty-five minutes or an hour is the limit. If I get that kind of delay before I've even boarded the airplane, I will do anything I can to get to the destination I want to go to by some other route that I know is going to move. If I'm booked on American and next door is Delta going to the same place within half an hour, I jump. To maintain my option to be able to do that, I normally take all my baggage as carry-ons. If you have given them your luggage, you're trapped. The chances of getting that back and catching another flight are damned near impossible."

The Fictional Departures Board

Unfortunately Anderson's skepticism is well-placed. In many situations there is a tendency to string the passenger along. Delays are often tacked on in increments just small enough to make it appear not worth the trouble to find another flight. Your plane will be leaving in another twenty minutes, then another, then another. Whether airlines do this on purpose or just out of faulty information is immaterial. My own rule of thumb is **never believe the Departures board.**

If there is a delay, always talk directly to the agent at the gate. Don't just accept that the flight is late, find out why. Sometimes this will give you a clue which will inform your decision on whether to bolt or wait it out. If the agent tells you that a flight is late due to "late inbound equipment" it means, in plain English, that your aircraft is not in the airport. At this point the right question to ask is whether the plane has left its prior destination. It is also important to be able to use a little math and a lot of common sense.

A flight listed as sixty minutes behind schedule is going to be much more than an hour late if the aircraft is inbound from another city an hour away but hasn't taken off yet. Not only does the flight have to take off that very minute and make the one-hour trip, it also has to discharge passengers, load luggage and supplies, and reboard. Under these circumstances your flight is going to be at least an hour and a half late, and more likely closer to two hours behind schedule. This is an all-too-common situation on shuttle flights, where a problem early in the day will ripple through the entire schedule. For an airline that flies closely scheduled turnaround flights, there is often no way to make up the time.

A Sure-Fire Warning Sign

Although the airport Departures board can provide false reassurance about how soon a delayed flight is leaving, it does provide the executive traveler with the first indication of potential trouble on what you might otherwise believe will be a prompt departure. **Beware the departing "on time" flight without a gate assignment.** If you arrive at the airport at 7:20 A.M. for an 8:00 A.M. "on time" flight and no departure gate has been posted, your warning antennae should be twitching. Begin reviewing your *Skyguide* for flight options—a flight with no gate that close to departure time is a flight that does not have an aircraft.

Despite what the gate agent may say, even if the carrier can roll out another plane, a delay is all but inevitable. Meanwhile, as the airline is trying to maintain the fiction that your flight is on time, your best flight alternatives are fast disappearing. This is especially true on popular long distance routes, where competing airlines tend to bunch departure times together, vying head-to-head for your business. Provided that you're not tied down with checked baggage, now is the time to figure out a substitute flight, head for the phones (or get out your cellular phone), call another airline's toll-free reservation number, and book yourself a seat. Tell the second airline that you are already ticketed, then ask for the value portion of your flight coupon back (if you have surrendered it), have it endorsed by the gate agent to the second carrier before a huge backlog of disgruntled passengers piles up, and make your alternative flight.

Gone but Not Departed

The tendency of many airlines to fib about delays can sometimes work in your favor. It's not necessarily true that a flight which the Departures board lists as having taken off is really gone. The folks tracking departures don't monitor radio contact with the tower or wait to see the wheels lift off the runway before listing a flight as having departed. They are dependent on information they receive from the gate agents. If the gate has not reported the flight as delayed, the center that programs what you see on the board assumes an on-time departure and posts it as such.

Since minor delays in boarding generally are not mentioned, even if the Departures board says your flight has left, don't give up. If it's a matter of a couple of minutes, say eight or less, odds are your flight is still at the gate. I've made more than one tight connection on a flight that had theoretically already departed, but in fact was still boarding the last passengers.

Not All Standbys Are Created Equal

If you choose to stand by for a fully booked flight for which you have no reservation, is it worthwhile to check in as soon as possible and secure an early place in line? Maybe yes. Maybe no. If space does become available, assignment of seats to standby passengers is not necessarily accomplished on a democratic first-come, first-served basis. With standby flights as with delayed flights, paying full-fare for your ticket does entitle you to some privileges. Many airlines board standby first-class and business-class passengers first, followed by full-fare coach passengers, and then on down the financial pecking order from the most expensive (least discounted) tickets down to the cheapest. Some airlines also consider whether you are a member of their frequent flyer program in determining where you are in the standby hierarchy.

Being Bumped Is Different

Your passenger rights when you have been bumped from a flight are very different from your passenger rights if the flight has been delayed or canceled. You have consumer advocate Ralph Nader to thank for that. In the late 1970s Nader was holding a confirmed reservation and a ticket and was bumped from an Allegheny Airlines flight. He sued, claiming breach of contract. His experience eventually resulted in new federal protection for passengers.

In the United States, if you have a confirmed reservation (with your ticket earmarked "OK" in the status column) and your airline cannot offer you the seat you paid for on your flight, *and* you check in the prescribed number of minutes before flight time (usually twenty minutes before departure), you have been "denied boarding" and you are entitled to compensation as determined by the federal Department of Transportation. If you are late checking in, your right to compensation evaporates.

As the economic climate has deteriorated, the incidence of bumping has declined, simply because fewer flights are overbooked. However, it still occurs, particularly at peak hours (early morning and late afternoon flights from cities like Chicago and New York) and peak seasons (Thanksgiving through

New Year's, around Easter, and the beginning and end of summer). Keep an eye on major events, but consider the impact of less earth shattering ones as well.

It will surely be sticky getting in and out of Hartsfield Airport in Atlanta when the summer Olympic games are there in 1996, and you can count on an increase in bumping and overbooking. However, Logan Airport in Boston is a mess in May every year. Why? There is a heavy concentration of colleges and universities in the Boston area. Graduation ceremonies all seem to be scheduled on the same weekend. The mix of business travelers with arriving and departing students (many of whom have schedules in flux) is a recipe for delays, bumping, and overbooking.

Your Rights If You Are Denied Boarding

If you have been denied boarding, met the ticketing and check-in criteria, and your airline does not find another way to get you to your final destination within an hour of the original schedule (and most of the time this is impossible), your airline owes you money. Specifically, it must pay you the amount of your one-way fare (or half the cost of your round-trip ticket) up to a maximum of $200. If you arrive at your destination more than two hours late (a real likelihood), compensation is doubled. International flights inbound to the United States (even on a U.S. carrier) are exempted. So are charter flights and any flight using an aircraft seating fewer than sixty people. Other rules—or no rules—apply in other countries. Check before you leave.

Let's Make a Deal

Rather than pay out actual cash to those who have been denied boarding, many airlines prefer to offer free tickets to travelers who have already made the flight if they volunteer to be bumped to a later flight. When a flight is oversold, the airline asks passengers whether they might be willing to take a later flight. As a further incentive (some might call it a bribe), they are offered cash and/or another free ticket in addition to passage on a later flight. If an insufficient number of volunteers come forward at the first offer, the airline will keep sweetening the deal until the situation is resolved.

I have to assume that the executive traveler is not interested in cash or free tickets used as rewards to tempt passengers to surrender their seats on an overbooked flight. Vacationers and students (some of whom have made a cottage industry out of being bumped from what they know will be oversold flights in exchange for future tickets) are the passengers most likely to accept the airlines' offers. For the executive traveler, the goal is to avoid finding yourself on the wrong side of the jetway when your flight leaves the airport.

How Not to Be a Bumpee

The first rule to follow is **be early.** Arrive at the airport early. Check in early. Board early. It's preferable to get your boarding pass when you get your ticket, before you arrive at the airport. There are some people who like to wait until the last minute to get on the plane. I'm not one of them. (My wife is, however.) To me it is far preferable to board the aircraft early, stow my carry-on baggage, and settle into my seat. I get to hang my garment bag before everyone else jams theirs into the closet; I get to ask the flight attendant what the choice of meals is and register my preference. Sometimes I do work before takeoff; other times I just fall asleep. In Europe this technique sometimes doesn't work. On the continent many carriers board economy first, business second, and first-class passengers last.

Having a boarding pass with an assigned seat reduces *but does not eliminate* the possibility that two passengers will be assigned to the same seat. When this occurs, the bottom line is that on an overbooked flight, possession of a seat is nine-tenths of the law. No matter what I'm planning to do on the aircraft, if the flight is overbooked and I've boarded early, I'm the one who is sitting in the seat and it's the late arrival with the identical boarding pass who has the problem, not me.

A Thorny Issue

Bumping of ticket-holding passengers is a direct consequence of flight overbooking by airlines, which in turn is a direct consequence of multiple reservations by executive travelers, in short, people like you and me. Because we business travelers want—generally with very good reason—to keep our travel options open, we make a lot of reservations that we don't keep. Generally speaking, we don't cancel them, either because we don't have time or because we want to have an option in case the worst happens at the airport. This leaves airlines with a significant number of no-shows for each flight.

To offset the no-shows, airlines deliberately overbook their flights, generally by approximately ten to twenty percent, sometimes by a lot more. At peak times airlines can overbook by as much as seventy percent (which goes a long way toward explaining how two passengers can have boarding passes with the same seat number). "An MD-87 holds 133 people," says one top airline executive. "We will often book it to 180 people, but even so, more often than not it will push out of the gate carrying 110 passengers. Every so often we guess wrong, or one of our competitors has a mechanical difficulty or a cancellation."

Yield Management

The executive's description of deliberate overbooking is a precise thumbnail sketch of "yield management." This is your first of three McCormack seminars on the subject. In the airline business, yield management is the way air carriers deal with the evanescent value of an airline seat. Once the plane leaves the ground, the revenue that the carrier might derive from that seat is gone forever. From the airline's point of view, every empty seat is money out of pocket. In an industry wracked by deregulation and economic recession, where profits have recently dissolved into a sea of red ink, overbooking is an economic necessity.

Yield Management Horror Stories

In addition to deliberate overbooking, the other component of yield management is the intricate Rube Goldberg fare structure that gives passengers and travel agents both incredible bargains and financial nightmares—sometimes on the same trip. Yield management is the reason why you can fly the 3,000 miles between Los Angeles and New York on an advance purchase round-trip ticket for about the same fare as the 450-mile trip between Los Angeles and San Francisco if you buy a last-minute ticket.

Not only are fares illogical on a cost-per-mile basis, they always seem to be in constant flux. If you think that it sometimes appears as if airline fares change by the minute, you're not far wrong. Actually they may change by the second. Under the yield management system, airlines have the capacity to reprogram their computer reservations systems to accept as many as *200,000 fare changes a day.*

This process surely has its flaws, and the airlines are not always the beneficiaries. "It's a dark science," says Sandy Gardiner of British Airways, "and certainly not a perfect science." Gardiner told me that the blemishes in the yield management system were all too apparent at a conference of British Airways executives. "At one point in the conference our general manager for pricing walked up to the podium and asked how many fares we thought there were between London and New York. We all thought about it for a moment and concluded that there must be about fifty. He then took out a large roll of paper and threw it out. It unraveled itself clear across the room. He told us that the number was in the thousands."

The Revenge of the Travel Agents

Travel agents are among the victims of this lunatic pricing system. Their clients are always coming back at them after a trip with reports of a fellow passenger who paid less—sometimes a lot less—for a seat on the same flight. Until recently it was a hopeless battle. Not even the most conscientious travel agent could keep track of the myriad fare changes. In self-defense, some large-volume travel agents have resorted to guerrilla warfare against the airlines to try to beat them at their own game. They have purchased twenty-four-hour fare-checking programs (among the better-known systems are Maestro and Aqua), which continually monitor airline price structures.

If the travel agency's computer program spots a change in the airlines' computer fare listings and that change benefits a client, it automatically alters his or her reservation and grabs the reduction. These watchdog systems also check for changes in seat options. Maybe that bulkhead seat on the aisle between Seattle and Miami was not available when you booked your flight, but if it opens up after you've purchased your ticket, it will snatch it on your behalf, even if the seat clears at 3:48 A.M., your agent is on maternity leave, and you are in Budapest.

Individual Commando Action

You don't always need a travel agent to outfox the yield management system. I tip my hat to one California business traveler who had been booked on a 12:30 P.M. Southwest Airlines flight from Burbank to Oakland with a bargain fare of $59 round-trip. When a morning meeting ran late, he realized that he would not make his plane. The next flight out was a United flight at 2:15 P.M. He knew he wouldn't be able to match the $59 fare, but as a last-minute passenger, he was unwilling to get stuck paying $168, more than five times what one leg of his original round-trip ticket cost. The next best choice was a 6:30 P.M. United flight at $79, one way. The price was acceptable, but it meant he would be unable to keep his dinner appointment.

Undaunted, the intrepid businessman arrived at the United counter at Burbank at 1:15 P.M., purchased his ticket for the 6:30 plane, and asked whether there were any seats on the

2:15 flight. He was hoping that under yield management, some previously reserved discounted seats for the 2:15 flight had been released to the agents at the airport. However, the agent at the counter informed him that the 2:15 flight was now not only sold-out but overbooked—even his $168 seat was no longer available. Worse, the standby list was twenty passengers long.

The valiant businessman tried yet another approach. At 1:35 he called United's 800 reservations number and asked whether there were open seats on the 2:15 flight. To his astonishment, he was told that there were seats available. He booked not only a reservation in his own name, but one for an imaginary traveling companion as well, and got seat assignments. As it turned out, he had the entire row to himself. How much did he pay? $79.

What happened? Within twenty minutes the flight with no space available at $168 and a twenty-person waiting list had turned into a flight with empty seats at $79. Because an empty seat is lost revenue, United made a yield management decision that it was better to sell last-minute seats at $79 than not to sell them at $168.

Keep Checking

What is the moral of this story? **Never assume anything.** Keep checking fares, even after you have your ticket. Don't take no for an answer, no matter how long they say the wait list is.

The truth is that no airline really knows whether a flight is overbooked until boarding has begun. You can all but count on the fact that airlines will hold a block of a certain number of seats for high-volume travel agents, frequent flyer celebrities and bigwigs, airline executives, staff, and other users. As long as these seats remain on hold, they will show up in the computer system as occupied—sold, in other words. If these potential passengers don't use the space that has been reserved for them, the seats are released back to the airline at a certain point before the flight leaves. The time and date when these seats are released varies. If an airline tells you a seat is unavailable (or unavailable at a discount price), don't give up. Keep calling back. The discount ticket that was out of the question yesterday (or an hour ago) might be available today.

Surviving Baggage Claim

Have Purse, Will Travel

Every business traveler strives mightily to avoid checking his or her luggage. Sometimes the efforts to circumvent the limits on cabin baggage appear comedic. From the way Sarah Wooldridge, my London assistant, describes my appearance at the check-in, I'm sure that to some observers we may look like two overloaded Bulgarian spies. She claims that when I go into the terminal, I always have too much hand luggage. While I check in with my two briefcases, she is lurking behind a pillar with my garment bag. Airlines, particularly U.S. carriers, have become increasingly bureaucratic about the number of pieces of carry-on luggage that is permitted. It's a limitation which I think has the potential to work in favor of women. I've seen women passengers board the aircraft with two carry-on items plus a huge bag, which on most airlines should put them over the limit. They get away with it because that huge bag is technically a "purse." Since I'd been harassed about my garment bag and two briefcases, I asked the airline for the definition of a purse and was told that a "purse" has a strap and a zipper. If one wanted to be contentious about it, I suppose a male executive traveler could carry a small flight bag and call it his "purse."

Don't Surrender Your Valuables

Never pack anything in your checked baggage that can't be easily replaced. This includes your house keys, car keys, tickets for the next leg of the trip, driver's license, passport, and any other identification. It also includes obvious valuables like jewelry, cameras, furs, and electronic equipment, as well as valuable papers and documents. By valuable papers and documents, I mean not only negotiable stock and bond certificates, *but also:*

- the floppy disk containing the final manuscript of your novel
- the pictures of your newborn child
- the original receipts and other documentation you are carrying to your IRS audit
- the approved contract with your best client—the one existing copy bearing the penciled-in changes initialed by the CEO

Pictures, contracts, receipts, manuscripts, and computer files, although they are priceless to you, have no inherent value as far as the airlines are concerned and you will have a very difficult (if not absolutely impossible) time getting compensation for them.

What the Airline Owes You
If Your Bag Is Lost or Damaged

Not much.

Within the United States, an airline will provide lost or damaged baggage compensation up to a maximum of $1,250 per person—not per bag, per person. The airline is liable only for the *depreciated* value of your belongings, not for their replacement value—you won't get enough compensation to replace a four-year-old designer suit with anything more than a nice jacket off the sale rack at Macy's. Before they compensate you, it is likely that you will be asked to furnish purchase receipts for items you claim were in the bags in order to document their value.

Limitations on liability differ from airline to airline and are stated in something known as "Conditions of Carriage," an implied contract you buy into each time you purchase a ticket. Airlines curtail their liability in ways that may surprise even the frequent traveler. Because there is no U.S. government-mandated liability for carry-on baggage, many airlines exempt themselves from any obligation about it. The Conditions of Carriage for American Airlines clearly states, "American assumes no responsibility or liability for baggage carried in the passenger compartment of the aircraft." In other words, if another passenger walks off the plane with the garment bag that you carried onto the aircraft, American Airlines, like most domestic carriers, owes you no compensation whatsoever.

On U.S.-international flights, you get very little protection for lost or damaged luggage that you check in with the airline. Baggage is insured by the kilogram—$20 per kilo, or roughly $9 per pound—about what you pay for a good filet of salmon, but hardly sufficient to replace your business wardrobe. Rather than weighing each bag at check-in and recording that weight on your ticket, many carriers assume that each bag weighed the maximum they will accept—generally 32 kilos, or about 70 pounds. This makes the international liability limit just $640 per bag.

Outside the United States, the compensation you can expect to receive for lost luggage varies from airline to airline. Under the international Warsaw Convention, which governs these things, airlines are obliged to pay only trifling amounts per bag. Whenever you travel, therefore, make sure you have taken out adequate private insurance.

Excess Valuation Insurance

Depending on what business you are in, there may be occasions when checking luggage containing valuables cannot be avoided. Within the United States, if you are at your maximum carry-on limit and you are concerned about the safety of the items in your checked luggage, you can purchase excess valuation insurance from the airline. Most airlines don't publicize the service but it is available—you just need to be sure to check in a little earlier to complete the paperwork.

Although there are variations among airlines, the excess valuation premium costs approximately one to two percent of the value of what you are insuring, over and above the $1,250 liability limit imposed by the U.S. Department of Transportation.

For between $20 and $40, you can insure an additional $2,000 worth of your belongings. By taking out excess valuation insurance, you also give your baggage a very high profile with the baggage handlers and other airline staff. Your bags are specially tagged with an identification which indicates that your luggage is to get the kid-gloves treatment. It also puts any potentially larcenous baggage handlers on notice that your belongings are all but radioactive. Behind-the-scenes thieves know that if they tamper with "excess valuation" baggage they will incur the wrath of not just the passenger but the airline itself. On one occasion when I took out excess baggage insurance, as I was waiting at the carousel for my bags to come down the chute, an agent walked up to me and physically handed me my luggage.

If Your Baggage Goes Astray

We've all seen the forlorn individuals desperately searching various nooks and crannies of the baggage claim area for their luggage. We've also seen the same lonely suitcase making repeat laps of the baggage carousel with no one to claim it. How do you deal with the airline if your luggage is lost?

Very carefully. What you do, when you do it, and what you sign at the airport affects your ability to collect from the airline in the event that your bags are permanently lost.

Bureaucracy at Its Worst

If your baggage doesn't show up, it is once again time to call upon your relationship with the Special Services representatives, if they are present and available. If not, you will be forced to deal with the staff of the baggage claim office, who are considerably down the corporate hierarchy from the Special Services agents.

Invariably, you will be given a form to complete. Resist the temptation to carry on business as usual and complete the form in your office or at the hotel. Read it carefully. On some airlines, these forms are merely reports of lost or damaged luggage. Others also include a claim for damages against the airline. Insist on the latter, even if it means completing two separate documents. **Complete the form(s), even if the airline representative assures you that your baggage will be along on the next flight.** Describe your luggage and its contents as fully and completely as possible. Some battle-hardened travel veterans (who probably learned from bitter experience) even carry a snapshot of their luggage for just such occasions.

Make sure you get a copy of anything you sign, that the date and time of filing the form are noted in writing, and that you have the name, title, and telephone number of any airline employee you deal with. **Do not surrender your baggage claim tag** unless you get signed proof from the airline representative that custody of the tag has been transferred to the airline. If you must give them the tag, record all numbers on it—that tag is the *only evidence you have that you actually ever checked your baggage at all.* If possible, have a xerox made for the airline and keep the original yourself.

A few carriers will not accept the claim form until they have declared your bags irreversibly and irretrievably lost. However, the act of completing the form will help acquaint you with what you will need to furnish as documentation in case the worst happens. It will also offer an opportunity to build a bit of a personal connection with the baggage claim supervisor, who probably has all too many of these kinds of problems to deal with.

Damaged Goods

Almost as disheartening as missing luggage is the sight of a cardboard box or plastic tub coming down the chute, housing the mangled remains of what was formerly a suitcase—your suitcase. Here again, what you do and sign at the airport may affect your ability to collect from the carrier. If your bag has been damaged (incidental scuffs or smudges aside), the airline will pay for repairs or make the repairs itself. Repairs are utilitarian, not cosmetic—if the new green handle or bright orange zipper makes the bag functional, whether or not it matches the original leopard skin print is not a factor in determining compensation. If the suitcase can't be fixed, as is the case with missing baggage, the airline will pay for its depreciated value, not for the cost of a replacement.

Airline responsibility for damaged luggage is spelled out in the Conditions of Carriage, and varies from one carrier to another. Most impose a strict time limit on a passenger's right to claim compensation for damaged baggage or missing items from claimed baggage. This may well be one reason why baggage thieves are all too common—airlines have established a very limited liability and the passenger has very little recourse.

The time limit for filing a claim can be as long as twenty-four hours—or as short as no time at all. American Airlines signs off on your bags the moment you claim them and step out onto the curb. "Acceptance of baggage by the bearer of a claim check without filing a written complaint shall constitute evidence of delivery by American of your baggage, with all original contents, in good condition."

Clearing Customs

For the great majority of business travelers, the main aggravation of going through Customs and Immigration is the time it takes. We know the U.S. Immigration and Naturalization Service (INS) has no interest in us, and most of us will gladly pay whatever import duties we owe to Customs, provided that we can pay them quickly and get on with our journey.

A Show of Hands Through Immigration

Passport checks at New York's JFK Airport now can entail delays as long as ninety minutes. For frequent international business travelers, the INS has instituted a new way to speed your way through U.S. Immigration passport checkpoints. The system is based on the established scientific principle that everyone's hand is distinctive—not just the fingerprint, but the size and shape of the hand itself.

Called the INSPASS, the system entails making a photographic record of what your hand looks like. When your application is accepted, a three-dimensional image of your hand's size and shape is recorded onto the INSPASS card. When you return to the United States, instead of going through the conventional lines, you approach the INSPASS kiosk, and place your hand under an infrared measuring device. The measuring device then compares your hand with the image on file. If they match, you proceed on through. It takes less than a minute. The only downside is the potential for a more frequent renewal period. Because hands change over time, the INS expects to require new 3-D imagery every couple of years.

Dress the Part

Unless they have been on an overseas shopping spree, most business travelers have nothing to declare. Nevertheless, some people in the "nothing to declare line" are going to get stopped. How can you avoid being one of those people? Go through Customs—in any country—looking like what you are: an executive business traveler. The odds of your being stopped as a well-groomed respectable-looking person wearing a suit (and tie, if you're a gentleman) going through the "nothing to declare" lanes with a porter are infinitesimal. If you're under thirty, or look under thirty, the odds increase a little. If you don't have a porter and are on your own, the odds of being stopped increase a bit more. If you are a man and aren't wearing a tie, the odds go up again. If you're wearing torn or grungy jeans and a two-day stubble, the odds are almost fifty-fifty that you're going to get stopped. Add a surly expression, a beard and a ponytail, and/or one earring and it's almost a sure thing.

The Trojan Horse in the Three-Piece Suit

How well does dressing the part work? I've heard many stories of prosperous families returning to the United States from

European vacations with purchases that should have been declared and getting through without challenge. What's the strategy? The family sent three-piece-suited button-down Dad ahead through the "nothing to declare" line, carrying just his distinguished business traveler sangfroid, his briefcase, and a small suitcase. Ten or fifteen minutes later, Mom and the kids straggled through, carrying all the rest of the myriad suitcases with nothing in them but a few souvenirs and dirty laundry.

They've Seen It All

I suppose these families think they are clever enough, but I can't recommend their approach. Several years ago there was a highly publicized case of a socially prominent and very wealthy woman apprehended coming through Customs because she tried to avoid paying duty on some designer clothing she'd purchased in Paris. **If you're over the limit, declare it.** The duty isn't that great on most items. If you can afford the item, you should be able to afford the duty. Customs officials have seen most of the scams. Sewing "JC Penney—Made in the USA" labels into a bespoke pinstripe suit from Gieves & Hawkes on Savile Row doesn't work. Neither does scuffing up a new Hermes handbag to make it look "old." The downside of being caught in terms of hassle and embarrassment is far worse than the duty you have to pay.

Don't Get a Record

Suppose you *did* go on an overseas shopping spree? What if your clients or suppliers gave you a valuable gift? If you are a U.S. citizen, you are permitted to return from a foreign trip with a total of $400 worth of items for personal or household use. If the value of these items exceeds $400, you must declare the price you paid for them, or estimate their worth at the time of purchase.

If you don't know whether you've gone over the limit, one technique is to **declare something.** First of all, it's not worth getting caught. Once you've been apprehended trying to clear

Customs without paying duty, your name goes into a computerized record as someone for Customs to watch for coming into the United States. Pay the duty on your excess, which will be minimal. Provided that you are dressed in your executive traveler "uniform," as soon as you've exceeded the limit, made your declaration, and paid your excess duty, it's been my experience that Customs inspectors move you on quickly.

Barter and Volume Discounts
With Airlines and Hotels

With the deterioration in the economy, not just in the United States but in Europe as well, the canny executive traveler has many more opportunities to obtain negotiated discount price arrangements with airlines, hotels, and rental car agencies. All are based on repeat volume travel, often to the same destination or group of destinations.

Sometimes the arrangement is a volume discount. At IMG we work on this approach a lot. Because we send people regularly between Cleveland and New York, we are in a great position to deal with Continental Airlines or USAir for a bulk purchase of tickets at a pre-negotiated price, usable by any member of our firm. Buying tickets in this fashion may not always beat the rock-bottom special discount fare, but it does take the financial sting out of the emergency last-minute trip.

The downside is a certain loss of flexibility. In case of a delay or cancellation, negotiated tickets such as these are generally not transferable from one airline to another, and executive travelers may need to purchase a full-fare ticket on another airline if they need to change carriers. This is not such a tragedy. As I explained previously in "Above All, Get Your Flight Coupon," the unused negotiated fare ticket can be used on another trip (even by another member of staff). Even if you have to purchase a full-fare seat, you are not in any worse shape financially than you would have been without the pre-negotiated block of tickets.

How prevalent are negotiated tickets? If your company isn't already doing this, it's missing an opportunity. According to American Express Travel Related Services, fares paid by its business clients are dropping markedly. A recent seventeen-month period showed a ten percent increase in trips booked by its clients, but a fifteen percent decrease in fares. American Express found that most of the drop was not due to lower air fares, but rather to assiduous use of negotiated discount tickets, and also to corporate travel policies mandating coach-only travel.

Airlines which once relied on business travelers, especially those who travel for middle to large size corporations, as full-fare paying "cash cows" are finding that they now must offer substantial discounts to attract or maintain their market share. Airlines that refuse to bargain often find themselves out in the cold. Georgia-Pacific Corporation, for example, requested that its employees refrain from flying on Delta because it felt Delta was not giving the company enough of a break on its ticket prices.

We also make barter arrangements with airlines and hotels. If we're running a German tennis tournament where Lufthansa is one of the official sponsors, part of our compensation from the airline may be several hundred thousand dollars' worth of air fares for IMG. When American Airlines sponsors a gymnastics meet that we created, they may give us vouchers for $50,000 worth of air travel. If you take this approach, **make sure you can take full advantage of what you are being offered.** You can most assuredly make use of $50,000 worth of air fare on American Airlines. We call that Class A barter. On the other hand, $50,000 worth of hotel rooms in Pakistan—or even in Pittsburgh—may or may not be a good deal, depending on how much business you have there.

Sometimes a Bargain Isn't a Bargain

Sometimes these corporate policies are not too well thought out. At one time we had a company policy which dictated that if there was barter available, you had to use it. At first blush, it made a great deal of sense. However, strict application of the policy resulted in a situation where five IMG executives from our London office flew to Orlando, Florida, on American Airlines because we had a barter arrangement with that carrier. They went through $22,000 worth of barter when they could have purchased five British Airways London–Orlando tickets for about $3,000 ($600 apiece) because of a special promotion that British Airways was offering at the time.

Legal Services, Little Fried Onions, and Patty Melts, Medium Rare

You have to apply a certain amount of creativity and ingenuity to your barter arrangements. For example, if your law firm has offices in Century City in Los Angeles, you may be able to strike up a deal with one of the local restaurants. There's a Hamburger Hamlet right there on the Avenue of the Stars; it's a quality chain with restaurants in many major business cities. Why not approach them and say, "Look, you probably do $200,000 worth of legal work a year. If you give us $200,000 worth of lunches and dinners, we'll give you the legal work for nothing." Everybody wins—that $200,000 worth of legal time probably costs your firm about $60,000–$80,000, which is probably about what that $200,000 worth of ground beef, lettuce, tomato, and sesame seed buns costs the restaurant.

Lettuce, Toilet Paper, Air Fare, and Widgets

At IMG we have a relatively easy time making barter arrangements directly with the airlines because we can offer them useful business and promotional opportunities—sponsorship or a hospitality tent at a sporting event, good seats at concerts and tennis matches. However, even if your business can't offer "glamorous" barter possibilities such as these, you still may be able to strike up a deal through a "second-hand" barter arrangement.

Many airlines with excess capacity have reduced their overhead by making barter arrangements for travel credits with their suppliers—the firms who furnish their gasoline, their spare parts, their lettuce, and their toilet paper. If your firm does business with these suppliers, perhaps you can negotiate those air credits into your working relationship.

You and Your Hotel

When you call the hotel chain's 800 reservations number and ask the price of a room in, say, Chicago, do you take the first price they quote you?

If so, you're a travel chump.

Since the late 1980s, the world has been awash in vacant hotel rooms. Average occupancy rates in the United States for hotels and motels are currently less than sixty percent. In other words, on any night, there's an almost fifty-fifty chance that a room will be empty. So what?

Yield Management, Part II

So welcome to your second seminar in yield management. To an airline, every vacant seat in a departing aircraft represents money flying away. To a hotel, every bed that does not get slept in on a given night is money out the window. Indeed, for hotels it's worse, since they lose not only the cost of the room, but the prospective revenue from meals, room service, and, of course, those telephone charges.

To cope, hotels have started copying the airlines in dealing with their excess capacity. This means that unless you want to be in Pasadena for the Rose Parade at New Year's or New Orleans at Mardi Gras or anywhere there's a major event attracting large numbers of high rollers, you're going to be able to negotiate—or haggle, if you will.

Marxist Economics

Sometimes the yield management game produces Marxist consequences (not Karl, but Groucho). At a prominent Manhattan business hotel, an associate of mine observed a gentleman approach the front desk and inquire whether there was a room available for the evening. The clerk checked through his computer inventory and informed the prospective guest that he had a room available at $185. The man shook his head, saying the rate was too expensive, and turned to leave. Despite his behind-the-counter handicap, the younger and faster desk clerk caught up with the gentleman before he went through the revolving door and into the night.

"Sir?" he asked. "How much *would* you be willing to pay?" By the time the two had strolled back to the front desk, an agreement had been reached for a charge of $119 for the night.

How Do You Rate?

At most hotels each room has a number of different possible rates. At the Loews Anatole (a gargantuan conventioneer hotel) in Dallas, there are as many as nine different rates for each room. At other hotels, there may be as many as thirty different tariffs (not including eleventh-hour ad hoc negotiations like the scenario above). Many hotel chains are empowering their reservationists and desk clerks to be flexible when it comes to rates and discounts. Rates vary by day of week, season, number of advance bookings, and recent occupancy trends. What you pay also depends on how you made your reservation. Did you use an "800" number? Chances are you'll pay more.

This happens not just in the United States, but all over the world. Hotel rates are negotiable. You will get your best rate as an individual frequent guest or as one of a group of frequent stayers under a prenegotiated arrangement.

A New Relationship With Businesses

Michael Gray, manager of the Hyatt Carlton Tower in London, told me how his hotel negotiates with executive travelers. "The corporate market is demanding lower rates," he says. "In return for a discount, corporations are narrowing down their lists of approved hotels. Instead of authorizing use of one of ten hotels in London, now they are listing only six. If my hotel is going to be one of the six, I'm going to get some positive spinoff from the four that are dropped. We can afford to give a discount, because we are going to see our occupancy go up.

"If we're going to give a reasonable rate to that company, then that firm must do its best to increase our volume. The companies must guarantee a minimum volume so we know that the discounted price doesn't affect our ability to continue to provide service. For a really major volume user who would book several hundred room-nights a year, we're talking about discounts of thirty to forty percent, which is very good—for both of us. The Carlton Tower is prepared to work with companies on this basis, but there has to be a lot of respect and integrity between the corporation and the hotel in carrying out the agreement." In other words, if you deliberately overstate the number of room-nights to strike the best possible deal with the hotel, you will have a great deal of difficulty renewing your arrangement.

Toll-Free, but Very Costly

Hotel 800 numbers and airline 800 numbers are two very different things. **Beware of a hotel chain's toll-free 800 number.** There is no financial penalty for calling airline 800 numbers—air fares don't cost more when you deal with centralized reservations agents. However, there may be a considerable extra cost attached to calling a hotel's "toll-free" number. This is because airline yield management decisions are made at corporate headquarters, not at the departure gate, and hotel yield management decisions are generally made not by corporate overseers but by individual hotel managers.

"We like to promote our 800 number as a convenience to our guests in making their reservations with us anywhere in the United States or around the world," explains a Hyatt representative. "They quote the latest published rates," he says, "but each hotel manages its room inventory differently, and the national reservations folks don't always know as fast as we do when certain rooms and rates become available."

It's fine to use the 800 numbers for basic comparison shopping for the lowest "official" room rates offered among the major chains. Remember, however, that many telephone reservationists are paid on a salary-plus-commission basis. In short, they make more money when you pay more for a room. They also may have far less flexibility and authority to negotiate with you.

In addition to comparing "standard" rates, the 800 number is the easiest way to get the direct number of the particular hotel you are interested in. By calling the hotel itself, you can **deal directly with your hotel of choice.** Desk clerks don't work on commission, and they are closest to the general manager, who is responsible for decision-making about room rates. This arrangement also reinforces your own personal relationship with your hotel. "I like to deal directly with a couple of my favorite hotels," says Dove Audio's President and CEO Michael Viner. "I think I get better service. The hotels don't have to pay the seven or ten percent commission. They make more money and feel that you're more of a loyal customer."

Recipe for Saving Money, or
How to Grill a Reservations Agent

How do you get the best possible rate? **Keep asking questions.** Every hotel has a corporate rate. To get it all you have to do is ask, even if you're a corporation of one. Is there a weekend rate? At business hotels, this is often very inexpensive. If you're arriving on Thursday, could you get the weekend rate with an early check-in? Is there anything else less expensive? Always ask for the best rate available.

Sometimes you can do better just stepping up to the desk and asking for the best rate when you check in, even if you already have a reservation at a price you believe is reasonable. One canny traveler, who had reserved a room at a super special rate of $65 for a one-night weekend stay, noticed as he was waiting to check in that a departing guest was paying just $49 a night for his room.

Choosing not to reveal the fact that he had a reservation, he inquired with the clerk about whether there were rooms available, and asked for the cheapest room. He was quoted a rate of $39, $10 less than the departing guest, and $26 less than the rate he had been quoted on the toll-free reservation number. (In fairness, however, it should be noted that his original $65 rate had included a "complimentary" breakfast.)

Although this particular incident occurred at a Hilton hotel, it could easily have happened at any one of the other major chains, such as Sheraton, Hyatt, or Radisson, as well. During times of economic slowdown, and especially during slow seasons (like New York in August, or Minneapolis in the dead of winter), with every question you ask, your quoted rate could go down, often far below what you might expect. A $175 room at the Hyatt Regency in Washington, D.C., has been known to go for as little as $69 a night.

Ah, but air fare is air fare, and a room is not a room. How do you get the best room in the best hotel, and how do you use it to your best advantage? We'll talk about that in the next chapter.

Chapter VIII
Successful Travel Is an
Accumulation of Details

God is in the details.
Ludwig Mies van der Rohe

Mies van der Rohe, one of the masters of modern architecture, knew that command of the details was what separated simple yet interesting structures from monotonous grey boxes. A smooth and comfortable journey is no different. This chapter covers an assortment of details about various aspects of business travel. Taking care of these details greatly enhances your odds of having an agreeable and fruitful trip. If neglected, however, they can easily come back to haunt you, making your time away from home unproductive, uneasy, and unpleasant.

At the Hotel

Check-In Tips

There are few sights more disheartening to an arriving business traveler than a lone beleaguered clerk at the registration desk and a line that's thirty people long. Some business hotels are beginning to offer accelerated check-in for their frequent guests. It's still a very uneven process, however.

With or without "accelerated" check-in, you shouldn't have to stand in that line. You can speed the process yourself by doing a great deal of the check-in work over the phone before you ever arrive at the hotel. Start by giving the hotel your credit card number and making sure that the hotel knows what time you are due to arrive. Tell them that you need accelerated check-in and ask for help in avoiding the lines. It also helps, of course, to plan your arrival time off-peak, away from the crush of other arrivals.

Which credit card you give the hotel when you check in matters a great deal. **Use a no-limit card to check in,** such as American Express, even if that's not the card you will eventually use to pay your bill. If you check in with a Visa, MasterCard, Discover Card, or any card that has a credit line, the hotel blocks or reserves a healthy chunk of credit for your bill to protect themselves against absconding guests. This chunk will be far greater than your actual bill. You won't even know that they did it—until you get a nasty and potentially embarrassing surprise when your credit card is refused after you try to pay for a client dinner at Michael's or Aquavit or Harry's Bar & American Grill. It's a very simple matter at check-out time to alter the method of payment. The hotel just destroys one charge slip and prepares another.

Easy Come/Easy Go? Maybe Yes/Maybe No

Although many hotels have found ways to speed up the check-out process, expediting check-in has been slower in coming. Marriott and Hilton are now offering members of their frequent stay programs a chance to bypass the front desk entirely and check in at a special counter. All they need to do is present a credit card to receive a room key and check-in packet.

Does this speedy check-in pay dividends to the business traveler? It depends. Instant check-in is fine if you are staying at a hotel you know well and the staff is familiar with your preferences. It's also fine if all rooms in the hotel are more or less the same.

But do you *really* want to stay in a hotel where all the rooms are plain vanilla? In larger cities, not just in Europe but in the

United States as well, the older hotels are the most interesting places to stay. In better old hotels, all rooms, even at the same price level, are most assuredly *not* the same. Within a given hotel chain, the same level of accommodation changes markedly from property to property and one city to another. There is a big difference between a suite at the meticulously restored 19th-century Willard InterContinental in Washington, D.C., a suite at the rather stolid, glass-and-concrete block InterContinental in Frankfurt, and a suite at the up-to-the-minute Inter-Continental in Seoul, with wet bars in the room and a shopping arcade below.

Old Wine in New Bottles

Despite the potential benefits of frequent stay programs, I can't recommend loyalty to a particular hotel chain the way I can recommend loyalty to an individual hotel where you are well treated. More often than not, hotel chains manage rather than own the buildings with their names emblazoned on the canopy. In some cases, when the property changes hands or the hotel becomes otherwise troubled, what was formerly a Sheraton reopens with a great deal of fanfare as a Marriott after the soaps and stationery have been changed.

In very few cases is the hotel revitalized from top to bottom, so major building flaws, like slow elevators and bad water pressure, will remain. If the phone cords were short before, chances are they're still going to be short under new management. This happens not just with small run-of-the-mill properties but with large deluxe business hotels as well. The Pan Pacific in San Francisco was the Portman just a few years ago. Even New York's venerable Plaza, which for many years has been operated by the Westin chain, was once a Hilton property.

Hotel names can also be confusing to the executive traveler. The Ritz in Paris has no corporate affiliation with the Ritz in London or the Ritz in Madrid. The Ritz-Carlton chain operates none of these European Ritz hotels, nor the Carlton Tower in London.

Personal Service

What's the point? Cultivating a relationship with a particular hotel where the service is good and where the staff knows you and your preferences is a great way to get the most out of your business travel. Herbert Striessnig, general manager of the Savoy in London, said it best of all: **The best hotel in the world is the hotel where you're best known.**

British television personality Michael Parkinson, our long-time client, finds Mr. Striessnig's hostelry to be among his favorites because of its personal service. "When I was working TV-A.M.," he recalls, "a condition of the deal was that I spend a weekend at the Savoy, because I had to get up very early in the morning to do the program. The first night I stayed at the Savoy, I told the fellow at the desk that I wanted a wake-up call at 3:30 A.M. He was astonished—he'd never had a request like that before. At 3:30 I was awakened not by the telephone but by a man shaking my shoulder. I opened my eyes and there was this immaculate man in tails and a white stiff collar who said, 'Mr. Parkinson, I have to regretfully inform you that it's 3:30 in the morning.' That's a great hotel."

Play the Field

Because of changing ownership and management of hotels and the fact that most chains own many types of hostelries, **no single hotel chain has "the best hotel" or "the best hotel for you" in every city you visit.** Therefore, cultivating an exclusive or semi-exclusive relationship with a particular hotel chain based on its "frequent stay" program is not nearly as rewarding as developing a rapport with staff at a particular hotel. Play the field and stay in the hotel that best meets your needs. If that turns out to be the Four Seasons Clift in San Francisco, the Westin Plaza in New York, and the Hyatt Carlton Tower in London, I think the gains in service and comfort far outweigh any frequent stay benefits that have been foregone.

Room-by-Room Through the Crillon

I sleep in hotel rooms at least as often as I sleep in my own bed at home, so I'm choosy about my hotel accommodations, even at the Crillon. The first time my wife accompanied me to Paris, for the French Open tennis tournament, we were shown to what had become my customary suite at the Crillon. It had always been fine on previous trips, so I moved in without hesitation.

The suite was on the top floor and had a very big bedroom and a huge balcony overlooking all of Paris. However, it had just a tiny sitting room. It didn't take long to discover that the accommodation that was quite wonderful for one solitary traveler was impractical for two busy individuals. Once I had established my office beachhead, there was no real personal space for Betsy to call her own. We were constantly falling over one another, something which was not a problem when I was traveling alone.

The Crillon was full and moving was impossible so we muddled through, but I asked my London assistant, Sarah Wooldridge, to find out what my options would be for the next visit. With typical thoroughness, she looked at every suite in the hotel. She checked for detail and weighed the pluses and minuses of each room—this one's got a tub; that one has a large bed; this other is not near the elevator. The suite we settled on is very nice, but not nearly so impressive as the grand suite on the top floor with the balcony. It has more space in the sitting area and is very practical. Betsy has a place for all her tennis gear and a staging area of her own. So what? **The best room in the hotel is the one where you are most comfortable and productive, not the one which is most "prestigious."**

A Hotel Room Punch List

Am I suggesting that you go through all 3,000+ rooms of the Las Vegas Hilton before you settle in? Of course not. Some room requirements you can establish when you make your reservation. Noted travel writer Ian Keown came up with the business traveler's dream checklist for a hotel room—however, he was quick to add that he's never stayed in a room that's even come close to having all his desired attributes.

The Keown Test: The Perfect Hotel Room

Down to Basics
- Double bed (or larger) with a firm mattress and a choice of pillows
- Swiveling reading lamps with 75-watt bulbs for the bedside
- Bedside table with three-way lamps and a control console for lights, TV, radio, and drapes
- Real desk with swiveling, high-intensity desk lamp and a proper desk chair
- Armchair, ottoman, or sofa
- Coffee table that converts to a dining table
- Coffee maker with a selection of coffees and teas
- Well-stocked minibar with two-way loading cubicle
- Lighted closet with removable coat hangers for trousers, dresses, and skirts; a full-length mirror and a luggage rack
- Individual heating/cooling controls
- Double-glazed windows that open and close
- Do Not Disturb signs—and hotel help that heeds them
- Doorknob cards for ordering breakfast

Keeping in Touch
- Two-line telephones with message light
- Three telephone extensions, one each for the bedside, desk, and bath
- Notepad and pen beside each extension
- Voicemail or video message retrieval
- Teleconferencing capability
- Facsimile and computer modem capability
- Incoming calls that revert to the operator after five—not fifty—rings when the guest is out

- Telephone messages placed in the concierge slot and under the door
- Service for in-room rental of fax machines, personal computers, dictating equipment, cellular telephones, and beepers
- Accessible electrical outlets

That's Entertainment
- Clock radio with alarm and readable operating instructions
- Color television with remote control
- Cable television, including CNN
- Video player with inhouse movies available
- *TV Guide* or equivalent opened to the correct date
- Stereo system with compact-disc player—and CDs available
- Other essential—though less entertaining—information on your television screen, including airline flight information, the weather, and your ongoing bill

Cleaning Up Your Act
- Bathroom with separate shower stall and separate toilet
- Twin vanities, preferably in separate dressing area
- Bathrobes, and hooks on which to hang them
- Hairdryers
- Makeup mirror
- Adequate shelves for toiletries
- Faucets that are easy to operate, overhead showers with variable speed, and shower curtains that cover the entire shower
- Large bath towels
- Trash can that can be opened without stooping
- Toiletries, including shampoo and conditioner, bath gel, toothpaste, razor, toothbrush, and cotton balls or swabs

Safe and Sound
- Electronic card locks
- Double locking doors
- In-room private safe (preferably electronic)
- Adequate soundproofing—between rooms and between the room and the corridor
- Double connecting doors

- Drapes and curtains that shut out all the light
- Smoke detector and emergency evacuation directions

Hotel Services
- Evening turndown service, with fresh towels and a bottle of mineral water rather than candy or brandy on the pillow
- Twenty-four-hour room service that offers omelets anytime
- Room service order-takers who are not located among the pots and pans in the noisiest part of the kitchen
- Twenty-four-hour business center
- Health spa or gymnasium, sauna, and pool, which are open after normal business hours
- Concierge floor with private keys, complimentary breakfast and cocktails, local and international newspapers, and a lounge with telephones and quiet corners for mini-meetings
- All-day dining room—with no music
- Same-day laundry, dry cleaning, and pressing service available seven days a week
- Complimentary shoeshine
- Daily newspaper delivery to your room

I'm in agreement with Keown except on a few minor points:

- I hate the minibars and try to avoid using them;
- Hotel hairdryers are just not very good;
- I've learned *never* to trust hotel alarm clocks *or* wake-up calls;
- There should be a master switch by the door *and* by the bed; and
- Beware of shoeshines if you don't have an alternative pair of shoes.

The following are some explanations for my preferences:

Minibars

It always seems that a hotel staff member is trying to inventory and replenish the minibar at the very moment you are on an important phone call. Some newer hotels have now been engineered to permit restocking from the hallway, but I still find minibars to be a second cousin to pickpocketing or petty larceny.

Hairdryers

I don't know any woman with hair longer than mine who thinks that built-in hairdryers are any good at all. They usually generate too much wind (and noise) and not enough heat. "They're a disaster," agrees Raymond Bickson, general manager of The Mark Hotel in New York. "You can never control their speed, and they always seem to be placed in the most awkward positions, so you have to be Houdini to dry your hair."

Alarm Clocks and Wake-Up Calls

On a business trip, the downside of not getting up is too serious to contemplate. "Never, ever trust wake-up calls or the clock radio or alarm clock the hotel provides," counsels Graham K. L. Jeffrey, general manager of the Willard InterContinental in Washington, D.C., making no exception for his own establishment.

It's very sound advice. Far too many things can go wrong. If you have trouble programming your VCR, you will have trouble programming the clock radio, especially overseas, and especially if you're trying to do it when you're tired and jet-lagged. Assuming that you do figure out how to set it, you may find out that the alarm is broken—the hard way. The clock radio is routinely placed next to the bed. Even if it does go off at the right time, it's all too easy to reach out and turn it off without really waking up. As for wake-up calls, they're just too unreliable. Every experienced business traveler can tell a story or two (at least) of the wake-up call that arrived a half hour late—or not at all.

How do I get up when I travel? I have systems and backup systems. **Bring your own *battery-powered* alarm clock, set it yourself, and place it *across the room,* *not* next to the bed.** I also ask for a wake-up call, but Graham Jeffrey provided me with the best strategy of all—"Always place a room service order the night before, even if it's just for coffee," he recommends. "It's a great backup, and besides, you have to get up to answer the door."

Master Switches

Many hotels will put a master switch right by the front door, which is great when you're coming or going. One switch serves all the lights in the room. But what about when you're going to bed? You have to go to the front door, turn everything off, bark your shins, and stumble back to bed in the dark.

Shoeshines

Looking well-groomed on the road is important, and I admire the European tradition of setting shoes out overnight to be shined. However, take a tip from the experience of Robert Anderson, retired CEO of Rockwell International, and carry a backup pair of shoes.

"I was staying at the Churchill in London and put my shoes outside the door, as is the custom," recalls Anderson. "When I got up in the morning and went out to retrieve them, they weren't there. They were nowhere to be found. It doesn't sound like much of a disaster, but when you get up in the morning and want to go somewhere, you're stuck if you don't have your shoes. I'd only brought one pair with me. I finally had to get someone from the hotel to go out and get me some slippers so I could at least get to a store to buy some replacements. I reported the disappearance to the hotel detective, and when I got back to my room that night after dinner my shoes were back in my room. I was baffled. 'What the hell happened?' I asked him.

"'We apologize for the inconvenience, sir,' he told me. 'We found your shoes down on the third floor in one of the laundry rooms, behind a pile of laundry.'

"It was a very strange place indeed for shoes. 'How did they get there?' I asked.

"'We have an old sheik staying with us, and he's a bit deranged. He goes around at night and steals shoes. We found about half a dozen pairs there, sir, mostly wingtips but a few tassel-loafers as well.'"

Be Finicky About Your Hotel Room

Whatever your expectations when you book your reservation, it's up to you when you are shown to the room to make sure that you are getting what you requested. Too many business travelers are too tired to notice room details when they arrive. Often you are so relieved by the time you finally reach your hotel room that you are insufficiently meticulous about checking it thoroughly. Not me. Don't accept the room to which you are shown without a careful look around. **It will never be easier to change your hotel room than before you've slept in the bed or flushed the toilet.** This involves a careful examination of not only the room itself but the corridor, and rooms surrounding it.

The Itzhak Perlman Rule

Violinist Itzhak Perlman has come up with one of the most elegantly simple maxims for judging a hotel room from the outside. **Never accept a room if the door next to it doesn't have a number on it.** That unnumbered door is a guarantee of a less than restful stay. Almost invariably it leads to something noisy, such as the elevator, the dumbwaiter, the laundry room, the soda and/or ice machine, or the place where the vacuum cleaners lurk and chambermaids go to gossip.

Cleanliness Is Next to . . .

I'm particularly finicky about hotel cleanliness. In a recent Wyndham Hotels & Resorts survey, stale rooms was the leading complaint business travelers had about hotel rooms. Unless you accept rooms that smell or look unclean at home, you shouldn't accept them on the road.

Assuming that the room passes your initial test, consider the bedding, an important component of room cleanliness (and one which is entirely out of view when you arrive). At most hotels, blankets are not changed with each new guest, and not every hotel provides fresh pillows. For all you know, they could have been in the room for weeks, or used just last night by a profusely sweating conventioneer and his dandruff-prone spouse. Even if the room appears acceptable, there are ways to make sure that your accommodations are really clean. Unless you have great confidence that this is done routinely, **call housekeeping and ask for a fresh blanket and pillow for the bed.** Ask them to replace the spare blanket and pillow in the closet as well.

The Shower Test

Unless you will be hosting meetings in your room or suite, you may find that you'll spend more of your waking hours in your hotel bathroom than anywhere else. Low water pressure in the shower was the second leading non-service complaint of business travelers, according to the Wyndham survey. Ignore the impatience of the bellman waiting for his tip. This room deserves considerable attention.

To me, a great hotel must have a great shower. This means a plentiful supply of hot (but not scalding water). It also means that **the water must stay at a uniform temperature and pressure unless you yourself change it.** Most business travelers have tales of a near-death experience in a hotel shower—by either sudden scalding or the instant arrival of a new Ice Age. When you check your room in an unfamiliar hotel, turn on the shower.

The first thing to notice is whether this can be accomplished without a manual from the faucet manufacturer. All too many of these high-tech faucets have an all-in-one control, whereby the difference between on/off and hot/cold is a subtle adjustment in or out, left or right. There are teensy little arrows and microscopic lettering indicating which is which. I need my glasses to read, but I most assuredly do not wear them in the shower. Without them I must resort to guesswork to determine whether I'm going to freeze or broil with every turn of the knob (or stick or handle or button or dial). I'm sure some interior designer thought this looked quite modern and elegant, but to me it's a potential disaster.

Watch the shower for random fluctuations in temperature and pressure. What happens when you flush the toilet or turn on the tap? What happens when someone down the corridor or on the floor below you does likewise?

In general, **be more suspicious of bathrooms in older hotels than in newer ones.** Although older hotels may have been refurbished many times, only in the most thorough renovations are plumbing difficulties resolved. **Taller hotels are potentially more susceptible to plumbing problems than low-rise buildings.** Without booster pumps, most hotels taller than eight stories will have trouble with water pressure, particularly on the upper floors.

Who's got the best bathrooms around? The stately Biltmore in downtown Los Angeles vastly improved its water pressure in a recent facelift. The Savoy in London has shower heads on the ceiling and a supplemental water-pressure system. The Regent in Hong Kong and other Regent hotels (as well as the Grand in Washington, D.C., formerly a Regent property) are known for their large and well-appointed bathrooms, which are also equipped with shower temperature regulators.

Planning a Business Meeting
Away From Home

Making good use of your hotel or your chosen restaurant when you must host an out-of-town event involves careful planning. A lot of business travelers call up the hotel and say, "I've got twenty people coming for lunch. Arrange to have a private room. Goodbye." If that is the extent of your planning, you'll get what you deserve.

Take Advantage of Being the Host

There's a great deal to be said for being the host rather than the guest. Along with the privilege of paying the check, you get to decide who's invited and where you'll dine. Given the choice, I'm most comfortable in a dining ambiance that's quiet rather than noisy, roomy rather that crowded, responsive rather than difficult. Use your status as host to call the shots, but mind what shots you call.

The Three Business Meals of the Day

The first guideline to follow is **make the meal fit the occasion.** Business meals have always been tricky. Unlike office meetings, where you know you have gathered to discuss business, business meals are partly social, partly business—and the ratio between the two changes from meal to meal. In general business meals get progressively less business-like as the day wears on.

Breakfast Should Bustle

Breakfast doesn't eat up time. About forty-five minutes is standard. You can be comfortable with anyone—even boring strangers—within that time frame. I often have two breakfast meetings before 9 A.M. You don't have to apologize for setting a specific business agenda at breakfast and getting right to it. In fact, people expect and appreciate it. **Breakfast is for getting down to business.** You don't have to eat much, or plan too strenuously—muffins or rolls, juice and fruit and coffee and tea are about all that's required. Almost any business hotel ought to be able to make a good breakfast presentation of this sort. (If they can't, it's a very bad sign indeed. Find another hotel or restaurant for a lunch or dinner meeting, and another place to stay next time you're in town.)

Breakfast creates momentum in a business relationship. People don't seem to mind meeting once or twice a month for breakfast—if they know something positive will be accomplished. Lunch and dinner are much tougher to schedule. I particularly like breakfast for floating trial balloons—for piquing the other side's interest with a new idea and telling them, "You don't have to decide this at breakfast." Best of all, issues brought up at breakfast can be followed up the same day.

The Rules of Lunch

Lunch takes time. One of our executives contends that the First Rule of Lunch is **never have a business lunch with someone you have never met before.** He figures it's as risky as a blind date. By the time the appetizer comes around and you realize that the two of you have nothing in common, it's too late. You're trapped, and even a short lunch seems like forever.

Lunch also costs money, and depending on the food and drink you consume, lunch can destroy the rest of your day. Having said that, I must admit that I am nevertheless a proponent of the business lunch. **Lunch provides the perfect balance between business and pleasure.** Enjoying yourself is not frowned upon and getting something accomplished is also approved.

Lunch is also an effective shorthand of telling someone you like them, simply by the care and taste you devote to choosing the restaurant or other venue. Done well, lunch can create a friendly, intimate atmosphere where your guests drop their "game face." People are relaxed and more revealing of themselves. This makes them more vulnerable—and more receptive to your ideas.

Not everyone is a good lunch "date." Like my exec, I don't generally have lunch with people I've never met. I also don't have lunch with professional "luncheoneers"—people who dine out daily, whether there's a reason to or not. Neither pleasure nor business will result from such a lunch. And I don't have lunch simply to thank someone for doing business with us.

I try to have lunch with:

- People I already know;
- People I want to know better; and
- People who need to know me better.

Important lunches should be one-on-one. I seldom have lunch with more than one person at a time (unless I'm hosting a conference). With two or more guests, the psychological dynamics become more difficult to interpret or control, defeating one of the main purposes of lunch. And I will not turn to business at the table until the main course has arrived and the waiters have departed.

Supper Is for Solidarity

Dinner is the most social of business meals. It takes place after the business day in the twilight hours that most people regard as "down time." It is loosely structured and open-ended. It can be festive, relaxed, informal, and revealing.

Most significantly, dinner takes time, much more than lunch. In fact, the sheer amount of time required for dinner—anywhere from two and a half to four hours—implies that the people present know and like each other.

Frequently, business dinners involve not just the principal business clients or colleagues but their spouses as well. In short, **dinner is for bonding.** Dinner is for making personal connections, not making deals. If you're looking for a direct cause-and-effect connection between a meal and a sale, you won't find it at dinner. If your association has become sufficiently congenial that everyone feels comfortable having dinner together, don't spoil the relationship by discussing business matters at the table.

Lunch With a Stopwatch

When you are arranging a business meal, keep these functions in mind. Because of their length, dinners seldom have to be plotted out, since neither you nor your guests are likely to be going onward to another event. Breakfasts, with their limited agenda and abbreviated time frame of an hour or less, generally take care of themselves. If you are hosting a business lunch, however, it is important to orchestrate the timing of the meal.

When I have lunch served at my office, I tell my catering staff quite precisely how the timing of the meal will go. I get really specific: "People will be arriving at 12:30. I want you to take their drink order, and at ten minutes to one I want you to have the first courses on the dining room table. I want the service to move briskly. I want lunch to be finished by 1:30." **Be precise with hotel or restaurant staff that is catering a business lunch.** Failure to accomplish this is one of the leading reasons why business lunches fail to accomplish their objectives.

When we are hosting a lunch or a dinner meeting at a restaurant or at a conference center, I select the menu and wine myself. I let the hotel or restaurant know that I am particular about how the meal and the meeting will go. I'm very attentive to the timing of the meal. I don't want the food being thrown at us; on the other hand, I don't want to wait. I want the wine poured delicately, no more than half a glass at a time.

I give the schedule of the meal to my assistant and have her communicate it to the hotel or restaurant staff. If I don't do this, the meeting can be destroyed by interruptions. The moment we start getting heavily into a major topic, the waiters waltz in with the main course.

This may sound overly controlling, but I don't have any hard-and-fast rules. Each meeting is different. I've got to think about it beforehand and tell the staff, "This is how I'd like it to go." I'm amazed that a lot of executives—who otherwise want everything to go their way—don't do that.

Cover the Ends

We do table plans for all meetings, whether only IMG staff will be attending or whether there will be others present. **Never have an end with nobody at it.** A number of times you'll walk into a private room and there's nobody at the end. You've got to have balance to a table.

You also must make the most of your seating arrangements. I don't put people next to one another because they like each other—those people can have lunch together without me. You've got to mix people up. I routinely pair two people who don't really know one another (and even people who don't get along with one another) as table partners. Then they might actually talk to each other and begin to appreciate one another. It's wonderful to see how it works. The whole point is to get everybody together.

At a business lunch people get very agitated about table plans. Everyone is always very concerned about where they will be seated. **Never put out the place cards in the dining room beforehand.** Invariably people will sneak in, have a look, and try to change the seating. I have a trusted staff member put them out just before they open the room. Never, ever put them out earlier.

Leaving the Airport

Once you've landed, retrieved the luggage, and cleared Customs, sometimes getting transportation into the center of town can be a problem. I find that using limousines is worth the extra cost for me, since I get a lot of work done in them along the way, but I recognize that not all business travelers are in a position to have a private car, even if it would be productive for them to do so.

Peter Kuhn of my London staff has a solution that works well for him in Europe. "If you're going to one city frequently, make an arrangement with a taxi company whereby you can call them and have them meet you. That's my budget version of being met by the chauffeur. It gives you a very big advantage. You don't have to stand in line. You get to know people who are reliable. Sometimes you can get these people to run errands for you while you are at a meeting. Then they'll come back to get you in time to get you to the airport. It all works very smoothly.

They'll run a tab for you. It's a little more expensive than just hailing a cab, but it's worth it in terms of efficiency."

This kind of relationship can be developed in cities you visit frequently. At IMG we maintain a travel "book" that tells our executives how to get from the airport into the city, which cab or limousine services to look for (and which to look out for). It's even easier to do in your own hometown. If you have this kind of relationship with a limousine or cab company, they ought to be willing to make a stop at your office before heading to the airport to pick you up from a return trip. When they do that, they can pick up faxes, messages, or mail that you can sort through on your way back into town. If many employees in your firm do a lot of traveling, you also may be able to get a volume user's rate.

If You Have to Rent a Car

Until recently, in most major cities of the world (with the notable exception of Los Angeles), renting a car to do business has generally been unnecessary. Indeed, in densely developed cities like London, Paris, and New York, even if you know your way around, a rental car is an out-and-out liability. Increasingly, however, businesses are diversifying their locations out from the center of town and into the suburbs. Although partially a response to congestion, high labor costs, and other urban problems, the blossoming of the computer age has freed many more businesses from their dependence on the central city.

The U.S. computer and electronics complexes in the Silicon Valley south of San Francisco, the science-research firms concentrated in the La Jolla area of San Diego, and various paragovernmental "think tanks" in the Virginia and Maryland suburbs outside of Washington, D.C., are just a few examples of business centers that are conveniently reached by car, but are not well-served by buses, trains, or subways. Since almost everyone in these areas drives, cabs are generally expensive and inconvenient because there is little demand for them. Sometimes you can rent a car for a day for the price of a one-way cab ride from the airport.

The Long Test Drive

Almost all rental car agencies are affiliated with automobile manufacturers. Ford owns Budget. It also owns about half of Hertz (another quarter of which is owned by Volvo). GM owns National—and a quarter of Avis. Chrysler owns Thrifty. The theory among the auto makers appears to be that business people who rent automobiles are candidates for purchasing new cars. From your perspective you are renting a car. From their perspective you are paying for a very long test drive.

What's Available

In a soft economy, rental car agencies have been dueling heatedly for business, especially from executive travelers. All rental agencies offer the highway equivalent of frequent flyer programs, which give preferred business users a leg up on ordinary renters. National's is called Emerald Aisle; Hertz has #1 Gold. They court business travelers assiduously because executives are their ideal clients. They are potential car buyers. Their credit is good. They don't hot-rod the cars or take them into dangerous neighborhoods. They don't travel with small children who eat drippy chocolate ice cream cones in the back seat.

To attract business clients, the agencies have initiated perks programs and added other amenities designed to appeal specifically to the executive. Dollar Rent-a-Car has equipped all its luxury cars and about half its standard models with cellular phones. About twenty-five percent of Hertz's cars system-wide have cellular phones; however, these are concentrated at airport locations where business travelers are most likely to pick them up. The cost of having a car phone is rather reasonable—

about $5 per day—but the cost of using it can add up quickly. Cellular access is priced at roughly $1.50 per minute. Twenty minutes on the phone while stuck in traffic will cost $30.

The Name of the Game Is Speed

Based on surveys (and on reading their complaint letters), the one thing business travelers want most when renting a car is speed—not that the car should go fast, but that it should be able to leave the airport fast. Thus, the primary advantage of having a perks card with a car rental agency is acceleration— the ability to get out of the airport and back in faster than other travelers, and with a minimum of hassle.

With National's Emerald Aisle, business people select their own autos from a special lot rather than having a car assigned to them. The keys are already in the ignition. All they have to do is drive away. With the #1 Gold program at Hertz, renters take the shuttle to the spot where their car is waiting. The trunk is open, the keys are in the ignition, and the motor is humming. If it's cold out, the heater is on; if it's hot, the air conditioning is running. Just show your driver's license on the way out of the lot. Hertz claims to be able to get you out of even airports like New York's JFK and Chicago's O'Hare in five minutes or less. Avis's Preferred Service puts you right on the shuttle bus to the parking lot, where bus drivers take your information. By the time your shuttle arrives in the lot, the keys and rental agreements are in your car waiting.

Hierarchies Among Renters

As with airline Special Services programs, rental car agencies offer preferential (and all but completely unpublicized) "meet and greet" treatment to their most prestigious clients. Under National's "Emerald Elite" and Hertz's "#1 Platinum" programs, deplaning passengers are met at the gate by an agency representative and escorted to their vehicle, which is waiting curbside at the terminal. No counters. No parking lots. Avis has a "CEO" card for VIPs which provides the same kind of service.

All of these programs are highly restricted. You don't "qualify" for this status of service—it is conferred on you, like knighthood, by the rental agency. There are roughly 4,000 Hertz #1 Platinum members in the United States, but substantially fewer Avis CEOs and National Emerald Elite patrons. How do you get this kind of service? If you are truly a senior executive frequent renter and cultivate your personal relationships with one particular agency, your odds of becoming entitled to join these exclusive ranks go up substantially.

The Price of a Rental Car

Car rental rates have been inching up, in part because most travelers have finally gotten wise to the desirability of rejecting collision damage waiver "insurance" when they rent a car. With increasing numbers of drivers refusing CDW, rental car agencies have lost one of their most lucrative profit centers, and are trying to compensate by raising their overall rates. Within the United States, in general, **never accept collision damage waiver "insurance."** CDW is a "service" offered by rental car agencies which can add as much as thirty percent to the daily cost of the car. In some cities, desk personnel may try to intimidate the client into accepting the coverage by conjuring up scenarios of huge liabilities and potential lawsuits, but in choosing to accept this coverage, almost every driver is duplicating coverage he or she already has through his own insurance. You may also be covered through your credit card. Many major charge cards provide collision coverage for their cardholders. Check with the customer service representatives at your credit card company to make sure you are covered. If you rent a car overseas, the rules of the game may be different. If you are contemplating leasing a car in a foreign country, check with your domestic insurer to see what coverage you have.

How do you get a good car at a bargain rate? Many large corporations negotiate special deals for their employees who are on the road frequently. Some big-volume travel agencies are able to get special consideration for their clients as well. Can you get a bargain on your own?

Yield Management, Round Three

This is your third clinic on yield management. Rental car prices are incredibly location-sensitive. According to recent surveys, the cost of a midsize car with unlimited mileage averages $29 in Miami, $48 in Chicago, and $61 in New York. Better rates can be had on weekends than in the middle of the week. Perks cardholders get better deals (and better cars for the money) than occasional renters.

However, these "average" costs mask wide price fluctuations. Car rental agencies, like hotels and airlines, continually realign their prices to account for changes in season, day of the week, convention traffic, general inventory, and the need to keep up with what competitors are offering at the next counter in the arrivals terminal. **No one car rental agency is consistently cheaper in all parts of the country than another.** Just because Budget had the best deal in Orlando last week doesn't mean that it has the best deal in Cleveland this week. As is the case with hotels and air fares, **never take the first quote offered. Keep asking questions.** Look in the newspapers to find out what specials and promotions are being offered by the rental agencies. Often these are the cheapest deals around. You won't get the cheapest rate unless you ask for the cheapest rate, and even then the agent may not be able to find it. Like the airlines, car rental companies have thousands of rates in their computer system. To help the telephone reservations agent locate the good deal you found in the paper, you must **be prepared to quote the rate code** listed in the ad (often in microscopically fine print).

With yield management in rental car prices, just as with yield management in air fares and hotel rooms, the differences in price are not always rational from a business executive's point of view. If you want to pick up a car in one location and leave it in another, sometimes there is a dropoff charge; other times it's free. There can be a $75 dropoff charge to pick up a car in Seattle and leave it in Portland, but no charge to pick up a car in Portland and leave it in Seattle. **Some of the best deals are eleventh-hour bargains.** Many experienced business travelers holding confirmed reservations with one agency will walk up cold to the counter of a rival and ask point-blank for the best deal. If you are on a late-arriving flight and the agency is sitting on an oversupply, you may find yourself driving off in a $27,000 car for $34.95, with free mileage and a car phone thrown in for good measure. It never hurts to ask.

Some Potential Pitfalls

Travelers who try to take advantage of a bargain rate that was publicly advertised and then try to piggyback other reductions (such as AAA membership discount or coupons received when frequent flyer miles are cashed in) generally find that the added discounts are not applicable to already diminished prices.

Even status car renters have to be prepared to do some old-fashioned dickering, both before picking up the car and after. It's not uncommon for bargain rates that were confirmed by phone to be unavailable or "not in the computer" when you arrive at the check-in counter. **Always have your confirmation number with you.**

One of my associates missed a return flight from New York to Los Angeles when Avis personnel at Kennedy Airport insisted he owed over $750, including a hefty dropoff charge, for a week's use of a Lincoln Town Car. Originally it had been a really great deal—the car had been rented to him at Dulles Airport in Washington, D.C., with unlimited mileage and free dropoff at JFK for $150.

The New York agent insisted that her counterpart in Washington had made a mistake. The dispute continued so long that my associate was confronted with the choice of either making his plane or correcting the invoice. It was a close call, but in the end he decided that solving the $600 misunderstanding on the spot was more important than making his plane. This is a good point to emphasize, not just with rental cars but with travel in general: **When you must dispute a bill, it's a lot easier to win your case in person and before you've paid it than to try to get your money back after the fact,** especially when you're on the other side of the continent—or on a different continent entirely. However, it's also important to watch your credit card statement when the charge does come through. Sometimes your bill will contain an unwarranted post-departure "adjustment."

Special, Just for You

When you step up to the car rental counter in the arrivals terminal, for a nominal charge (say $5) you may be offered a chance to upgrade the car you have reserved to a larger, more luxurious model. **Beware the "special" upgrade offered at the check-in counter.** Sometimes the offer is legitimate; often, however, you are going to pay $5 to be upgraded to the same make and model of car you would have gotten anyway.

Why? If the agency is sold out of the class of car you reserved, it would have given you a free upgrade to the next available category (from midsize to full-size, for example). If you rent cars frequently, familiarize yourself with the makes and models you prefer and what category they fit into—compact, midsize, full size, or luxury. Do you want to pay to upgrade your Chevy Caprice from a midsize to a full-size vehicle? If possible, ask to see the car you would get without the "special" upgrade, or at least get a full enough description of the vehicle so that you know that it exists (make, model, license number).

Don't be too quick to present your frequent flyer-related upgrade coupon, either. If the agency is out of the car you reserved, you were going to get one free upgrade in any event. Wait till you see what car you are actually going to be offered before you offer them your upgrade. At that point you can either save your coupon for another occasion or use it for a two-class upgrade this time. If you do upgrade to a better class of car, **make sure that the model of the car is the only thing that's more expensive.** You know that the bigger car is going to use more gas, but check carefully to see that the cost per mile (if there is one) does not increase along with it.

Watch Your Gas Gauge

Almost all rental car agencies maintain that they send you out of the airport with a full tank of gas and ask you to return the car in the same condition. Business travelers, anxious to get on their way, can sometimes forget to check, either coming or going. This can be expensive. **Check the gas gauge before leaving the airport.** I've been given cars with just a quarter tank of gas, or less.

Are You Filling a Tank or a TANK?

Although expensive, the surcharge wouldn't have been nearly so galling if the total cost of about $50 (for eighteen and a half gallons) hadn't implied that the gas tank on the rented Chrysler held almost thirty-seven gallons. Ask the agent when you rent the car how many gallons the tank holds. **If you don't fill the car up yourself when you return it, be prepared to pay a sizable (and perhaps illogical) premium.**

Cab Sense

There isn't a business executive alive (including me) who hasn't been ripped off by a cabbie in some part of the world. How often this happens to you as a frequent traveler depends on how highly developed your cab sense becomes. Cab etiquette and cab larceny varies from one country to another. In some cities (New York, Rome, Mexico City) cabs are infamous; in others (London, Tokyo, Stockholm) they are notoriously excellent. In Rome, drivers often conduct themselves as if they were auditioning for a spot on the Ferrari Formula 1 racing team. Fortunately, most of them are pretty proficient and you arrive white-knuckled but in one piece.

Aside from the not inconsiderable problems of exorbitant fares and reckless driving, the main danger to the business traveler of using cabs is leaving briefcases, luggage, and other belongings in the cab after you get out. It may take some practice since your primary view of him will be largely of the back of his head, but **make a habit of noting the appearance of your driver, his name, and ID number.** If you do leave something behind, at least you have some information to go on. If you leave your briefcase in a cab in New York and all you know is that the taxi was yellow and the driver didn't speak English very well, you've just described eighty percent of the cabs in Manhattan.

In New York, the three most frequent problems are lack of facility in the English language, geographic ignorance, and an industrial-strength case of Big Apple rudeness. To be fair, you can also find salt-of-the-earth native New Yorkers who will assiduously seek out the best route through midtown traffic, and explain why they are going via this route, not another, all the while cheerfully giving you their opinion (whether you solicit it or not) about everything from hot stock tips to local politics or the lowdown (and point spread) on the Knicks, Giants, Mets, and Jets. If you find yourself in a cab piloted by one of these endangered species, sit back and enjoy it as a quintessential New York experience.

In Mexico City, the cab meter, if there is one, is an ornament. In some cities, particularly in the developing world, cabs without meters are common. If you choose to get into an unmetered cab in any city, **negotiate the fare before you set foot in the cab.** Once inside the cab or at your destination, you are in no position whatsoever to bargain.

In any city there are some commonsense ground rules that will minimize your cab problems. **Know "about" what your cab ride should cost.** $10 may get you "about" five miles in Baltimore, two miles in Los Angeles, twenty feet in Tokyo, two feet in Zurich, and halfway to Laos in Bangkok. Guidebooks and newsletters track what a cab ride should cost in major cities. If you are leaving a meeting in unfamiliar territory and need to call a cab, ask your business associates what the approximate cost might be. Be aware, however, that getting stuck in a traffic jam can be expensive (even in Bangkok), since the meter keeps running. If traffic is stalled and it's just a couple of blocks to your destination, pay your fare and walk the rest of the way. You'll get there faster, and it will be cheaper, too.

Foreign Exchange Without Foreign Intrigue

Unquestionably, western Europe is far more rational about this process than the United States. In Europe, currency exchange at a bank or other financial institution is an everyday occurrence, with rates posted prominently for all to see. You may have to shop around to get the best deal, but all your options are pretty much out in the open.

In the United States, it's a chore to even discover what the exchange rate is, and many banks are reluctant to make the transaction. To add insult to injury, there's often a hefty service charge to boot. If you're trying to dispose of the last few francs left over from a trip to Paris, the service charge in the United States can be so high that you may as well not bother.

But wait—do you really want to get rid of that last $50 worth of francs? Are you never going back to Paris? Is no one in your firm ever going back to Paris? If representatives of your firm do a lot of transatlantic or transpacific travel, your company may wish to set up a multi-currency "petty cash" drawer for just such leftovers.

The amount to be maintained is not large—about enough for the fare between the airport and the hotel in town. This can be a lifesaver for redeye flyers. More than one of my associates has arrived in a foreign airport at the crack of dawn (or in Italy at almost any time, since bank holidays there are frequent), and suddenly discovered that he was technically "broke" because he'd forgotten to bring a bit of local currency along. It used to be the case that the worst rates of exchange were found in the airports, since exchange houses there were able to take advantage of these sorts of desperate travelers who had neglected to plan ahead and were in effect stranded without any usable currency.

Now, however, all is not necessarily lost at the airport. Many airports now have automatic teller machines (ATMs) linked to international networks like Plus or Cirrus. In Singapore you can get a better Singapore dollar/U.S. dollar exchange rate through a Plus ATM than you can by using a credit card or going through a local bank. Although the global banking network is growing, this knowledge, however, does you absolutely no good personally unless you **remember to bring a list of addresses of foreign banks with ATMs that accept your card.**

Suppose you really do want to get rid of all that leftover foreign exchange before you leave? After you **make sure you have enough to tip the hotel staff, pay your way to the airport, *and* pay the departure tax,** empty your pockets and apply the contents to your hotel bill, and put the rest on your credit card.

Sleuthing Your City

Knowing what cabs cost is a small part of sleuthing your city before you get there. Especially if you are headed to a city for the first time, research your destination with the same zeal you employ to research a potential business partner (or a challenger).

If many members of your organization travel, make sure that everyone benefits from the experience of his or her fellow employees. At IMG we do this by keeping a book of approved hotels and cab companies, and a listing of restaurants where we've had positive experiences. We also encourage well-traveled executives to disseminate any advice they've picked up on their travels that can increase an executive's efficiency or save the company money. The following is a typical memo, distributed to our worldwide executives, written by a senior executive after a business trip to Tokyo. He had some insightful thoughts about getting from Narita Airport to central Tokyo:

Executives traveling to Tokyo should be aware that getting from Narita Airport to central Tokyo can be trying and time-consuming. If you're not careful, it can also be the most expensive cab ride in the world. Visitors have the following four options (listed in descending order of cost-effectiveness) from Narita to Tokyo:

- **Airport Limousine:** This is a large, very comfortable bus, with guaranteed seating for everyone, that makes frequent trips to bus terminals in central Tokyo and direct trips to many of the city's hotels. Cost: ¥2100, or $20.
- **Train:** A train called the Narita Express leaves from the airport terminal to Tokyo central station, approximately every sixty minutes. This train service is by far the fastest, most reliable way to go between Narita and Tokyo. Its one-hour travel time equals the best that a bus or car can achieve in light traffic. The same trip by bus or car can take two or three hours in heavy traffic, which, of course, does not affect the train. Cost: ¥2205, or $21 to Tokyo; ¥2310, or about $1 more to Shinjuku.
- **Taxi:** An ordinary taxi departing from the taxi stand at Narita is convenient if you have an out-of-the-way destination or are traveling with a lot of luggage. Cost: approximately ¥17,800, or $170.
- **Hire Car:** This is a phenomenally expensive cab ride. The vehicle is an ordinary automobile, driven by a uniformed driver, and covers the distance no faster than a bus or taxi, and usually slower than the train. Depending on whether the driver speaks English, the cost varies between $500 and $600 one way.

The savings this sort of cost-conscious advice represents, multiplied by the dozens of cities our executives visit annually, can be considerable. But it doesn't have to be so formal. Any travel insights from any returning traveler should be encouraged. For some reason many executive travelers jealously guard hard-won knowledge gleaned in their experiences, even from their associates. **Share your travel knowledge.** If you are in a position to do so, insist that others do likewise.

Chapter IX
Creative Variations on
Executive Travel

Had I but world enough and time I should travel everywhere by train,—but another condition is that the year would have to be no later than 1938.
        Keith Waterhouse, *The Theory and Practice of Travel*

All of my most stimulating early travel experiences were on trains—in exactly the golden age of train travel before World War II that Waterhouse yearns for. My dad took me a number of times on the Twentieth Century Limited and the Commodore Vanderbilt. Most exciting of all, however, was our annual winter trip to the Gulf Coast of Mississippi. My parents took me out of school for a week on one end or the other of a vacation and we traveled to Mississippi on the exotically named (to me at least) Panama Limited.

I was a true train freak. I counted down the days and hours till we were to leave. I looked forward to this trip so much that I memorized the names of all the stations—in order—all the way from Chicago to Jackson, Mississippi. I took special pride in calling them out before the conductor did. There were a lot of them, even before we traveled halfway through Illinois. After we left Chicago there was:

Kensington,
Harvey,
Homewood,
Madison,
Monee,
Peotone,
Manteno,
Bradley,
Kankakee,
Chebanse,
Clifton,
Ashkum,
Danforth,
Gilman,
Onarga,
Buckley,
Loda,
Paxton,
Ludlow,
Rantoul,
Thomasboro, and finally
Champaign—

all in a space of 126 miles.

I've been a train lover ever since, and assiduously seek out those remaining trains that evoke the bygone era, not necessarily in ambience but in service and comfort. Although I find the Orient Express a bit overdone, I take the sleeper to St. Andrews from London when I travel to the Dunhill Cup in Scotland. I use the Bullet Train from Osaka or Nagoya to Tokyo when I am in Japan. Right now my favorite is the Blue Train, which runs between Johannesburg and Cape Town, South Africa. The food is first rate, as is the onboard wine cellar. What makes it even more special is the fact that many of the accommodations have not only bathrooms but bathtubs as well. The train travels over the Karoo Desert and stops in Kimberley, the diamond mining town. When you awaken the next morning, you are in the wine country of Paarl River Valley north of Cape Town, which is South Africa's answer to the Napa Valley.

To be sure, as an executive traveler you may have to differentiate between taking a train just to experience the train and taking a train to get where you're going, but trains are just one example of the many ways in which the routine aspects of business travel can be altered to make the experience more enjoyable. Some are actually more efficient and more cost-effective than the conventional way of doing things. For example, the opportunity to stay at a unique, historic, or out-of-town hotel often compensates for additional transportation time with charm and lower cost. Moreover, as greater numbers of businesses leave urban centers for suburban locations, some of these hotels can actually have a proximity advantage.

Also increasingly common in the realm of business entertaining is the use of resort hotels for client or staff meetings. By providing a pleasant atmosphere—a retreat from the usual office surroundings—executives can foster a positive environment for deal-making and problem-solving. The classic example of this sort of variation is the annual sales meeting, which is designed both to reward sales representatives of a company and to make more pleasant a tough dialogue about projections and sales expectations.

In this chapter I will discuss innovative ways to travel, out-of-the-ordinary places to stay, and novel ways to hold meetings, all of which demonstrate how mixing business with pleasure rewards the traveling executive, not just personally but professionally as well.

Innovative Ways of Getting There

Trains: Slow, Inconvenient, and Expensive?

Everyone knows that "modern" trains are slow, inconvenient, and expensive, especially in the United States.

Not necessarily. Indeed, the time and trouble inherent in fighting your way to and from the airport sometimes makes the train a much better deal. Marvin Bush agrees. "My image of going from Washington, D.C., to New York is rushing to

National Airport, placing your bag carefully above your seat, and having twenty other people cramming theirs on top of yours. When you land, everybody is hurrying up to wait to get out of the airplane. There's a great deal of pushing and shoving.

"I take the Metroliner. I can make phone calls from the train. I can spread out my work or my reading. I've got elbow room. I can write letters. I don't know anyone who can sit on that shuttle and get any real work done. It's a three-hour trip— that's door-to-door."

Time Is $$$

That's fine for a guy like Bush who can spend the extra time, right?

Maybe if you're in a peculiar sort of business in which you go from an airport conference at LaGuardia to an airport conference at Washington National, taking the shuttle is preferable. But if you're going from midtown Manhattan to inside the Beltway, my money's on Marvin.

A Shaggy Train Story, or Marvin vs. The Shuttle

Let me describe a hypothetical race between you and Marvin leaving from midtown Manhattan and ending on the Capitol steps. We'll assume you both leave Rockefeller Center at the same time.

Marvin takes a five-minute, $6 cab ride to Penn Station. He gets on the train. It leaves.

You get into a cab headed for LaGuardia, crawl across the Triborough Bridge and get stuck in a traffic tie-up on the Grand Central Parkway. The trip costs you $30. You make the plane, barely. It sits on the ground for at least twenty minutes waiting for clearance before taking off.

Marvin sits in comfort in the club car on the train, with complimentary meals and wine, hot towels, and real service.

He makes phone calls and does some paperwork. He's been on the train for over an hour before you've even left the ground.

You are sitting in a flying bus. After being delayed on departure, you are also delayed in a holding pattern on approach. Eventually you land at Washington National, where you wait an extra fifteen minutes for your luggage. You finally get a cab into the city.

Marvin and the Metroliner pull into resplendent Union Station, in the heart of Washington. He and his luggage get off the train at the same time. He hops a waiting cab.

You show up at the Capitol, frazzled and desperately in need of resuscitation, about five minutes *after* Marvin, who magnanimously offers to buy you some gin-enriched therapy at the Old Ebbitt Grill. "And by the way," he says, putting a comforting arm around your shoulder, "I was able to hold a teleconference with our attorneys in the office while I was on the train. We've reviewed all the changes to our contract that you asked for. You and I can discuss them over cocktails. . . ."

To add insult to injury, Marvin paid about half as much for his travel experience as you did. To be sure, at offpeak travel hours when the airports are not congested, you might beat Marvin timewise into Washington. But not for long. Amtrak is planning to introduce high-speed trains on the New York–Washington corridor, which will tip the scales even further in favor of train travel.

What's the moral of this shaggy train story? **Sometimes the best alternate airport is the railway depot.**

Remember the Tortoise and the Hare

There's also a follow-up lesson to be learned from this example. The corollary is that **it's not always how fast you get there, but what shape you're in when you arrive.** Not that Marvin Bush would take advantage of you, but if you are foolish enough to negotiate with Marvin after he's scraped you off the ceiling of the Old Ebbitt Grill, you may find yourself agreeing to more than you might have otherwise.

Trains: You Have to Sleep Somewhere

We have an executive named Bev Norwood with us at IMG. At one point he was doing work in Europe, and needed to spend three days in Paris and two in Barcelona. The conventional business traveler would have set up his schedule to work first in one city, then fly to the other.

Not Bev. He bought a Eurailpass and began his work schedule in Paris. He worked in Paris all day Monday, got on the overnight train to Barcelona, had a good meal and a good night's sleep on the way, did a day's work in Barcelona on Tuesday, got on the overnight train to Paris, spent the day in Paris on Wednesday, got back on the train to Barcelona, worked in Barcelona on Thursday, got on the train for the last time, and returned to Paris to finish up the week on Friday.

Did he spend a lot of money on travel? It's true that his Eurailpass was more expensive than one round-trip air fare between Paris and Barcelona. However, he saved the cost of four nights of hotel rooms in two of the most expensive cities in Europe, so IMG came out way ahead. Bev Norwood came out way ahead, too. It goes without saying that he had a dandy travel experience. Moreover, because train stations are more centrally located than airports, he also saved a lot of time and was much nearer to where he was going to be doing business during the day. In addition, he spared himself all the hassle involved in getting between the city and the airport, and he most assuredly impressed his boss with his attitude about cost cutting.

Pablo Casals and Me

After a late meeting with the International Olympic Committee in Lausanne, I had to be in Barcelona the next day. Geneva has the nearest airport serving Lausanne, but there was no flight I could make to Barcelona that would get me there on time. To solve it I took a tip from Bev and took a sleeper train from Geneva called the Pablo Casals.

I didn't expect much, but it was the only way I could fit the trip to Barcelona into my schedule. It was a wonderful trip, just two or three stops along the way, with terrific service. I had a comfortable room complete with shower and internal telephone. I gave the porter my passport, so I was not awakened at the border crossings in the middle of the night. He even provided a very timely, gentle, and genteel telephonic wake-up call in my compartment. After a hearty breakfast, I arrived in Barcelona at 9 A.M. in fabulous shape.

The Grand Gesture

Kerry Packer is the wealthiest man in Australia, the owner of the Channel Nine television network and a good friend of mine. While I was in Melbourne doing television commentary on the Australian Masters golf tournament, he called and asked me to join him for dinner. Kerry was in Sydney. I said, "Well, I'd be delighted, but it's going to be a late supper. I won't be finished on the air till 4:00 P.M. It's an hour and a half to the airport. The earliest flight I can catch is the 6:30, which gets into Sydney at 8:00. After waiting for my luggage, I won't see you for dinner much before 9:00 P.M."

This was not what he wanted to hear. "Nine?" he sniffed. "That's too bloody late. I'll send the chopper and the jet for you."

I finished my commentary at 4:00 P.M. as scheduled. After that, things moved with military precision. I jumped into a golf cart and headed for the fifth hole, where the Channel Nine helicopter had landed. The chopper took me to the private terminal at Melbourne Airport, where Kerry's personal jet was waiting for me. We took off immediately and landed in Sydney at 6:30. A limousine waiting at the steps of the jet delivered me to Packer's flat at 7:40. I expected to sit down promptly and tuck into dinner with my friend. Ludicrously enough, however, Kerry himself did not arrive until 9:00—the same time I would have arrived on his doorstep by less extraordinary means!

This story is quite a spectacular example of a creative variation on traditional business travel, but very few of us can travel the way Kerry Packer does. Even if you don't own your own helicopter and private jet, however, sometimes you can still find a creative and stimulating way to get there.

Exotic Car Rentals

There are some people who love cars as much as I love trains. If you have to arrive somewhere in style, consider renting something other than a run-of-the-parking-lot four-door sedan. Agencies that specialize in exotic car rentals are located primarily in parts of the world where the car is still king, such as Los Angeles. Zipping (or rather slogging) around Manhattan in a large Mercedes that you yourself are driving brands you not as a moneyed sophisticate but as:

- An out-of-towner with a profound sense of masochism;
- A chauffeur with the night off; and/or
- A prime carjacking prospect.

Although they are most assuredly more expensive than your basic Ford or Chevrolet, fancy wheels like Mercedes, Lexus, or BMW, or a sporty Corvette or even a Jeep, may be worth the extra cost to make a distinctive impression on a client. Depending on your timing, you may also be able to negotiate a special deal with the rental car agency. Even if you can come up with a relatively reasonable cost, I'd recommend clearing this sort of rental ahead of time with the powers that be in your office—this is not an expenditure you want to spring on your company as a little surprise when you return. Know in advance how much a conventional rental car would cost—if having the hot car will really make your trip, offer to pay the difference. You should be aware, however, that some insurance policies and credit card backup coverage exempts exotic or otherwise unusual rental cars. Make very certain you are covered before you decline the collision damage waiver.

The Changing Face of the Business Trip

The changing face of the business trip goes hand-in-hand with the changing face of what used to be the typical vacation. The classic two-week American vacation, generally in summer when the kids are out of school, is as extinct as the stegosaurus. Instead, executives are taking mini-vacations, often by adding a weekend or a few days to a business trip. A recent survey commissioned by the Omni hotel chain found that eighty percent of frequent travelers took a family member on an extended business trip within the past two years.

I find this an altogether positive trend. **It's OK to combine business with pleasure.** Before the chorus of "harrumphs" from the ascetics in Accounting about "frivolous travel," "paid holidays," and "vacation business trips" swells to a crescendo, I should quickly point out that this process pays dividends not just for the business traveler but for his or her company as well.

Saturday Night Fever, Part II

Although the refreshed and invigorated executive is a corporate asset that cannot be quantified, it is much easier to put a dollars-and-cents value on the ticket price reduction that results from a Saturday-night stay. Staying over a Saturday entitles the traveler to what is known as an "excursion fare," which is often far cheaper than a weekday coach seat, even one that is deeply discounted. Hewlett-Packard, among other corporations, encourages its traveling executives to take trips that include a Saturday night layover, but it does not insist that they do so.

Since this policy went into effect, use of excursion fares for business trips is up by fifty percent at Hewlett-Packard. Does this mean that HP is fomenting family separation during what is traditionally family time, all for the sake of corporate profit? Not necessarily. A discount fare with a Saturday-night stayover is likely to be a great opportunity for a mini-vacation.

For example, if you are going to New Orleans from Chicago for a three-day business trip, regular coach air fare departing Monday, returning Thursday is about $785. With a Saturday-night stay, the fare drops to as little as $258. Who would you rather see in the office on Monday morning—the guy who had to come back Thursday night, or the guy who spent the weekend in the Crescent City with his wife and saved the company $527?

Weekend Hotel Bargains

I'm not suggesting that the organization pick up the tab for the executive's weekend getaway, but even the hotel portion of the extended stay may offer cost-saving possibilities for the business traveler and for the parent company. As we discussed in Chapter VII, hotel prices in this economy are anything but firm. This is especially true at business-oriented hotels, many of which are likely to be virtually empty over the weekend.

Over and above whatever special corporate or frequent-stay rate the business traveler can negotiate, if you extend your trip to depart on Sunday rather than Thursday, those extra couple of weekend nights are likely to be a bargain. As an inducement, many hotels will even give the executive traveler the super low weekend rate for the entire length of his or her stay. To further sweeten the deal, they may throw in other amenities like free parking and/or free breakfasts. (Find something wrong with that, Accounting!) As with most other hotel discounts, however, **you gotta ask,** sometimes more than once.

Out-of-the-Ordinary Places to Stay

Of Hotels, Inns, and Dormitories

Most executive travelers have seen enough sterile "modern" hotels to last a lifetime. Far too many business hotels are merely "in" their cities, not "of" them. From the architecture to the amenities, there is a sameness about them that was probably intended to be comforting but turns out to be monotonous instead.

Don't stay where you get the feeling that you could be anywhere. If it seems that you might be able to relocate the hotel to another city in the next time zone without any noticeable difference in what goes on inside the building, you are far less likely to enjoy your trip.

Don't stay where you get the feeling that you could be anyone. All other things being equal, I much prefer staying in an older, smaller hotel with interesting architecture, a unique sense of place, and personal service to staying in a newer, larger hotel where I'm just a name and a room number. By "all other things," I mean primarily plumbing and telecommunications. However, small interesting hotels where the staff calls you by name, with good plumbing and phones that work, are not hard to find. Almost every major city offers charming alternatives to the standardized cookie-cutter business hotel, generally at about the same price, if not substantially less than what you would pay otherwise.

For example, in Seattle you can stay in one of the 865 rooms of the twin towers of the Westin (oft likened to a pair of corncobs by the locals), wait forever for your luggage (and for the elevators), and get lost amidst the proms and weddings if you extend your visit over the weekend. Or you can be coddled at the Alexis in Seattle's lively historic district, where 54 rooms ring a sheltered courtyard and the ambience is like that of a private home. The Alexis offers complimentary continental breakfast, shoeshines, the morning paper, a steam room (that you can reserve just for your own use), and a restaurant that attracts not only business travelers but local epicures as well.

In St. Louis, the traditional business hotel is Adam's Mark, all 910 rooms of it. It's a fine first-class business hotel that provides everything an executive traveler could need. However, you don't give up much if you stay at the half-timbered Seven Gables Inn, twenty minutes from downtown St. Louis, in Clayton, which is a business and financial center in its own right. Affiliated with the Relais et Chateaux group of hotels, the Tudoresque, turn-of-the-century Seven Gables has all of thirty-two rooms, an award-winning restaurant with a marvelous wine list, a real concierge, plus fax facilities and audio-visual equipment.

Not Just the Fax, Ma'am

I have the same experience visiting Toronto. It's hard to argue with the overall excellence of the Four Seasons Toronto—with 600 rooms, it's amazing how attentive and alert the staff is. But

I have a soft spot for the Sutton Place Hotel, where the staff is equally attentive but the size (180 rooms) is much more accommodating for a traveling executive who wants to feel at home.

Hotels like this are not exceptions. They exist all over the United States, and are even more common in Europe. In Stockholm, for example, which I visit regularly for the Nobel Awards ceremonies in December, I tend to stay at the 320-room Grand Hotel, not only because it is a first-rate business hotel, but also because a lot of the Nobel activities revolve around it. The convenience is irresistible. Visiting at another time of the year, however, I might prefer the more intimate confines of the Victory Hotel, just five minutes from the Grand, in a 500-year-old building in Old Town. With a treasure trove of nautical antiques filling each of its forty-eight rooms, plus a Michelin-starred restaurant and world-class wine cellar, the Victory makes a trip to Stockholm special. **You can recharge yourself by selecting a hotel with more to offer than just business facilities.** Finding hotels like these takes a little more work, but that's where planning comes in, as I discussed in Chapter II.

The Last Resort

Many conferences and conventions are held at resorts; however, these hotels can sometimes function as excellent places to do business. A good example is the Claremont Resort Hotel in Oakland, California. The Claremont is a splendid old Victorian dowager of a building, fully restored, situated on a beautifully landscaped twenty-acre site, with a pool, comprehensive health club, ten tennis courts, and large well-appointed rooms.

If you are meeting with representatives from the University of California or from a Berkeley- or Oakland-based business, the geographic advantages of the Claremont are clear. But is it the most convenient hotel to stay in if the majority of your appointments are going to be in the Transamerica Pyramid or the Embarcadero in the heart of San Francisco?

Hardly. It takes about thirty-five to forty minutes to get into downtown San Francisco from the Claremont. Does this knock it out of the running as a place to stay? Perhaps, but think about it. If you do have to do business in the city, you're not going to be spending very much more time getting there than locally based executives who commute in daily from Berkeley, the Oakland Hills, Walnut Creek, or any of the other prosperous Alameda County suburbs.

Do any of the people you will be dealing with live nearby? If so, it won't be inconvenient for them to stop by and have a drink on the way home from the office. Offer them a little tour of the historic old hotel. (The Claremont has a bit in common with local landmarks in many cities, in that most residents have seen it as they drive by, but very few of them have actually been inside the building.) Or invite them to come and play a few games of tennis—if your spouse will be joining you for all or part of the trip, make it a game of mixed doubles.

What's happened here? By staying "out of town," you've given yourself an opportunity to strengthen and personalize your business relationship with the people you came to see. Your own trip has also become far more enjoyable. All of a sudden that off-the-beaten-track hotel has become an asset rather than a liability, and that forty-minute trip into San Francisco is getting shorter and more worthwhile all the time.

Novel Ways to Hold Meetings

If you think this sounds far-fetched, it's not. More and more business is being done in nontraditional ways and nontraditional locations. People doing everyday business are always posturing. They put on their "game face" or their "negotiating face" in the office. Even at a conventional business lunch they are likely to be on guard and maintain their facade. However, if you put people in unfamiliar territory, especially unfamiliar territory which is also fun or interesting, they are far more likely to drop their game faces and relax. When people are comfortable, they will be far more receptive to whatever you're trying to talk to them about.

One of my favorite techniques is to **shake people up**— nicely, of course. Introduce them to places they

- Have never heard of;
- Would never go to on their own;
- Would never think of in a business context; or
- Would never associate with you.

This goes not just for hotels but for restaurants as well. Most business meals are held at places known to be "safe and predictable" by those organizing the event. Alas, they are usually known to be "safe and predictable," and hence not very interesting, to others attending as well.

Neutralizing the Environment

When you do business in nontraditional ways, it serves to **neutralize the environment.** By neutralizing the environment, you have given yourself the edge and "disarmed" your counterpart. Not that all business relationships are adversarial, but almost inevitably one of you will be more comfortable on a given turf than the other.

Better it should be you. In his struggle to adapt to that new environment—which he is actually going to like—your counterpart or potential business client comes to like you in the process because you are approaching a business relationship in a different, unexpected, and refreshing way.

The Lube 'n Tune Lunch

How do you neutralize the environment? You have to be ingenious about it, and unafraid to consider possibilities that are a little offbeat—or maybe even very offbeat. Find a venue for lunch or dinner that's not necessarily a restaurant. Find a venue for a meeting that's not necessarily an office. In New

York you might take a walk in Central Park and have lunch at the Zoo. Former race car driver turned immensely successful transportation entrepreneur Roger Penske once invited his bankers to his Pennsylvania headquarters for lunch. Where did he serve the flawlessly prepared gourmet meal? In his immaculate garage.

No Breakfast at Tiffany's? How About Dinner at Gump's?

Other examples of this kind of creativity abound. Gump's is a renowned gift and housewares shop in San Francisco. Like the cable cars, columnist Herb Caen, and Irish coffee at the Buena Vista Cafe, it's a venerable and very San Francisco institution. Gump's is famous for its china and crystal departments and for its elaborate room displays. A few of the better hotels in San Francisco have developed a relationship with Gump's whereby business executives can host meetings and dinner parties catered by the hotel, but held in the display rooms of the store after hours. I don't know a San Franciscan who wouldn't jump at the prospect of having a private dinner at Gump's. Could the same arrangement be made with Harrod's or Fortnum & Mason in London or Fauchon in Paris? You'll never know unless you ask. This is the kind of assignment that a good concierge loves to undertake. (Remember to give them enough time to set it up.)

One-on-One in a Rowboat

There's a wonderful place in Seattle called the Wooden Boat Museum on Lake Union. It's not a hot museum frequented by tourists, but it's not a dusty, static display, either—there are about forty boats there that you can rent and take out on the lake. One enterprising business acquaintance of mine asked a potential client to meet him at the Wooden Boat Museum for lunch. He picked up a couple of great sandwiches and some terrific microbrewery beer from a nearby deli, ushered his quarry into a boat, and rowed around the lake for a while.

Although I believe in unorthodox venues for business lunches, I found this to be somewhat beyond the pale. A rowboat? My friend explained his reasoning. "I didn't do this out of the blue," he said. "I knew the guy liked boats—he keeps a sailboat at his weekend place in the San Juans.

"I also knew that by the time we got to a restaurant, got a table, talked about the weather, his wife, my wife, his kids, my kids, what the specials are for the day, the Mariners and the Seahawks and the Supersonics, the mess at Boeing, and the rest of the small talk, I'd have about eight minutes to get my point across. The deal I was proposing was a bit complicated. Eight minutes just wasn't going to do it.

"I knew he was comfortable on a boat. I needed his undivided attention. On the boat I had an unbelievably captive audience. It was perfectly private. There were no interruptions. We relaxed and had lunch. On the boat I had as much time as I needed."

He made the deal.

The Eight-Minute Man

My friend came up with a delightfully ingenious solution. If you read "The Rules of Lunch" in Chapter VIII you will find that he actually followed them to the letter, but on his own terms. In the process, however, he highlighted a real problem with the business lunch. It's very true that **the real time you will have to make your pitch is often ten minutes or less.** Save the charts and the overhead projections and the aerial photography for a breakfast meeting or for a separate presentation in a conference room. **Don't turn lunch into a lecture. You defeat the purpose of lunch by overburdening it with exhibits and paperwork.**

Beating an Unhasty Retreat

With impeccable meteorological logic, January sales conferences are held in Honolulu, not Hartford, and July corporate strategy and budget meetings convene in Nantucket, not New Orleans. It's a foregone conclusion that company retreats and business conventions will be held in vacation-like resorts during times of fair weather—sunny, not rainy, warm, but not hot.

If it is your responsibility to plan one of these conferences, I urge you to use the same kind of creativity that you would in planning a smaller business lunch. You will find that a bit of ingenuity deepens the experience for the participants and often pays financial dividends as well.

Scout for Package Deals

Belt-tightening has cut sharply into conference and convention travel, giving you even more clout for negotiating discounted air fare and hotel rates. Some airlines and hotels have joined forces (including Hyatt and United Airlines) to offer discounted fares and nightly rates at excellent hotels.

Watch for Last-Minute Possibilities

Booking in advance is not necessarily a guarantee of a bargain. Sometimes even a popular destination will end up with a hole in its schedule, either because the economy is lethargic or because of a cancellation. If the group you are planning for is small, you may find yourself with an eleventh-hour windfall.

Playing the "High Season" Game—and Winning

Many if not most resorts have rates that fluctuate by the season. Off-season rates can be as little as half (or less) the going rate at the height of the "fashionable" period. In tropical and subtropical locations, summer is outré, winter is fashionable, and you will pay through the nose to be there during the holidays. In cooler or mountainous retreats, the seasons are reversed. However, it takes nothing but a little common sense (and perhaps a bit of recollection of personal experience) to realize two important but somehow not quite obvious facts:

- Weather doesn't turn from good to bad overnight; and
- Even "high season" is no guarantee of good weather.

For the conference planner, seasonal weather fluctuations and seasonal hotel rates are an opportunity, not a problem. If you study hotel rates and weather trends carefully, you are likely to discover windows of opportunity (generally on the "shoulders" or just before or just after the peak season) when the weather is terrific and the prices are reasonable.

Even Off-Season Has Its Charms

I'm not recommending Florida during October (prime hurricane season) or Rancho Mirage in the heat of August, but **don't overlook the attraction of some locations in their least popular seasons.** During the summer, many skiing destinations are covered with wildflowers and offer terrific hiking, fishing, and/or boating, as well as a plethora of empty hotel rooms. By the same token, the area around Santa Fe, New Mexico, believed to be at its most fashionable in summer during the opera and chamber music festivals, is fascinating as well as beautiful under a dusting of snow in the winter with a piñon pine fire in the fireplace.

Give Good Lunch

The common thread running through all these examples is to be inventive and play against the hackneyed approach to executive travel. Positioning yourself as an executive who "gives good lunch"—a person who can share more than speeches and memos with your colleagues and business associates, and who repeatedly comes up with original venues for business meals and meetings—has always been good business.

Chapter X
Pace Yourself, Reward Yourself, Invigorate Yourself: Health, Exercise, and Relaxation

An important part of the *Hit the Ground Running* attitude is finding ways to keep your energy level at a maximum. As I have already discussed in previous chapters, the smart business traveler is not afraid to take a nap in the afternoon in preparation for an evening of meetings, and he or she often will find time for a game of golf or a few sets of tennis. If you are working at 110 percent, you need to relax. You have to renew your energy and you need to set goals with self-motivating rewards. For some travelers, a short jog or a brisk swim in the morning is part of a regular at-home regime that helps them keep their equilibrium. If you include it in your schedule, you can do it without endangering business appointments.

Simply staying healthy on a trip is an aspect of business travel that is too often neglected. Depending upon the distance traveled, many travelers give their biological systems some abrupt shifts and shake-ups. In this chapter I will give you my common-sense tips on how to maintain health and energy levels; how to adjust to time and climate changes; and how to beat the toughest physical problem long-distance travelers face: jet lag. Diet, vitamins, water intake, sleep patterns, and meal schedules can be important factors in maintaining focus and stamina.

There are many avenues of tension relief and relaxation. Smart business travelers should explore all of them—from stretching exercises on the airplane to utilizing exercise facilities in various hotels around the world—until they find the ones that work for them. Depending upon age level, not every traveler needs intense aerobic activity—a good brisk walk through a scenic park or historic part of town can serve double duty as exercise both for the body and for the psyche of the *Hit the Ground Running* traveler.

Find Your Own Rhythm—and Dance to It

I cannot emphasize too often that effective business travel is really an extension of an effective business life. If you establish a routine for yourself that works at home, try to maintain it on the road. Eliminating exercise or moments of relaxation from your schedule ultimately does not contribute to your effectiveness.

I set a fast pace for myself and enjoy it. Staying busy means staying vital and engaged with life. I freely admit that there are mornings when the alarm clock goes off at 4:30 A.M. and it is not an inspiring sound. But as soon as I am caught up in the action of the day, I feel energized. When I hit my stride, I anticipate the meetings on my schedule, enjoy my accomplishments hour-by-hour, and look forward to moments of reward that I always include.

There are people who will start work at 7 A.M., and then work through dinner with no time off to get something done in three days. The same agenda might take me six days, if I only worked in the mornings and made phone calls and took a nap in the afternoons and had social dinners. **Whatever your customary pace is, stick to it.** Some people will fly into San Francisco and get it all done in three days and get out. Others would like to see a little of the town and work a little less frenetically, either because they are more effective that way or because they prefer it.

Keep Your Eye on the Ball

If you do try to have an intensely programmed business trip, make sure you aren't losing your effectiveness in the process. As Christopher Lewinton puts it, "There can be a tendency to confuse effort with results when you travel. I look at my effectiveness and the *quality* of the decisions I make—which is the thing that really matters. We all have different mechanisms, different body rhythms. I don't find that hopping the redeye does any good for me at all. I work better after having gotten a good night's sleep in a bed. It's no use hopping an overnight flight and pretending that I've gained those hours. I haven't, really."

In sports, the concept of pacing is well-established. No marathon runner will survive long by sprinting from the starting line. Jockeys will plan different strategies for races of different lengths. Boxers vary greatly in how they approach a fight. And many coaches will tell you that pacing is the secret to winning the game.

Too many people just allow life to happen to them. An astonishing number of executives allow their business—and by extension, their business travel—to "happen" in a similar way. **Whatever pace you prefer, set it deliberately and stick to it.** I have already discussed the importance of participating in the details of your business travel and organizing your daily schedule. But there is a subtle aspect of your daily planning that only you can determine, and this is your own sense of rhythm or pacing.

As I hope you have understood by this point in the book, the concept of *Hit the Ground Running* means to arrive at your business destination in motion—with your schedule planned efficiently, your business tools at hand, and yourself in command of this valuable time out of the office. It certainly does *not* mean to dash off the airplane like O.J. Simpson in those ads and to keep running madly through an overbooked series of appointments. What I do, and what I advocate that the smart traveler should do, is to determine a series of goals for a trip, make a schedule that will fulfill those goals, and carefully plan the details that will enable you to move through that schedule efficiently and energetically. To achieve your goals on any given trip, you must pace yourself.

To keep your adrenalin flowing and keep your energy focused, **find the rhythm that works for you.** If that rhythm requires some "down time" for rest and relaxation in mid-afternoon or a pre-dinner jog, then plan for these activities. Write them into your schedule. If you don't feel good unless you have started your day with a workout, then include a workout among the priorities on your daily travel itinerary. Don't just hope you will "find" an hour. Recognize your needs—both physical and psychological—and include them in your plans. You will be healthier and happier for doing so.

Finding the Health Club That Meets Your Needs

Michael Gray, General Manager of London's Hyatt Carlton Tower, told me that he has been amazed at how important health clubs have become to a hotel from a marketing stand-point. "Quite a few people said to me that their traveling executives will choose a hotel simply on whether it's got a health club or whether it hasn't. It's really one of the primary criteria. The interesting factor from the hotelier's point of view is that very few of those people are actually using the fitness fa-cilities. The majority of our Carlton Tower health club users are outside members. We average just twenty people a day from our hotel guests, which is very small. People pack their swim-ming gear, running shoes, etc., and rarely find the time to use them. The use of the club at our hotel is included as one of our general services. There is no extra charge, yet usage is still sur-prisingly low."

In recent years, many hotels have added fitness centers or health clubs. But they vary widely in size, sophistication, and cost to guests. What some hotels call a "fitness center" is noth-ing more than a converted closet with an inexpensive station-ary exercise bicycle and a few weights. For example, the Sheraton Boston Hotel and Towers advertises a "health/fitness center." In reality, the "center" consists of three Lifecycle machines, a set of Universal weights, a Jacuzzi, and a large indoor/outdoor pool.

At the Four Seasons hotel chain, however, well-equipped and staffed fitness centers are a priority. "If you don't have a good fitness center, your guests will know right away," claims Charles Ferraro, vice president of operations for Four Seasons. "A good health club has become an expected amenity." A few years ago they spent $3 million on the health club at the Four Seasons in Washington, D.C. In Los Angeles, the Four Seasons facility has four Stairmaster machines, six stationary bicycles, and three treadmills. In addition, if you prefer to sweat in private, they have a Stairmaster that can be put in your room, upon request.

An aspect of health clubs that hotels are beginning to appreciate is qualified staff. "You need good supervision at a hotel," says Tom Pheil, health spa manager at Loews Santa Monica Beach Hotel. "The biggest problem at a hotel health club is guest ego. That's the most important reason why a hotel fitness center needs certified trainers to be there. We've had guys come in who have never rowed before on a rowing machine and they set it for the Olympic level. Or people who have never exercised hard lose their balance and fall off the treadmill. It can be dangerous." Good trainers can be helpful for more experienced exercise enthusiasts, too. At the Plus One Fitness Clinic in New York's Waldorf-Astoria, personal trainers are available to go running in Central Park with visitors who are apprehensive about running alone.

If your workout requires more specialized high-tech equipment than most hotels provide, you will want to plan ahead and stay in a hotel that has a fully equipped gymnasium nearby. If you already belong to a club that is part of one of the large chains, such as Bally's, you can usually arrange to use facilities in other cities for free or a nominal charge. Bally's has ties with some 400 different gyms and clubs in the United States, (800) 547-2750. If you are a member of a club affiliated with the International Racquet Sports Association, you will find clubs with tennis, racquetball, and squash courts in several countries.

I am always interested in new golf courses or good tennis courts near my hotel. I have found that golf, tennis, and other sports associations will help you locate facilities in cities where you are traveling. There are frequently specialized guides for hiking, jogging, or bicycling available in different areas. To accommodate your exercise needs, you have to make a few telephone calls, but it will be well worthwhile for the health of your next trip.

My friend, Robert Anderson, former CEO of Rockwell International, sums up the argument for exercise pretty well: "I think exercise helps most executives on a trip if they make time for it. Most business trips are usually pretty pressured, but one thing you can always find time to do is your exercise—all you need is an hour. Most hotels have made great improvements in this area in the last few years—it used to be that to get any exercise you had to run around the halls. People are beginning to recognize that they really need their exercise, just to feel better, to do the job well."

Other Forms of Relaxation

Although I am an advocate of exercise for relaxation, I recognize that many people prefer less strenuous ways of taking their minds off business and shedding their stress. Both Betsy and I enjoy bringing new books with us when we travel. Reading books is usually a late evening pleasure for me, because there is just no time during the rest of the day. (I also like to inquire if the hotel television system receives ESPN or CNN.)

A number of my executive friends have become enthusiasts for books on audiotape and will carry boxes of cassettes or CDs and a Walkman on their trips. Lots of people in an airplane are wearing headsets for the movie or the programmed music, so no one pays any attention to another passenger who is happily "reading" *War and Peace* with his or her eyes closed. (Some even arrange to have reports or information from their offices put onto cassettes so that they can absorb the material without reading.)

The idea of meditation conjures up mysticism and New Age religions for some people, but I know many business travelers who find that meditation exercises are an effective way to deal with tensions, focus energies, and just relax. If you close your eyes and meditate in your office, there is always the lurking concern that someone will think you are "sleeping on the job." In the privacy of your hotel room, you have an opportunity for refreshment that many people claim is more revitalizing for them than a nap. Of course, half the people on airplanes are sitting there with their eyes closed. Maybe more of them are meditating than we know!

The Global Traveler's Greatest Health Threat: Jet Lag

The bad news is that there is no cure for jet lag. The good news is that there are lots of things you can do to mitigate the effects of zipping your body through time zones too quickly.

There are entire books on the subject of jet lag, yet no one has been able to pin it down. Some researchers say that for every time zone you cross, it takes one day to adjust your body clock. Unfortunately, business travelers can't wait around for their circadian rhythms to catch up. They suffer the familiar agonies of insomnia, fatigue, aching muscles, and headache. If they are lucky, their jet lag will not induce more extreme symptoms, such as disorientation, memory loss, gastric distress, heart-rate problems, reduced reflexes, or lowered immune response (which can lead to many other medical complications).

A curious aspect of the jet lag problem which none of the scientific studies address is that most people suffer jet lag more severely traveling in an easterly direction than they do heading west. For example, business people traveling from New York find that they are hit with more symptoms of jet lag going to Europe than upon returning. Same number of time zones, same distance—but there is no explanation for the difference in experiences.

Many Japanese corporations and a few American companies have corporate policies requiring employees to wait one full day after a transcontinental trip before entering into business negotiations on behalf of the company. Sir Christopher Lewinton agrees. "In the decision-making process, I try to build a gap between traveling and making a decision. When you travel a lot, your gyroscope flips a little and you need to ground yourself again and stabilize. Providing the decision can wait a day or so, I'll tend to wait to make a commitment.

"There's an element of being persuaded that you're a real man—that you can come off an airplane and make a decision straightaway. I think that's nonsense. When I'm pressed, I'll say, 'Wait a minute! Tell me what the penalty is for deciding this tomorrow rather than today.'"

This makes sense if you have the time. All too often, however, I don't. Frequently I am moving through time zones so many times a week that if I stopped to adjust at each destination, I would never have time for business. I am not immune to jet lag. But I have developed ways to reduce the initial symptoms to a manageable level and to recover my body clock quickly. Needless to say, I make no claims to medical authority, but here is what works for me:

Mark McCormack's Rules for Taking the Lag Out of Jet Lag

1. Hit the Ground Running
The smart traveler will plan every step of the departure, the flight, the arrival at the airport, the trip to the hotel, and the schedule after arriving, so that he or she already is caught up psychologically in the destination's time zone before departing. Set your watch to your destination's time. Think about your activities upon arrival. Give your mind every chance to tell your body what will be expected.

2. Drink Large Quantities of Water
If you don't want to bother with bringing your own bottled water, try to persuade a flight attendant to give you a bottle right after takeoff. Dehydration is often responsible for many symptoms described as "jet lag." Most of the medical experts will tell you not to drink alcohol or caffeine on the flight because it will exacerbate the effects of dehydration. I don't follow this

advice strictly. I enjoy having a few glasses of wine in the evening or with dinner and I find that maintaining this simple ritual makes me more comfortable. But I drink lots of water, too.

3. Exercise

I suppose this rule could be a subsection of Rule Number One, Hit the Ground Running, because I literally believe in taking a vigorous walk (not necessarily a "run") as quickly as possible after arrival—unless you are arriving at an hour which dictates immediate sleep. I exercise a bit in the airplane whenever I am not sleeping. Get up, stretch, walk around the cabin, touch your toes, and generate some circulation in your body. Some flight attendants are downright hostile about passengers being out of their seats for any reason. Ignore them. Claim you need to use the rest room and take your stroll.

4. Eat Lightly—On Your Own Schedule

Order special meals of fruit or salads and try to eat them approximately when you would normally be eating in your destination time zone. This, of course, can be difficult because airline service often is organized around the timing of inflight movies and will allow no individual flexibility. To circumvent this problem, you can carry your own food and eat it on your own schedule or simply skip most of what is being served on the airplane. (This is not difficult to do if you are sleeping through the food service anyway.)

5. Give Your Body Time Zone Signals

Patterns of illumination and social behavior tell your body what time it is, too, according to scientists at the Argonne National Laboratory. This translates into emphasizing the obvious. If you are arriving at your destination in the daytime, get out and be active in sunlight as much as possible. When you sleep, be sure your room is quiet and has good blackout drapes or you use a sleep mask. Do not stay up later than you normally would simply because you know that you are ahead a few time zones.

Gary Player offers an insight that combines several of these rules: "I'm very averse to coffee, to caffeine, but coffee has been one of my great saviors. I don't drink coffee ever while playing in golf tournaments or in general. But when traveling, when I arrive at my destination in the morning, obviously my time sense is screwed up. I have a cup of coffee to jolt me up and keep me awake. One of the secrets of good traveling is to get off the plane and get on the local clock as though there is no time change. You've got to almost brainwash yourself. It's like golf. Never think about the putt you missed. Think about the one you're going to make. Never think back to what the time was where you were coming from. Think about what the time is where you are now." [Researchers confirm Gary's intuitive idea about having a cup of coffee upon arrival. The methylated xanthines in caffeine help to reset the body clock.]

Readers who are interested in a more comprehensive scientific look at the jet lag problem may want to look at *Overcoming Jet Lag* (Berkley; 160 pages, $6.95) by Dr. Charles F. Ehret and Lynne Waller Scanlon. Dr. Ehret is the director of the Argonne National Laboratory, 9700 South Cass Avenue, Argonne, Illinois 60439. If you send him a SASE, he will send you a wallet-sized copy of the anti-jet lag program he has developed and a reading list on the subject.

All of my suggestions about jet lag may be irrelevant soon, however. Scientists at the Oregon Health Sciences University in Portland are well on their way to developing a jet lag pill. They have discovered that the body's circadian rhythms are controlled by a hormone called melatonin produced by the pineal gland. Melatonin (playfully dubbed "the Dracula hormone") is stimulated by darkness and acts directly on the brain's timing center. A tiny dose of this hormone will fool the body into believing that it is time for bed. So, in the near future, we may just have to pop a pill to reset the body clock.

Fear of Flying Is Not Just Erica Jong's Problem

Novelist Erica Jong wrote a sexy book called *Fear of Flying* several years ago, and *FOF* has been the subject of jokes ever since. But, according to surveys, one out of every six persons harbors a serious, deep-seated fear of getting in airplanes. Often this fear manifests itself in excessive drinking and eating or other nervous behaviors. Sometimes it is mistaken for jet lag. If you secretly suffer from fear of flying and are worried that this will affect your business opportunities, get help. Several airlines and private clinics run modestly-priced weekend and evening programs to deal with fear of flying. They claim a high rate of cures, and any travel agent should know where to contact one of them in your area. There is also a generally useful little book, *How to Fly* (Corkscrew Press; 160 pages, $5.95; (800) 345-0096) by Natalie Windsor, with tips on the fear of flying.

Dr. McCormack's All-Purpose Traveling Medicine Chest

Travelers heading to the major business centers will generally find pharmacies available with the usual array of over-the-counter remedies. But if you wake up in a hotel room at 3 A.M. feeling lousy, you will wish you had brought along a few items. Here are my suggestions for a compact, all-purpose traveling medicine chest:

- All prescription medicines you are taking (bring prescriptions to satisfy Customs agents)
- Aspirin, Tylenol, or mild pain-killer
- Rolaids or antacids of some sort
- Pepto-Bismol
- Cold/flu remedies
- Eye drops
- Laxative
- Lomotil or other diarrhea remedy
- Band-Aids of various sizes
- Small scissors
- Antiseptic ointment
- Bug repellent
- Anti-fungal foot powder
- Sleeping pills or sedative
- Sleep mask
- Earplugs

- Small packs of tissues for emergency toilet paper and that head cold that's just leaving or just coming on
- The name and phone number of your physician at home
- The name and phone number of someone in the city where you are staying who can speak for you if you are incapacitated
- Your international vaccine record
- Your blood type and allergies

Sometimes You Feel Like You Are What You Eat

I advocate adventurous eating, but because travelers are particularly susceptible to nervous stomach troubles, jet lag, and exhaustion, they should use some good sense when dining out. Too many travelers find that the expense account is an invitation to gluttony. This is bad economics and bad dietary sense. My friend Bill Fugazy, chairman of the board of Fugazy International, observes: "Most people find business travel very tiring. The reason is that they drink too much, eat too much, probably don't get enough sleep, and never exercise on the road. The excess liquor and food is very bad for your constitution."

Worse than overeating can be eating foods prepared in ways your stomach is not equipped to handle. For example, the classic French haute cuisine can be loaded with buttery, egg-enriched, creamy sauces. Many a self-diagnosed case of "Montezuma's Revenge" turns out to be hot Mexican peppers and spices wreaking havoc in a gringo stomach. Be cautious of the same zingy problem with certain dishes of Chinese, Indian, or Thai food.

Worth a warning of its own is MSG or monosodium glutamate, which many Chinese restaurants sprinkle all too generously into soups, rice, and dishes of all sorts. MSG (like soy sauce) is high in sodium and may affect blood pressure. This substance can have even more unpleasant side effects for many diners, including headaches and nausea. Most waiters in Asian restaurants are familiar with the problem and will respond to a request that the chef leave out the MSG.

Be moderate in your consumption of alcohol even if your clients are not. Many Americans who travel in Europe are surprised to discover that wine and the pleasures of the table in general are much more a part of life there than they are at home. This does not necessarily mean that you should completely abstain. It means that you should maintain the same reasonable drinking habits that you have at home.

Whenever I hear cautions about drinking on business trips, I am reminded of the first time I met the great Olympic skier Jean-Claude Killy in the summer of 1967. (The next year in Grenoble, he swept away three gold medals.) We had lunch at a good restaurant in Geneva with my friend Hank Ketchum, who draws the Dennis the Menace cartoon strip. After we sat down, Killy ordered a glass of red wine. Somewhat naively I expressed surprise that he would be drinking wine while in training for the Olympics. In response, he smiled warmly and asked me, "Would you rather I drink milk—and ski like the Americans?"

Bloom Where You're Planted

Several years ago, the tennis press reported that "Andre Agassi hates Paris." Richard Evans, formerly of the London *Sunday Times*, reported that Agassi absolutely detested the City of Light, one of his very favorite places on earth. Why? Evans went on to explain that Agassi had a trainer with him all the time, and that every night he sent him out for burgers and french fries from McDonald's. The two of them would sit in front of the TV in the room eating burgers and fries with his brother and his coach. Evans wrote, "How can he hate Paris when he's never really been there?"

The simplest and most gratifying way to enjoy your trip to another city is to discover the pleasures of the city you are visiting. Although some cities are more pleasurable than others to visit, virtually no major business center is completely devoid of charm. To reward yourself for being on the road, **you must get out and see some of the city you are visiting.**

What's in My "Go To" Files

I maintain "go to" files on cities I visit or expect to visit. For places that I know well, such as London and New York, I've kept most of the generalized knowledge of the city in my head. I find that I am much more experimental with restaurants than I am with hotels, so that much of my filing deals with eateries. My files are a collection of clippings from travel newsletters and from magazines, as well as recommendations passed on to me by friends, business colleagues, sports and entertainment personalities, reliable hotel concierges, and other restaurateurs. Restaurateurs are, of course, a tough group to please. As such, when they have good things to say about a restaurant that is not their own, I pay attention.

I do, of course, keep track of extraordinary hotels that associates and staff members have told me about. Up until now, my way of sharing this information has been by means of the Notes and Comments section of my newsletter, *Success Secrets*. The following Destinations section, however, represents the accumulated "head knowledge" and file clippings from my own travels, as well as from IMG staffers and other business executives.

Don't think this is everything you need to know, however. Follow the current travel newsletters and magazines. I have a complete set of the most current Zagat restaurant surveys, which are compiled not by reviewers and critics but by actual diners. Get a good guidebook or two. How do you know which guides you prefer? **Read what they have to say about your home town.** If they make your city sound like a place you've never been to and are raving about restaurants you know to be second rate (or closed), that should cause you to suspect their input about other cities as well. However, you should know that the same individual (or team of individuals) doesn't write each volume in the series.

You should also know that for many parts of the world, travel books are outdated by the time they reach the bookstores. Don't expect the cab ride or *prix fixe* dinner to cost exactly the same at the time of your visit as it did when your guide was published, even if it's brand new.

Monitor the weather for a few weeks before you leave. Make sure you have a decent map of the city where you're headed. Visit an international magazine stand and pick up the local paper.

For the executive traveler, the keys to finding health, pleasure, and relaxation while traveling are moderation, exercise, and a willing spirit. **Be adventurous.** No matter how many times you've been to a city, **find ways to make your travel experience fresh for yourself each time.**

Check to see if there are interesting places, museum shows, or other cultural events scheduled during your visit. This can be both an opportunity and a warning. If you find yourself headed for Paris during the Paris Air Show or the spring or fall fashion showings, there won't be a decent restaurant reservation in the city. Gather as much input as you can. The next section summarizes some of the best knowledge in my "go to" files, but please remember, **if you leave for a business trip carrying nothing but this book, you haven't followed my advice.**

DESTINATIONS

Mark McCormack's "Go To" Picks and Tips
for Major American and Worldwide Business
Destinations

Amsterdam

Relentless business growth has pushed Amsterdam well beyond its tourist image of charming merchants' homes lining concentric rings of canals. Although there is no central business area anymore, location as well as physical splendor still make the **Hotel de l'Europe** the best choice for executive travelers here. A slightly more off-beat choice in a quieter setting would be the **Pulitzer**, where twenty-four interconnected canal houses form one of Europe's more unique hotels.

Best small hotel (and toughest to book): **Ambassade**.

Local secrets: **Sama Sebo** (Indonesian) and **Keyzer's Bodega**.

Most adventurous dining: **Halvemaan**.

For discreet business lunch: **Excelsior** (in the Hotel de l'Europe).

Best French cooking: **Dikker & Thijs**.

Best seafood: **Imko's** in the fishing port of Ymuiden (20 minutes southwest of town).

Best brasserie: **Luxembourg**.

Best hotel restaurant: **La Rive** (in the Amstel Hotel).

For serious business discussions: **Bistro Klein Paardenburg** (terrific food in the discrete ambiance of a converted coachmen's house, 15 minutes south of town).

Best diversion: **Rijksmuseum Vincent van Gogh**.

Medical emergencies: **Central Doktersdienst** (020 664-2111) for doctor listings; **Tandarts Bemiddling Bureau** (020 627-5815) for dentists. For hospitals: **Onze Lieve Vrouw Hospital** (020 599-9111) and the **Vrije University Hospital** (020 584-9111).

Business tip: Taxis can be phoned (677-7777) to any location and are remarkably quick and reliable.

Atlanta

Immediately after General Sherman burned Atlanta in 1864, they started rebuilding the city, and they haven't stopped yet. This is the focal point of the New South, headquarters for twenty-two

Fortune 500 companies, and home base for Delta Airlines. Southern hospitality and Confederate pride still reign here, and the business climate could not be more positive. With the 1996 Olympic Games just down the road, Atlanta continues to add to urban landmarks, such as the Peachtree Center and the Omni complex. Many new businesses have settled in suburbs outside the city core, so check a map before you choose your hotel.

If you can afford the time and the tariff, the **Ritz-Carlton Buckhead** is a landmark of gracious luxury and lives up to its position as the flagship hotel in the chain. It also boasts an outstanding restaurant, **The Dining Room**. Its sibling **Ritz-Carlton Atlanta** is clearly the top choice downtown (as well as home to a 4-star restaurant and power breakfast spot called **The Café**).

The European touch: **Swisshotel Atlanta**.

Best Oriental touch: **Nikko Atlanta**.

Best convention hotel: **Westin Peachtree Plaza**.

Gourmet dining with a view: **Nikolai's Roof**.

Best Italian: **Veni**, **Vidi**, **Vici**.

Steakhouses: **Chops**, **Bones**.

Best seafood: **The Fish Market**.

Best Chinese: **Chopstix** (on Roswell Road).

Best French: **Ciboulette**.

Southern cooking: **Horseradish Grill**.

Local favorites: **Pano & Paul's**.

Don't miss seeing: **The Atrium in the Atlanta Marriott Marquis**.

Evening entertainment: **Atlanta Underground**.

Hot new restaurant: **Nava**.

Best health club: **The Atlanta Health and Racquet Club**.

Best jogging: **Piedmont Park** or the **Chattahoochee Park**.

Peace and quiet: **Atlanta Botanical Garden**.

Medical Emergencies: **Medical Association of Atlanta** (404/881-1714); **Georgia Dental Association** (404/636-7553).

Business tip: If the pace of discussions seems slow or negotiations appear to be tied up by social amenities, be patient. Southern traditions of trust and friendship mean that personal warmth is more important than a slick presentation. They've seen carpetbaggers here before.

Barcelona

Barcelona was a great place to visit before the 1992 Olympics. But hosting the Games dramatically forced it to become an international showcase. There are several world-class hotels here now, but the gold medal still goes to **The Ritz**. Not so far behind in terms of panache are **Condes de Barcelona**, the stylish **Rivoli Ramblas**, the **Hotel Arts**, situated on the seafront of the Olympic Village and overlooking the Olympic Harbor with many good restaurants within walking distance, and the new **Rey Juan Carlos I**.

Best weekend retreat: **Hostel de la Gavina** (90 minutes away on the Costa Brava).

Best seafood: **Botafumeiro**, **El Cangrejo** (in the Olympic Harbor).

Power lunch: **Neichel** and **Via Veneto**.

Best brasserie: **Brasserie Flo**.

For gourmets (and worth the effort): **Eldorado Petit** (15 minutes by car) and **Hispania** (45 minutes north in Arenys de Mar).

Best bargain dining: **Senyor Parellada**.

Best-kept dining secret: **Passadis del Pep**.

Local watering holes: **José Luis**, **Network Café**.

Best hotel gyms: **Hotel Juan Carlos I**, **Meliá Barcelona Sarria**.

Best jogging: **Carretera de les Aigues**.

Best tennis: **Real Club de Tenis Barcelona**.

Best golf: **Real Club de Golf el Prat**, next to the airport.

Best diversions: Touring the buildings by the architect **Gaudi**, unique to Barcelona; the **Miro** and **Picasso** museums; the **Boqueria food market**.

Medical emergencies: Doctors and hospital: **Hospital Clinic I Provincial**, (323.14.14). Dentist referrals: **Institut Dexeus**, (418.00.00); **Amesa**, (302.66.82).

Business tip: Set your watch to Barcelona time. Evening meals begin around 10 P.M. here, and smoking cigars in restaurants is regarded as a delightful pleasure, not a socially abhorrent ritual.

Berlin

Although I had few business reasons to visit Berlin regularly in previous decades, that is changing rapidly with reunification. With the Wall gone, Berlin will continue to pursue its rightful place as Germany's premier business and cultural center. Hotels, already at an acceptable international standard, will surely improve. For old-world charm and crack efficiency, the **Bristol-Kempinski** has its advocates (rightfully so), but I prefer the **Grand Hotel** in what used to be East Berlin for elegance and its up-to-the-minute modernity.

Best small hideaway hotel: **Schloss Hotel Vier Jahreszeiten** (a grand villa in the exclusive residential area of a Grunewald).

Best restaurant for serious business: **The Grand Slam** at Tennis Club "Rot-Weiss."

Best Italian: **Ciao.**

Best French: **Paris Bar.**

Best international meeting place: **Fofi's.**

Best Thai: **Thai Palace.**

Best Indian: **Kashmir Palace.**

Best Mexican (very casual): **Tres Kilos.**

Best fitness facilities: **Grand Hotel.**

Best tennis: **Tennis Club "Rot-Weiss."**

Best golf: **Golf Club Berlin Wannsee.**

Best jogging: **Tiergarten.**

Best bar: **Bar am Luetzowplatz.**

Business tip: Berliners are among the most impatient people on earth, but it's a lifestyle choice, not rudeness. So don't take the locals' haste personally. They won't waste your time with small talk and will give you a straight answer instantly.

Boston

In ambiance and adherence to tradition, Boston is America's most London-like city. The obvious difference is size. Boston is one of the most compact American cities and easy to navigate (Logan Airport is only 15 minutes from downtown). Choosing a hotel here is less a function of where your meetings are held and more a function of what part of town suits you. (However, first-time visitors should keep in mind that there are really two Boston business centers now—the traditional downtown and the clutch of high-tech companies along Route 128 north of town. Plan accommodations accordingly.)

The perennially splendid **Four Seasons** would remain Boston's hotel of choice even if it didn't also happen to have the best location—overlooking the Public Garden and Boston Common. **The Bostonian** is a distant second, but worthy if you need to be close to Logan Airport. The Water Shuttle is the number-one way from airport to downtown. The ride takes eight minutes.

Boston's huge student population is reflected in the casual style of many of its restaurants, which cater more to young people and academics than the usual business clientele. That's a plus if you are tired of formal, overstuffed, and over-priced dining salons.

Best hideaway hotel: **The Charles Hotel** in Cambridge.

Best Italian: **Davio's**, **Il Pannino** (North End).

Best Spanish: **Dali**.

Best hotel dining: **Aujourd'hui** (in the Four Seasons), **Seasons** (in the Bostonian).

Best American cooking: **Biba**, **Grill 23**.

Best bistro: **Sonsie**.

Heartiest meals: **Olives**, **Hamersley's Bistro**, **Jasper's**.

Best for serious business: **L'Espalier**, **Bay Tower Room**.

Best food-to-price ratio: **La Famiglia**.

Best franchises: **Legal Sea Foods** (for fish), **Morton's** (for steaks).

Best Chinese: **Mister Leung**.

Best pizza: **The European**.

Best meals in Cambridge: **Harvest, Michela's, Rialto**.

Local secrets: **Jae's Bar and Grill, St. Cloud's, Providence**.

Best gym: **Boston Athletic Club**.

Best jogging: **The Esplanade** along the Charles River, **Castle Island** (South Boston).

Best golf: **Stow Acres** (public), **Ocean Edge, Tara-Ferncroft** (resort courses), **The Country Club** (private).

Best tennis: **Mt. Auburn Club, Longwood Cricket Club**.

Medical emergencies: Call **Beth Israel Hospital** (617/735-5356) for doctor referrals. **Massachusetts General Hospital** (617/726-2000) has a dental clinic.

Business tip: Don't arrive or depart form Logan Airport in the early morning (7 to 9 A.M.) or late afternoon (5 to 7 P.M.) rush hours, when the Callahan and Sumner tunnels that connect the airport to Boston jam up.

Brussels

For a city that is the geopolitical center of Europe and the third busiest convention city in the world, where executive travelers outnumber tourists four to one, Brussels has a remarkable dearth of world-class hotels. The newest additions—the **SAS Royal** and the ambitious **Conrad**—are certainly elevating local standards. My personal preference has always been the **Hilton** because of the great location, the first-rate executive floors, and the 24-hour rooom service; the **Cafe d'Egmont**, which offers the best venue for a business breakfast; and the reputable **La Maison du Boeuf**, one of the best restaurants in the city.

Business entertaining here is another matter. The restaurants and cafes are superb, both at the high and low ends of the price scale. The Grand Place, Brussels's majestic town square, houses many fine restaurants in its 400-year-old guild houses. First choice here should be **La Maison du Cygne**, but it would be a pity for any visitor to ignore some of the wonderful establishments in Brussels's environs.

Best hotel value: Junior suite at **The Amigo**.

Best cafe: **Le Cafe Metropole**.

Best bar (upmarket): **De Ultieme Hallucinatie**.

Best bar (downmarket): **Falstaff**.

Best leisurely lunch: **La Villa Lorraine** (in the Bois de la Cambre).

Best truffles: **La Truffe Noire**.

Best light meals: **L'Ecailler du Palais Royal** (on the picturesque Place du Sablon), **Sheltema**.

Most dazzling dining decor: **Le Barbizon**.

Best way to impress your guests: Take them to **Bruneau** or **Comme Chez Soi**.

Smartest wine list: **La Manufacture**.

Local secrets: **La Quincaillerie** (excellent seafood at modest prices in a former hardware store); **Brasserie Georges** (seafood bistro); **L'Amandier**.

Best golf within 60 minutes of town: **Le Zoute** (an inland links, site of Piaget Open).

Best golf in town: **Royal Golf Club of Belgium** at Ravenstein.

Best tennis: **Royal Leopold Club**.

Best gym: **Golden Club** (on Place du Chatelain).

Best jogging: **Bois de la Cambre**.

Chicago

Perhaps I'm biased because I was born and raised here, but Chicago has always struck me as the perfect big city for business. It's large and prosperous, but easy to navigate. It has the best airport connections through O'Hare, a constantly growing lineup of solid business hotels (to handle the heaviest volume of trade shows and conventions in the United States), and a rich crop of restaurants. It's also surprisingly pretty along Lake Michigan.

With my perennial favorite, the Mayfair Regent, closed, top hotel honors go to the **Ritz-Carlton** and its sister **Four Seasons** for service and lakeside views. Keep your eye on the newly renovated

Whitehall, which is bringing the elegance of a small European hotel back to town.

Best breakfast: **The Original Pancake House (Wilmette)**.

Best dining concept: The half portions at **Gordon**.

Most spectacular setting: **Riva** at Navy Pier.

Gourmet shrine: **Charlie Trotter's**, **Le Français**.

Best Italian: **Tuscany**, **Carlucci**.

Best Mexican: **Topolobampo**.

Best bargain: **Sole Mio**.

Best Greek: **Papagus Greek Taverna**.

Best Chinese: **T'ang Dynasty**.

Best Midwestern cooking: **Prairie**.

Best Rich Melman restaurants: **Hat Dance** (Mexican), **Un Grand Café** (French bistro), **Shaw's Crab House** (fish), **Maggiano's** (Italian).

Best hotel restaurants: **The Seasons** (in the Four Seasons), **The Dining Room** (in the Ritz Carlton).

Power lunch: **Nick's Fishmarket**.

Best burger: **Biggby's Bar & Grille**.

Best pizza: **Pizzeria Uno**.

Best golf: **Kemper Lakes** (amazing public course in Hawthorn Woods).

Best tennis: **Mid-Town Club**.

Best jogging: **Lakefront along Lake Michigan**.

Best gym: **East Bank Club**.

Medical emergencies: For dentist referrals, call the **Chicago Dental Society Emergency Service** (312/726-4321). Hospitals: **Northwestern Memorial** (312/908-2000) or **Rush-Presbyterian-St. Luke's Medical Center** (312/942-5000).

Business tip: Despite its big-city dimensions, Chicago is at heart a warm, friendly Midwestern town. A warm, friendly Midwestern attitude is most winning here.

Cleveland

Cleveland—where I started my career, raised my children, and maintain our company's world headquarters—has enjoyed a marvelous renaissance in the last ten years. A spate of new hotels and adventurous restaurants has livened up the business district. Restoration of the Warehouse District and night life in the Flats has helped Cleveland gain such attractions as the Budweiser Grand Prix and the Rock 'n Roll Hall of Fame. It is also one of the most convenient business centers. The airport is sleek, uncrowded, and nearby. The downtown business center is compact and sanely organized—with almost any appointment within a few minutes by car. Even the gleaming new ballpark, Jacobs field, is just a short walk from all the central hotels.

Best hotel: **Ritz-Carlton**.

European hideaway: **Baricelli Inn**.

Best convention hotels: **The Marriott at Society Center** and **Stouffer Tower City Plaza**.

Gourmet dining: **Sammy's in the Flats**.

Best bistro: **Johnny's Downtown**.

Best Italian: **Giovanni's**.

Best French: **La Pomme**.

Best American: **Piperade**.

Best hotel dining: **Ritz-Carlton**.

Best lunch: **Café Sausalito**, **Ninth Street Grill** (both in the Galleria).

Best franchises: **Morton's of Chicago**.

Best burger: **Hecks**.

Evening entertainment: **Cleveland Orchestra** (winter) and **Blossom Music Center** (summer).

Best jogging: **Metro Parks**.

Best golf: **Fowler's Mill**.

Best tennis: **Thornton Park** (Shaker Heights).

Don't miss seeing: **Jacobs Field**, **Gund Arena**, and the **Rock 'n Roll Hall of Fame**.

Medical emergencies: **University Hospitals**.

Business tip: Most people aren't aware of Cleveland's Rapid Transit System that can get you from the airport to the heart of downtown in twenty-five minutes for $1.50. One of America's great bargains.

Dallas/Fort Worth

Yes, some people still do wear Stetsons and cowboy boots to the office here, but don't let the drawl and the unusual dress code fool you. J.R. was not entirely a figment of some TV producer's imagination. There are plenty of exceedingly bright, capable business people in the Metroplex (as they refer to the Dallas/Fort Worth area), and sharp negotiators need to stay on their toes.

Before this city went bust in the late 1980s, it had enjoyed a long period of boom, and there are many signs that Texas will bounce back quickly as the nation recovers. For the business traveler, this is a comfortable, hospitable city with the advantage of being American Airlines's home base. (I advise you to "fly against the hub," but there's a difference between a hub and the home base. American clearly has the greatest choice of flights into and out of DFW.)

There's no doubt that my first choice of hotels is still the **Mansion on Turtle Creek**, which gives new meaning to the concept of service in American hotels. If your business is out in the North Dallas district, **Lufthansa's Grand Kempinski** is the best bet. And in Ft. Worth, the most efficient spot is the **Worthington**.

Best dinner: **The Mansion on Turtle Creek**, **The Riviera**, **Star Canyon**.

Best business lunch: **Lawry's Prime Rib**.

Best Tex-Mex: **Joe T. Garcia's** (FW), **Mario's Chiquita**.

Best French: **St. Emilion** (FW), **The French Room** in the Adolphus Hotel.

Power breakfast and brunch: **The Promenade Room** at the Mansion on Turtle Creek.

Texas BBQ: **Sonny Bryan's Smokehouse II** (in Dallas's West End District).

Jogging: **White Rock Lake area** (good weather), **Northpark Shopping Center** (bad weather).

Nighttime local color: **Billy Bob's Texas** (in the Stockyards).

Fitness center: **Worthington Hotel** (FW), **University Club** (Westin Hotel in the Galleria).

Artistic gem: **The Kimbell Art Museum** in Ft. Worth, **Dallas Museum of Art**.

Boots to bring home: **Shepler's** (in Arlington).

View: **The revolving lounge atop the Hyatt Regency** on Reunion Boulevard.

Medical emergencies: **Prologue** is a free referral service for doctors and dentists at (214/256-2283).

Business tip: A Texas twang may be contagious, but don't go native and try to emulate the locals—either in speech or in dress. If you want to win friends as an outsider, say something nice about "America's Team," the Dallas Cowboys, but make sure you can tell Emmitt Smith from Leon Lett.

Denver

For all its frontier history, Denver is clearly an American city of the future. Strategically located at the intersection of lines drawn from the four corners of the United States, the "Mile High City" also boasts the world's largest airport—Denver International. In addition to oil and mining, microelectronics, computers, and cable television are among the flourishing businesses here. The population growth has spread comfortably out around the suburbs, leaving the city with a stable population hovering around a half million people for the last decade. (That translates into a generally comfortable downtown traffic flow, too, even during rush hour.) Aside from the smog problems, the city is a clean, comfortable, and efficient place to do business.

There are plenty of good business travelers who would not consider any place to stay in Denver other than the **Brown Palace Hotel**. I have been equally happy, however, at the more intimate **Oxford Alexis Hotel**. Now part of the small Seattle-based Alexis chain, this lovely Victorian boasts a first-rate health club, and is within walking distance of historic Larimer Square and the Denver Center for the Performing Arts.

Business breakfast: **Ellyngton's** at the Brown Palace.

Best restaurant: **Strings**.

Best Rocky Mountain cuisine: **Buckhorn Exchange, The Fort**.

Best steak: **Morton's of Chicago**.

Best French: **Tante Louise**.

Best pizza: **Saucy Noodle, Beau Jo's**.

Best Mexican: **Las Brisas, Las Delicias**.

Local secret(s): **Cafe Paradiso, Mel's Grill, Aubergine, Napa**.

Best Italian: **Ciao Baby**.

Best golf course: **Fox Hollow, Arrowhead**.

Health club: **One Denver Place** (Downtown), **Greenwood Plaza** (SE Denver).

Jogging: **Cherry Creek Bike Path** or **Washington Park**.

Information on nearby skiing: **Colorado Ski Country**.

Don't miss: **The Tattered Cover**, one of the best bookstores in the USA.

Medical emergencies: **St. Joseph Hospital's Med Search** (303/866-8000); **Center Dental Associates** (303/592-1133).

Business tip: Taxicabs are the most efficient means of transportation within the metropolitan area (but don't try to hail them—they prefer to work from cab stands). If your business takes you into the suburbs, you would be wise to rent a car at the airport.

Dublin

Dublin is the most genteel of cities, in part because it is barely industrialized and more focused on service and light industries such as computers. It is also one of the friendliest towns, and as tourism here increases, the hotels and restaurants will surely improve. The **Shelbourne** remains the traditional hotel of choice in town, although the newish **Conrad** and **Westbury** seem to have all the essentials that executive travelers need. The real prizes, however, are the spacious suites at **The Towers** annex of **Jurys** and the elegant tranquility next door at the **Berkeley Court Hotel**.

Best hideaway: **The "K" Country Club Hotel** (thirty minutes southwest in Straffan).

Best weekend retreat: **Ashford Castle** (three and a half hours away in County Mayo).

Best French dining: **Les Frères Jacques**.

Top business lunch: **Le Coq Hardi**.

For gourmets: **Patrick Guildbaud**.

Best Irish meal: **Locks**.

Best seafood: **The Kish Restaurant** (in Jurys).

Local secrets: **Cookes Café**, **Roly's Bistro**.

Best match of setting and food: **La Stampa**.

Best Italian: **Kapriol Restaurant**.

Worth the drive: **The King Sitric** (seven miles away in the fishing village of Howth).

Best jogging: **St. Stephen's Green**.

Best golf: **Portmarnock Golf Club** and the new **Links Portmarnock**.

Best tennis: **Elm Park Golf and Sports Club**.

Best diversion: **The Abbey Theatre** (theatre is Dublin's greatest strength).

Medical emergencies: For doctors: Every hotel has its own arrangement with a local doctor. For dentists: **The Park Clinic** (01/285-3666); **Dental Hospital** (01/679-4311). Hospitals: **Blackrock Clinic** (01/283-2222); **Mater Private Hospital** (01/384-4444).

Business tip: The Irish love to entertain and be entertained. Don't be surprised if you find yourself carrying out certain negotiations on the golf course or in a bar/restaurant. Also, although punctuality is the rule during business hours, after hours is more relaxed. If you are invited to someone's home at 8 P.M., you won't be expected before 8:30.

Edinburgh

Edinburgh's most charming feature for business travelers is also its most exasperating: It doesn't have an international airport. That's charming if, like me, you usually travel there from London. That lets me go there by train. But if you're flying from another part of the world, you have to touch down in Glasgow, 50 miles (and a £45, 70-minute taxi ride) away.

Top tier business hotels in the center of town are limited to two. My first choice has always been the spacious and gracious **Caledonian**. But the recently refurbished and equally well situated **Balmoral** is a worthy rival.

Top hideaway hotel: **Prestonfield House Hotel**.

Best weekend retreat: **Gleneagles** (one hour north of town and easily the finest inland golf resort in the U.K.).

Best restaurant for serious business: **Pompadour** (in the Caledonian).

Best Italian: **Cosmo's**.

Best French: **Pierre Victoire** and **L'Auberge**.

Best bargain: Lunch at **Le Marche Noir**.

Best weekend brunch: **Cafe Royal Oyster Bar**.

Best seafood: **Skipper's Bistro**.

Authentic tavern: **The Canny Man's**.

Local secrets: **Martin's Restaurant**.

Worth the drive: **La Potiniere** (twenty-five minutes east of town; advance reservations essential).

Best golf: **Dalmahoy**.

Best tennis: **Craiglockhart**.

Medical emergencies: Hospitals: **Edinburgh Royal Infirmary**.

Business tip: Be aware that local bank and commercial holidays may differ from other major U.K. cities.

Frankfurt

The best travel feature in Frankfurt is its airport, which is not only Europe's busiest but is also its most convenient (only six miles from downtown). Although the **Steigenberger Frankfurter Hof** in town is a worthy hotel, in recent years I've been content to stay at Europe's best airport hotel, the amazing and enormous **Sheraton** which can accommodate any business need and meeting you can throw at its expert staff.

Best getaway: **Schlosshotel Kronberg**.

Best combination of food and knockout setting: **Brükenkeller**.

Best French cooking: **Erno's Bistro**.

Best Chinese meal: **Regent**.

For special events: **Humperdinck**.

Best German cooking: **Rotisserie** (in the InterContinental).

Best hotel (and airport) restaurant: **Papillon** (in the Sheraton).

Worth the drive for a meal: **Gutschänke**, **Neuhof,** and **Die Gans**.

Best Italian: **Gallo Nero**.

Best-kept dining secret: **Maschanz**.

Best gym: **Health Club in the Arabella Grand Hotel**.

Best golf: **Golf Club Niederrath**.

Best tennis: **Tennis Club Bad Homburg**, oldest tennis club in Germany.

Best jogging: **Museumsufer**, along the Main river.

Medical emergencies: For doctor/dentist referrals call the American (069/75304) or British (069/7204060) consulates.

Business tip: In a city devoted to banking, it's not surprising that Frankfurt keeps banker's hours (i.e., 9 A.M. to 5 P.M.). Even restaurants shut down around 10 P.M. If you don't know your way around, get organized privately with your business contact.

Geneva

Geneva is such a prosperous city—replete with first-rate lodging and dining—that it's easy to forget it has a population of only 160,000. That smallness makes it one of the most pleasant and efficient business centers. It also frees executive travelers to move freely in and out of town to take advantage of scenic Lake Geneva.

With the steady flow of international executives coursing through the city, Geneva's hotels have an instinctive feel for what business travelers are looking for. Although you can't go wrong with the **Beau Rivage**, the **Hôtel de la Paix**, or **Les Bergues** (all spectacularly situated on the water), when in town I prefer **Le Richemond** which seems to be in a class of its own.

Top lodging outside Geneva: **La Reserve**.

Best weekend retreat: **Royal Club Evian**.

Best hotel restaurants: **Le Gentilhomme** (in Le Richemond), **Le Chat Botté** (in Beau Rivage).

Best pastas: **Roberto**.

For special dinners: **Parc des Eaux-Vives**.

Best restaurant bargain: **Jet d'Eau** (Eaux-Vives).

Best dining in outskirts: **Café de la Place** (Plan-Les-Ouates).

Local secrets: **Auberge Communale** (in nearby Onex), **Le Patio**.

Best golf courses: **Royal Club Evian**, **Golf Club Divonne**.

Best tennis: **Tennis Club de Genève**, **Tennis Club Les Eaux-Vives**.

Best skiing: **Verbier/Valais** (two hours' drive or one and a half hours by train), **Chamonix** (one hour's drive, in France).

Business tip: Here, more than anywhere else on earth, *be on time.*

Hamburg

In no other city does one hotel so thoroughly outdistance the competition as the **Vier Jahreszeiten** does in Hamburg. For sheer grandeur, comfort, attentive service, and catering to every and any whim, this is certainly the best hotel in Hamburg, in Germany, probably Europe, and quite possibly the world.

Best small hideaway hotel: **Garden Hotel Pöseldorf**.

Best restaurant for serious business: **Haerlin** (in the Vier Jahreszeiten).

Best seafood: **Fischereihafen**.

Best traditional German feast: **Mühlenkamper Fährhaus**.

Best Italian: **Il Gabbiano** (formal), **Paolino** (casual).

Best Chinese: **Peking Enten Haus**.

Best bar: **Old Fashion Bar**.

Best after-hours venue: **Simbari**.

Best nouvelle French: **Le Canard**.

Local secrets: **Schlachterbörse**.

Best golf: **Hamburger Golf Club Falkenstein**.

Best tennis: **Club an der Alster Rothenbaum**.

Best gym: **Kaifulodge**.

Best jogging: **Außenalster**.

Business tip: Hamburg is the most British of German cities—in tradition and pace. Dynasties with several hundred years of history behind them dominate the town. Locals love to meet over lunch or dinner and they prefer to take their time. You will not impress people if you are in too much of a hurry here.

Hong Kong

Hong Kong is all about commerce and pace. It is noisy, crowded, bustling, and top-heavy with atmosphere and sensory distractions. When I visit, I want the opposite extreme: a hotel that specializes in serenity and comfort.

Hong Kong has more exceptional hotels than any other city in the world. **The Peninsula** (which has just recently been renovated and looks better than ever) on the Kowloon side of the harbor will not disappoint the most exacting traveler. It is perennially listed among the top twenty hotels in the world. But my regular retreat on Kowloon is **The Regent**, for its sleek elegance and spectacular harbor-side vistas. On the Island side, in the financially-oriented Central area, the **Grand Hyatt** and the **Island Shangri-La** are great hotels but the clear winner is **The Mandarin Oriental** for its veteran staff and unerring style. (Describing these five hotels in ten words or less is a gross injustice to them; only a handful of establishments around the world rise to the level they achieve every day.)

Best hotel restaurant: **Plume** (in the Regent).

Best out-of-town waterfront restaurant: **Stanley Oriental**.

Best high tea: **Grand Hyatt**, **The Peninsula** (great tradition).

Best hotel health club: **The Shangri-La**.

Best Continental cuisine: **The Mandarin Grill**.

Best steaks and chops: **The Regent Steakhouse**.

Best Italian: **Va Bene**.

Most fun French: **Michelle's** at the Fringe.

Best "Yum Cha" (Dim Sum): **Luk Yu Teahouse** (sit downstairs for a trip to old colonial Hong Kong).

Best Chinese: **Man Wah** in the Mandarin Oriental hotel, **One Harbour Road** in the Grand Hyatt (Cantonese), **Great Shanghai** in Tsim Sha Tsui (downmarket), and **Hunan Garden** (spicy) at Exchange Square.

Best restaurant view: **Cafe Deco** (on the Peak).

Most nostalgic setting: **The Veranda** (Repulse Bay).

Best diversion: **Ride the Peak Tram to The Peak overlooking the harbor**, eat outside the Peak Cafe and enjoy the view and wander through Hong Kong's wealthiest neighborhood.

Best English pub: **Carnegie's**.

Best nightclub: **JJ's** in the Grand Hyatt.

Best indoor swim: The marble-columned pool at **The Mandarin**.

Medical emergencies: Doctors and dentists: Ask at your hotel. Hospitals: **Hong Kong Adventist Hospital**, (2574-6211); **Queen Mary Hospital**, (2819-2111).

Business tip: Though taxis are cheap, they are sometimes hard to find during rush hour. Taxis can also get stuck in the tunnel traffic if you are trying to cross the harbor. It is often faster and more convenient to use the Star Ferry or the MTR (Hong Kong's subway system) instead.

London

London is so vast in size that it is absurd to offer a quick-hit list of its best lodging and dining. For top-tier hotels, all the guides will direct you to the Savoy, Connaught, Dorchester, and Claridge's (perhaps the Ritz, Berkeley, and the newish Lanesborough as well). But to hit the ground running in London, your hotel strategy should begin and end with location, not status. In other words, no matter how partial you may be to the Savoy in London's West End, if all your business activities are 30 minutes away in Knightsbridge, you're better off making friends with, say, the **Hyde Park Hotel** or the **Hyatt Carlton Tower**. I'm particularly fond of the latter. Before we opened up a London office and I acquired a home nearby, I literally conducted all my business from my room in the Carlton Tower or from a booth in its exceptional **Rib Room**.

London restaurants have long since shed their reputation for dullness. The London dining scene rivals New York or Paris and is even more varied and dynamic. Every cuisine can be found here.

Best classic French: **Tante Claire**.

Best Indian: **Bombay Brasserie**.

Best Chinese: **Mao Tai**.

Best Nouvelle Chinese: **Zen Central**.

Best Thai: **Khun Akorn**.

Best fish: **Poissonerie de l'Avenue**.

Best English food: **Simpson's** in the Strand.

Best pub: **The Australian**.

Best cocktail hour: **Blake's**.

Best off-the-beaten-path meal: **Le Caprice**.

Best hotel dining: **The Connaught**.

Best tea service with view: **The Park Room, Hyde Park Hotel**.

Best Italian: **Santini's**.

Best Italian (downmarket): **Trattoo**.

Best burger: **Drones**.

Best presentation: **Mosimann's**.

Best steaks and chops: **The Guinea**.

Power lunch: **The Savoy Grill**.

Best weekend lunch: **Cliveden**.

Best roast beef: **Rib Room** (Hyatt Carlton Tower).

Best sushi: **Suntory**.

Best Spanish: **Robato's**.

Best pizza: **Pizza Express** on Earl's Court Road.

Best brasserie: **Langan's**.

Best private clubs: **Annabel's**, **Mark's Club**, and **Harry's Bar**.

Best celebrity watching: **The Ivy**.

Best Lebanese: **Al Hamra**, off Curzon Street.

Most underrated restaurant: **The Greenhouse**.

Best gym: **The Peak** (in the Hyatt Carlton Tower).

Best tennis: **David Lloyd Tennis Club**.

Best golf: **Stockley Park**.

Medical emergencies: 24-hour Dental Emergency Service: (081/677/8383); £6 reference. Casualty departments of hospitals offer free treatment in case of real emergency; try **University College Hospital** and **Charing Cross Hospital**.

Business tip: Check bills to see whether service is included—or ask—before you tip; you may be tipping twice as much as you wish or as the service merits.

Los Angeles

Los Angeles is so immense and culturally diverse that there's no appropriate symbol for the city—unless it would be an automobile (presumably a convertible equipped with phone and fax machine), which is the only suitable method to get from one spot to another here. Meetings should be scheduled with careful attention to a road map to avoid wasting time shuttling between distant corners of the city.

Although the **Beverly Hills Hotel** is my L.A. "home," when it closed for a three-year renovation, my first choices for world-class service (and a relatively central location) became **The Peninsula** and the ever-splendid **Four Seasons**. For a more remote hideaway on luxurious grounds, there is the **Hotel Bel-Air**.

The Los Angeles restaurant scene is rich but volatile. Restaurants open and close with blinding speed but the following are in the midst of long runs.

Best French California cuisine: **Patina**, **Citrus**.

Best Provencal cooking: **Pinot Bistro**.

Best Wolfgang Puck restaurants: **Chinois on Main** and **Granita** (thirty minutes up the coast in Malibu).

Best Japanese: **Matsuhisa**.

Best Pacific Rim cooking: **Chaya Brasserie**.

Most opulent: **Rex**, **Il Ristorante**.

Best pizza: **Spago**, **Orso**.

Best burger: **Fatburger**.

Best Mexican/Best margarita: **El Cholo**.

Best hot dog: **Tail o' the Pup**, **Pink's**.

Best Chinese: **The Mandarin**.

Best steak house: **Morton's of Chicago**, **The Palm**.

Local secrets: **Il Giardino**, **Saddle Peak Lodge**.

Best breakfast: **Patrick's Roadhouse**.

Best setting: **Four Oaks**.

Best Mediterranean: **Campanile**.

Best Italian: **Valentino**.

Best golf: **Malibu Golf Course**.

Best tennis: **The Tennis Place** on Third Street.

Medical emergencies: For doctor referrals, call **Physicians Referral Service** (310/483-6122); for dentists, **Dentists Referral Service** (310/380-7669). Hospital: **Cedars-Sinai Medical Center** (310/855-5000).

Business tip: Say something nice about L.A. Residents, who invariably have emigrated here from somewhere else, have an inferiority complex about L.A. They are so used to hearing wisecracks about the surreal lifestyle they have chosen that they are pleased (perhaps shocked) when a visitor praises some aspect of L.A. other than the weather.

Milan

For a town that is Italy's financial center and clearly all business, Milan is not deep in great hotels. Constant trade shows ensure that the best-situated hotels are fully booked (so reserve far in advance). The standard executive amenities (good phones, 24-hour room service, etc.) are often lacking in so-called business hotels. And staff and service can be spotty.

My lodging strategy has always been: Don't take chances. Stick with the best (and damn the cost; you'll pay nearly as much at second-rate hotels). My first choice remains the **Principe de Savoia** for its spacious rooms and over-the-top elegance; the location on the busy Piazza della Repubblica is a nuisance only if you travel by foot. Its sister hotel across the square, the **Palace**, is no less venerable. **The Pierre** is a small ultra-modern favorite with American executives and tourists. The brand-new superb 98-room **Four Seasons Milan** is very popular with executives, in and out of the fashion industry, due to its excellent service and location in the heart of the fashion area.

If you don't dine well in Milan, you either haven't done your homework or need to get new friends. But be aware that lunch, not dinner (when Italians prefer to spend time with their families), is the optimal time for a working meal.

Best reason to commute from Lake Como: the palatial **Villa d'Este** (thirty-three miles north of Milan). A world-class resort this close to town should not be ignored.

Best by reputation: **Gualtiero Marchesi**, the Michelin three-star where nouvelle Italian cuisine was invented.

Best pasta, best waiters: **Alfio**.

Best way to impress your guests: **Santini**.

Best Bice: The original **Bice**, progenitor of super-successful clones in Paris, New York, Tokyo, etc., is here.

Best reason to drive thirty minutes to eat: **Antica Osteria del Ponte** (book far in advance).

Best Milanese cuisine: **Grand San Bernardo**.

Best takeout: **Peck**, the nonpareil gourmet food store, is also a nonpareil restaurant for business.

Best cappuccino: **Cova**.

Best fish: **Da Giacomo**.

Smartest lunch: **Biffi Scala**, **Girarrosto Toscano**, and **Boeucc**.

Liveliest dinners: **Giallo**, **Bricola**, and **Osteria del Binari**.

Best pizza: **Rosy e Gabriele**.

Best golf: **Golf Club Milano** (in Monza Park).

Best tennis: **Circolo Tennis Milano**.

Best diversions: **Soccer at San Siro Stadium**, **fashion shows** (twice a year).

Business tip: Pan-European travelers should beware the impenetrable fog at Milan's Linate Airport between November and March which can cause massive delays. Best time to land or leave is between 11 A.M. and 3 P.M. Long-haul flights usually leave from Milan's other airport, Malpensa, where fog has less impact.

Miami

There are at least four Miamis. There is Latin Miami, with its huge Cuban expatriate community (more than fifty percent of the Miami population is Spanish-speaking). Retirement Miami and Tourist Miami co-exist side-by-side on Miami Beach. And then there is Business Miami: gateway to South America, Central America, and the Caribbean. This last Miami is the second largest financial center in the United States. It boasts the world's largest cruise port and the second busiest airport in the country. This is truly the land of sunshine and money.

Your trendy friends may tell you about the colorful delights of Miami Beach's Art Deco district—but save that traffic-clogged, noisy, youth-oriented area for a vacation (if that's your idea of a vacation). The smart business traveler will stay at **Mayfair House** in Coconut Grove, where there is plenty of local color, along with efficient business service.

The power center: **The Grand Cafe** of the Grand Bay Hotel.

If you have the time and the tariff: **The Turnberry Isle Yacht and Country Club**.

If you must be on Miami Beach: **The Alexander Hotel**.

Best Art Deco dining: **Chef Allen's**.

My Favorite: **Mark's Place** (naturally).

Best stone crabs: **Monty's**—less frenetic, but just as good as the famed **Joe's Stone Crabs**.

Best Italian: **Baci**.

Best Spanish: **Casa Juancho**.

Best French: **Café Chauveron**.

Hot Cuban: **YUCA** (Young, Upwardly-mobile Cuban Americans).

Trendy breakfast: **The Newsstand Café** on Miami Beach.

Business cocktails: **The Oak Room** at the Hotel InterContinental.

Health club: **The Hotel InterContinental** even has its own jogging track.

Jogging: **Miami Beach** itself is great beach jogging. For more solid turf, try the trails at **David T. Kennedy Park** or **Margaret Pace Park**.

Medical emergencies: **Dade County Medical Association** (305/324-8717); **East Coast Dental Society** (305/667-3647).

Business Tip: Nowhere outside of Paris will you find a more style-conscious business community than in Miami. If you have the flair and know your client, go for the light-colored linen look. Otherwise, stick to cool, expensive, Italian tailoring.

Montréal

The first thing to remember about Montréal is that it is a French-speaking city with some English-speaking citizens—not the other way around. The luxurious **Le Westin Mont-Royal** (formerly Le Quatre Saisons) hotel is my lodging of choice in Montréal. Just down the road is its rival, the **Ritz-Carlton Kempinski Montreal**, a European-style, smart-looking hotel near McGill University. Not surprisingly, Montréal is densely populated with very good French restaurants, but the city's huge immigrant population guarantees that almost every imaginable meal is possible here.

Best Italian: **Le Latini**, **La Sila**.

Best seafood: **Costas**, **Milos**.

Best steaks: **Moishe's, Gibbey's.**

Best traditional French: **Les Halles.**

Best watering hole: **Whisky Café.**

Best Chinese: **Tai Kim Lung, Piment Rouge.**

Best dinner with a view: **Tour de Ville** (Radisson Gouverneurs), **La Saulaie.**

Best dinner in the outlying areas: **L'Eau à la Bouche.**

Best bistro: **Chez Gauthier.**

Best lunch: **Mas des Oliviers, Chez Julian.**

Best burger: **Il Était une Fois.**

Local secret: **L'Express.**

Best fitness facilities: **Le Westin Mont-Royal hotel** (Gymtech).

Best tennis: **Nun's Island, Mirabel, Le Sporting Club du Sanctuaire.**

Best golf: **Royal Montréal Golf Club** (private).

Medical emergencies: Doctors: **Montréal General Hospital**, (514/937-6011); **Royal Victoria Hospital/Emergency**, (514/843-1610). Dentists: **Côte-des-Neiges Dental Centre**, (514/731-7721); **Emergency Dental Services**, (514/875-7971).

Business tip: Winters are brutal in Montréal, so keep in mind the elaborate underground network that connects most office buildings and hotels downtown. (Underground is also the setting for some of the best shopping in North America.)

New Orleans

It's easy to understand why New Orleans is a favorite city for visiting Europeans. Not just in the Vieux Carre (what locals call the French Quarter) but throughout the city, New Orleans still bears the charming imprints of its time as both a French and Spanish colonial headquarters. The town and its residents take pride in the fact that they were "civilized" and cosmopolitan at a time when most Americans were country bumpkins. Indeed, when President Thomas Jefferson sent James Madison to negotiate a small real estate deal with Napoleon in 1803, all he really wanted was New Orleans. The Americans were amazed when he offered up the entire Mississippi River basin as the Louisiana Purchase.

They don't call it "The Big Easy" for nothing. Life moves at a different pace here, and long lunches, even business lunches, are the norm. Mention the concept of a "power breakfast" and you will be met with either incredulous stares or outright laughter. New Orleans moves on its ears and its stomach. Jazz and good food are not accessories to life; they are the essence of the city itself.

Best of the best hotels: **The Windsor Court** (a little bit of England).

Business hotels: **Fairmont, Omni Royal Orleans** (excellent concierge service).

Best small hotel: **Maison de Ville and Audubon Cottages, Hotel St. Louis**.

Don't miss dining at: **Commander's Palace**.

Classic Creole: **Antoine's, Galatoire's** (no reservations).

Nouvelle Orleans cuisine: **Emeril's, Nola**.

Business lunch: **Mr. B's, Royal Orleans**.

Rising star: **Bayona, Gabrielle**.

Best place to walk off a meal: The iron lace estates of the **Garden District**.

Best jogging: **Along the Mississippi in Woldenberg Park**.

Best Dixieland: **The Second Line** jazz club.

Best R&B: **House of Blues**.

You'll be glad you packed: **Extra shirts**. With the heat and humidity, you may go through them quickly.

Medical emergencies: **Tulane Medical Center** (504/588-5263); **New Orleans Dental Association** (504/834-6449).

Business Tip: The best restaurants can book up early, and a dinner reservation at a popular place like Commander's Palace can be hard to come by. However, these places do often hold out a few tables for locals. Use the clout of your concierge, or better yet, the clout of your local business associate, to make reservations on short notice.

New York

To enjoy New York, you must first stay sane in New York. That requires a measure of tolerance—for the confusion, noise, rudeness, and delays. Once you accept those conditions, you are in the world's most exciting city.

The bulk of New York hotel rooms for executives can be found in the midtown grid between 42nd and 59th Streets (the **St. Regis** and the **Peninsula** are tops here) where most of the gargantuan conventioneer hotels I abhor can be found. Better choices can be found uptown in the quasi-residential calm of the Upper East Side. **The Carlyle**, **The Lowell**, and **The Westbury** have their proponents. At the **Mayfair Regent**, there are four telephone lines into each room, local calls are free, and room service is from Le Cirque. First choice within our company's ranks, though, is **The Mark**.

I've long thought that the smartest dining strategy for New York (and London, Los Angeles, San Francisco, and Paris, too) is to not patronize a restaurant until it's two years old—when it's no longer "hot" and you can actually enjoy yourself. I also prefer restaurants one notch below in price and pretension to the familiar axis of Lutece, Le Cirque, La Cote Basque, and the Four Seasons.

Best lunch: **Arcadia**.

Best Southwestern cuisine: **Mesa Grill**, **Arizona 206**.

Best bistro: **Jo Jo, Les Halles**.

Best Mexican: **Zarela**, **Rosa Mexicano**.

Worth going to Brooklyn: **The River Café**.

Best seafood: **Manhattan Ocean Club**, **Le Bernardin**.

Best steaks: **The Palm**, **Peter Luger** (Brooklyn).

For gourmets: **Aureole**, **Bouley**.

Best $22 burger: **"21."**

Best wine list: **Montrachet**.

Best pizza: **Patsy's** (Brooklyn), **Mezzogiorno**.

Best theatre-district meal: **Orso**.

Best tapas bar: **Solera**.

Best deli: **Carnegie Deli**.

Best elegant lunch: **Lespinasse** (St. Regis Hotel).

Best Italian: **Remi**, **Le Madri**, **Il Mulino**.

Best hotel dining: **57-57** (in the Four Seasons).

Best-kept secrets: **Rosemarie's**, **Zen Palate**, **Ferrier**.

Where New Yorkers eat: **Union Square Cafe**, **Gotham Bar & Grill**.

Best gym: **New York Athletic Club**.

Best jogging: **Central Park** (during daylight).

Best golf: **Arrowood** in Westchester County.

Best tennis: **Roosevelt Island Racquet Club**.

Medical emergencies: Doctors: **Affiliated Physicians of St. Vincent's**, (212/775-1218); **Central Park West Medical**, (212/769-4321). Dentists: **Concerned Dental Care**, (212/696-4979). Hospitals: **Beth Israel Medical Center**, (212/420-2000); **Mount Sinai Hospital**, (212/241-6500).

Business tip: Before you enter a cab, know where you're going and how to get there. (The rudeness of New York cab drivers is a hoary myth—because few cab drivers speak English well enough to be rude—but they can be geographically illiterate.)

Paris

There are so many faux Parisian establishments around the world (the type that bill themselves as "a little bit of Paris in the heart of—") that when I find myself actually in Paris, I aggressively seek out the quintessential Parisian places and experiences that could not be replicated in any other city.

To hit the ground running in Paris, you must first surrender to Paris. It took me years to realize what this meant. I used to resent the high cost of everything in Paris, until a friend taught me to think of the outrageous prices as a "value-added surcharge" for all the things that make Paris special—the sidewalk cafes, the public gardens, the richness of the architecture, the late-evening light in summer. That makes the steep bills easier to bear. (Also, Hong Kong, London, Tokyo, and Stockholm, among other cities, are now easily as expensive as Paris.)

Any listing of Paris's best hotels leads off with the familiar quintet—the Ritz, Crillon, Bristol, George V, and Plaza Athenée. Of these five, my favorite for years has been the **Crillon** because it is not living on its exalted reputation but continually surpassing it.

It is difficult to get a bad meal in Paris. If your intention is to impress a business associate at dinner, you're certainly welcome to the established temples of gastronomy—e.g., Joël Robuchon, Taillevent, Tour d'Argent, Apicius, etc. But unless you take a perverse pleasure in bragging about how much you spent for a meal, you can easily get more bang for the buck elsewhere in Paris.

Best weekend retreat: Gerard Boyer's **Les Crayeres** in Rheims.

Best distraction: **Musée d'Orsay**.

Trendiest hotels: **L'Hôtel**, **Novanox**.

Smartest hotel choices on Left Bank: **Lutetia**, **Montalembert**.

Best jogging: **Parc Monceau**.

Best hotel gym: **Royal Monceau**.

Nearest great golf course: **St. Germain en Laye**.

Best tennis: **Racing Club de France** (for members), **Paris Country Club**.

Best English-language bookstore/newsstand: **Brentano's**.

Best bistros: **Chez Géraud**, **Benoit**.

Best cheese shops: **Barthelemy**, **Androuets**.

Fastest waiters: **Le Divellec**.

Best seafood: **La Maree**, **La Cagouille**, **Prunier**.

Best "event dining": **Le Pré Catelan**.

Best Italian: **Il Cortile** (in Hotel Castille), **Gabriele**.

Friendliest meal: **Duquesnoy**.

Most imaginative meals: **Michel Rostang**, **L'Ambroisie**.

Local secrets: **Le Recamier**.

Best takeout: **Fauchon**.

Business tip: Do not try to hail a taxi on the street London-style. You must go to a taxi stand.

Rome

Visiting Rome can offer as many frustrations as pleasures. It is a chaotic city that rewards the traveling executive who plans well ahead and double-checks everything. Front-line hotel options range from the great rooms and tradition at the **Grand** to the greenery and privacy of the **Lord Byron** to the international glitz at the **Majestic**. My favorite hotel is the **Hassler-Villa Medici**, managed by Swiss and perfectly situated at the top of the Spanish Steps.

Best reason to commute from outside Rome: **Posta Vecchia**, a beautiful hotel within the Principe Odescalchi in the village of Palo on the Roman seaside.

For gourmets: **Il Moro**.

Best pasta, best waiters: **Augustea**.

Best hotel dining: **Relais Le Jardin** (in the Lord Byron).

Best way to impress your guests: **Alberto Ciarla**.

Best reason to drive thirty minutes to eat: **Vissani**, brilliant Italian cooking in the small hamlet of Civitella del Largo in Baschi (Orvieto).

Toughest to book: **Felice**.

Best Roman cuisine: **Cecco er Carrettiere**.

Best takeout: **Franchi**.

Best cappuccino: **S. Eustachio**.

Smartest lunch: **Mastro Stefano**.

Liveliest dinner: **Il Matriciano**.

Best pizza: **Picchioni**.

Best golf: **Acquasanta**.

Best tennis: **Circolo Tennis Parioli**.

Best diversions: **Vatican Museum**; the **beach at Fregene** on the Roman coast in summer and in winter.

Local secrets: **Porta Portese street market on Sunday mornings**.

Business tip: Cooperative Airport is a private taxi service (Tel. 65010858) that provides punctual taxi service with large comfortable air-conditioned automobiles to and from the airport to center city for the reasonable fixed price of Lit. 60.000. A great way to avoid being fleeced.

San Francisco

San Francisco is my favorite city (I'm not alone in this opinion) and I go out of my way to visit here. If you want to know what the rest of America will be thinking and doing three years hence, come here first.

Although it's hard to argue with the perennial excellence of the **Four Seasons Clift Hotel,** and aficionados of "boutique" hotels seem to gravitate to the **Prescott Hotel** or the **Compton Place Hotel**, for location, staff, and relative tranquility my first choices are **The Mandarin** and the **Ritz-Carlton**.

As you would expect of a city that starts most of America's dining trends, San Francisco has a spectacular and seemingly inexhaustible restaurant scene, not just within the city proper but an hour away in the Napa Valley and over the Golden Gate Bridge in Marin County, too. Being adventurous here rarely disappoints.

Weekend retreat: **Silverado Country Club** (in Napa Valley).

Best hideaway resort in Oakland: **The Claremont Resort**.

Best Mexican: **Cafe Marimba, Guaymas** (on the water in Tiburon).

Power lunch: **The Big Four**.

Best hotel dining room: **The Dining Room** (in the Ritz-Carlton).

Best brasserie: **Stars, Bix, Roti**.

Best Sunday brunch: **Perry's, Green's**.

Watering hole: **Moose's**.

Best Mediterranean cuisine: **Square One**.

Best California Chinese: **China Moon Cafe**.

For gourmets: **Zuni Cafe, Chez Panisse** (in Berkeley), and **Fleur d'Lys**.

Best French: **Masa's, Rubicon**.

Best Italian: **Ecco**.

Worth the drive: **The Lark Creek Inn**.

Best ambiance: **Fog City Diner**, **Boulevard**.

Best burger: **Hamburger Mary's**.

Dining in Napa: **The French Laundry, Mustard's Grill, Tra Vigne, Kenwood Bar & Grill, Brava Terrace,** and **Rutherford Bar & Grill**.

Best gym: **YMCA** (financial district), **Club One**.

Medical emergencies: Dental: **San Francisco Dental Office** provides 24-hour emergency service. Hospitals: **San Francisco General** (415/206-8000).

Business tip: September to November is the best time to visit, but schedule early to beat the convention and trade show rush.

Seattle

As a gateway city for the Pacific Rim and an attractive corporate home in its own right, Seattle has become a more frequent stop for the business traveler. Yes, it rains here—or at least drizzles—often enough to maintain this city's reputation for precipitation. So come prepared. Also, take extra precautions about vitamins and rest, because the damp climate can trigger an annoying cold even in the heartiest visitor.

The corporate style is casual here, but until you have established enough rapport with your clients to drop the formalities, punctuality and suit-and-tie apply.

The **Alexis Hotel** is the definition of what a small, elegant business hotel should be. It's my first choice in this city. Ask for a room with a balcony overlooking the courtyard. The Alexis also houses **The Painted Table**, which features first-rate Northwest cuisine.

Traditional favorite business hotel: **Four Seasons Olympic**, which has old grandeur, excellent service, and one of the city's best restaurants, the **Georgian Room**.

Best of the large hotels: **The Westin** (although the elevators can be slow).

Local favorite: **Metropolitan Grill**.

Best French: **Rover's**.

Best Pacific Northwest: **Dahlia Lounge**.

Just out of town: **The Salish Lodge**, overlooking Snoqualmie Falls, is a memorable spot to stay or dine, if you can take the time.

Spectacular bookstore: **Eliot Bay Book Company**.

Best Japanese: **Nikko** in the Westin Hotel.

Charming secret: **Campagne**.

A toss-up for best seafood: **Ray's Boathouse, Elliot's Oyster House, Fullers, McCormick's Fish House**.

Best ambiance: **Adriatica Cucina Mediterranea**.

Most prestigious private club: **The Rainier Club**.

Spare time adventure: **The Seattle Art Museum**.

Medical emergencies: **Valley Medical Center** (206/228-3450); **Seattle-King County Dental Society** (206/443-7607).

Business tip: Don't get caught in the horrendous rush hour traffic on I-5. Seattle loses a lot of its small-town charm with this big-city problem.

Stockholm

The dominant element in Stockholm is water (and not just because it rains a lot here). The city sits on a string of fourteen islands on the Baltic. So, everything beautiful and interesting here is either near or on a body of water. I'm not sure where Stockholm picked up the reputation for being a cold, bland city, but it is a false impression. I've been visiting Stockholm regularly since the mid-70s heyday of our client Bjorn Borg and always do so with eagerness. Everything here is expansive and slightly larger than normal scale—like a restaurant with vaulting ceilings, oversized chairs, and the tables spread far apart. I never feel cramped in Stockholm. Yet with its centralized business area, it is an easy town to navigate.

Most of Stockholm's hotels fall into the standard international executive class—reliable and efficient. By far the best is the **Grand**, marvelously situated on the water and in the heart of everything. **The Diplomat** is an up-and-comer among executives who yearn for a less hectic atmosphere.

Best hideaway hotel: **Victory Hotel** (a deluxe, antique-filled, one-of-a-kind jewel in Stockholm's Old Town).

Best weekend retreat: **Grand Hotel Saltsjöbaden** (a gorgeous 19th-century castle just ten miles away on the Baltic).

Best restaurants open on Sunday night: **Bistro Jarl** and **Östergök**.

Best for a serious business dinner: **Paul & Norbert**.

Best seafood: **Wedholms Fisk**.

Best burger: **Eriks Bakficka**.

Best business lunch: **Eriks** (in old town).

Best game dishes: **Den Gyldene Freden**.

Best hotel dining: **Grands Veranda** or **French Dining Room** (in Grand Hotel).

Small jewel: **Min Lilla Trädgård** ("My Little Garden").

Best-kept secret: **The Leijontornet** (Lion's Tower) restaurant in the Victory Hotel.

Best golf: **PGA European Tour Course** and **Ullna Golf Club** (thirty minutes from town).

Best tennis: **Royal Tennis Club**.

Best gym: **Sturebadet**.

Best jogging: **Djurgården** park.

Best diversion: **A boat trip to one of the islands** (e.g., Utö or Sandhamn) in the Stockholm archipelago.

Medical emergencies: Call the **Karolinska sjukhuset**.

Business tip: Unless you are a passionate sailor, obsessed with everything nautical, do not be lured into booking a cabin on any of the boat hotels anchored in Stockholm's harbor; the novelty will wear off very quickly.

Sydney

Sydney is the most nonchalant international business center. With its breathtaking harbor and beaches, it is a perfect combination of San Francisco and Rio de Janeiro. Yet there was a time in the 1960s and

'70s when I hated visiting here. The hotels were ancient, the food was terrible, international phone calls were impossible to complete, and other than the friendly citizenry, some nice golfing, and pleasant weather, there was little comfort or joy to be found here.

Fortunately, no city in the world has transformed itself more dramatically for the business traveler in the last twenty years than Sydney. Qantas, the national carrier, is one of the world's great airlines. There's a healthy choice of hotels that cater to executives. And the restaurant scene is vibrant.

The Regent, which continues to merit its reputation as the best hotel in the Southern Hemisphere, is my first choice here, though it is getting a healthy challenge from the **InterContinental**, the **Ritz-Carlton**, the **Sheraton on the Park**, the **ANA,** and the ambitious **Park Hyatt**.

Top business restaurant: **Restaurant 41**.

Best wine list: **Treasury** (in the InterContinental).

Best tourist trap: **Doyle's on the Beach**.

Best Italian: **Tre Scalini**.

Friendliest service: **Beppi's**.

Best Chinese: **Imperial Peking** (Circular Quay).

Tastiest/healthiest cuisine: **The Pier**, **Rose Bay**.

Best garden setting: **Lucio's**.

Local secrets: **Rockpool**, **McLeay Street Bistro**, **Cicada**.

Best jogging: **Centennial Park**, **Botanical Gardens**.

Best dining tip: **Stick with local wines**. Though aggressive marketing has certainly made Australian wines familiar to British and American travelers, the local reds and whites taste five times better here.

Best golf: **The Australia Golf Club**, **The New South Wales Golf Club** (with a member or by prior arrangement only—write first before departing).

Best tennis: **White City** (with a member or by prior arrangement only—write first before departing), **Paddington**, **Rose Bay**.

Best diversions: **Darling Harbour**, **Cottage Point Inn**, **Hawksbury River,** and **harbor cruises**.

Medical emergencies: Doctors: **Women's Medical Centre**, (02/231-2366). Dentists: **Dental Emergency Services** and **Central Dental Laboratory**, (02/211-1011). Hospitals: **St. Vincent's Hospital**, (02/339-1111); **Sydney Hospital**, (02/228-2111).

Business tip: Australians do not always tip for services provided and are sometimes perturbed by visitors who insist on tipping (the accepted maximum is 10 percent) because it tends to ruin the system for them.

Tokyo

Tokyo may be the toughest city on earth in which to "hit the ground running." It is sprawling like London, but the unfamiliar language and local customs make it a challenge for Western executives who do not do their homework.

Again like London, there are many top-notch hotels here, but choosing one should be dictated by location. Though people I respect swear by the modern opulence of the **Seiyo Ginza** and the unalloyed excellence of the **Hotel Okura**, for service and convenience, I remain loyal to the **Capitol Tokyo**.

Tokyo has more bars and restaurants than any city in the world. Western diners will notice an interesting irony in the restaurant scene here. Though Japan may block imports of Western-made technology and consumer goods, that has not stopped Tokyo from aggressively importing restaurants and dining trends from the West. Some of the best restaurants I've tried in recent years are Tokyo outposts of proven winners from the U.S., Italy, and France.

Best Classic French: **Le Maestro, La Rochelle**.

Best Italian: **Enoteca Pinchiorri**.

Best hotel dining: **New York Grill** (in Park Hyatt).

Best Chinese: **Suienshuka**.

Local secret: **Hôtel de Mikuni**.

Best American franchises: **Spago**.

Best French franchises: **La Tour d'Argent, Maxim's**.

Best Italian franchises: **Chianti, El Toula**.

Best sushi: **Kyubei**.

Best pizza: **Tant Tant** (in the Tokyo Department Store/Main Building).

Best diversion: **Kabuki Theatre**, **Sumo wrestling**.

Best golf: **Kuni Country Club** (public—Prince Hotel).

Best tennis: **Shinagawa Prince Hotel**, **Tokyo Hilton**.

Best jogging: **Imperial Palace**.

Medical emergencies: For doctors, **Tokyo Medical & Surgical Clinic** (03 436-3028); for dentists, **Yanagisawa Dental Clinic in the Capitol Tokyo Hotel** (03 581-4511).

Business tip: The Japanese do not tip for services rendered, save for a chambermaid in an inn or for special appreciation. A ten percent service fee in hotels and restaurants is usually included.

Washington, D.C.

Perhaps because our nation's capital is overrun with tourists year 'round, the natives make a special effort to separate themselves from the "visiting yokels." They can be clubby, and here, much like Paris or New York, it pays to establish yourself as an "insider." How? By having a reasonable knowledge of the business hotels and restaurants described below, and by staying in touch with the daily political buzz—usually found in the pages of *The Washington Post*. Parking is such an expensive nuisance in this city (when you can find it) that taxis are the sensible mode for most business travelers. Or take the Metro; it's very clean, safe, and efficient, and has stops near probably everywhere you want to go except Georgetown. Either dining or cabbing, you will do well to spend a quiet fifteen minutes familiarizing yourself with a city map. Washington's primarily radial layout is confusing and you can save yourself a lot of disorientation by remembering a few landmarks in the four major quadrants.

Four hotels dominate in D.C., and all have fine business amenities: **The Four Seasons, The Park Hyatt, The Hay-Adams,** and **The Ritz-Carlton**.

Best weekend getaway: **The Inn at Little Washington** (in Washington, Virginia; book months in advance).

Tradition and class: **The Jockey Club** at the Ritz-Carlton.

Power breakfast: **The Adams Room** of the Hay-Adams or the **Melrose Room** at the Park Hyatt.

Best steaks: **Capital Grille, Morton's of Chicago, The Palm.**

Best Italian: **Galileo, Bice.**

Fun Italian: **Café Milano.**

Best meal in Georgetown: **Provence.**

Local secret: **Pesce** (small seafood market and restaurant, wine only).

Southern homecooking: **Georgia Brown's.**

Spicy fun: **Jaleo.**

Best jogging: **Along the C&O canal path in Georgetown.**

Best exercise facilities: **The Fitness Center** at the Westin Hotel.

Peace and quiet: **Dumbarton Oaks Gardens & Museum.**

Medical emergencies: **Doctor Referral Service** (202/994-4112); **Dental Referral Service** (202/547-7615).

Business tip: This may sound strange, but the frequent parades, motorcades, and demonstrations in Washington can ruin your day if you get stuck in traffic near them. Often your hotel doorman or concierge will know of such troublesome events. It never hurts to check.

Zurich

Zurich is *the* city that most closely approximates the "hit the ground running" ideal. It may be the easiest city in the world to conduct business in. It is prosperous, compact, easy to move around in, and, as a major financial center, has a healthy respect for the primacy of commerce.

In a nation as reliant on tourism as Switzerland is and as obsessed with cleanliness, order, and efficiency, the excellence of Zurich's hotels should not be a surprise. Pride of place in my heart will always go to the **Dolder Grand**, an otherworldly retreat a few minutes from the center of town which, besides having its own golf course, tennis courts, ice skating rink, and sublime gardens, is also a state-of-the-art business hotel. The **Baur au Lac**, though indisputably one of Europe's great hotels, surprised me that it doesn't have 24-hour room service. If you're an early riser, don't expect coffee before 6 A.M. This is its only deficiency.

Best summer hideaway: **Ermitage** in Küsnacht (fifteen minutes away on Lake Zurich).

Weekend retreat: **The Park Hotel** at Witznau. (This placid chalet rivals Villa D'Este; closer to Lucerne than Zurich, but worth the ninety-minute drive for extended stays.)

Best business lunch: **The Grill Room** (in the Baur au Lac).

Best dining bargain: **Bier-Falken**.

Best restaurants on Lake Zurich: **Petermann's Kunststuben** and **Chez Max**.

Restaurants worth the drive: **Witschi's** and **Sihlhalde**.

For meeting over drinks: **Pacifico** and **Kronenhalle**.

Best pastas: **Tübli**.

For gourmets: **Agnes Amberg**.

Best light meals: **Nouvelle**, **Königstuhl**.

Best beers: **Bierhalle Kropf**.

Best golf: **Zumikon Country Club** (in suburb of Zurich).

Best tennis: **Grasshoppers Club**.

Best skiing: **Laax** (a drive of one and a half hours), **St. Moritz**.

Business tip: As in Geneva, always be prompt.